*Detective Grogan of the LAPD
Took a Personal Interest in
Getting a Murder Conviction
for the Kyle Shooting....*

Grogan's fascination with the case began the moment he stepped into the dining room and sized up the situation. Here was a crime at least as interesting as any for which he had served as a consultant on *T.J. Hooker*.

Grogan quickly came to understand that the millionaire had been a hard-driving, competitive man's man in a world peopled by celebrities, ex-jocks, and glamorous women. Later in the investigation, he would say that he understood the victim "better than anyone."

Grogan initially conducted a routine burglary-homicide investigation. In reality, he was later to say, Bob Grogan determined that Kyle's death was a premeditated murder ten minutes after he walked into the house. In addition, he was convinced he knew who had done it.

Ulterior Motives

Suzanne Finstad

ST. MARTIN'S PRESS/NEW YORK

ULTERIOR MOTIVES

Published by arrangement with William Morrow and Company, Inc.

Library of Congress Catalog Card Number: 87-10981

ISBN: 0-312-91185-8   Can. ISBN: 0-312-91186-6

Printed in the United States of America

First St. Martin's Press mass market edition/July 1988

10 9 8 7 6 5 4 3 2 1

*For my brothers
and for Michael
with appreciation*

"Money does strange things to people."
—RICKY KYLE

PART
ONE

PART
ONE

1

AS THE HUNDRED AND FIFTY OR
so guests filed into the Sparkman-Hillcrest Funeral Home on a
hot Dallas morning in July 1983 to pay their last respects to
Henry Harrison Kyle, a sense of expectation was palpable. Five
days earlier, the sixty-year-old millionaire-developer's death had
made banner headlines in both Texas, where he had spent most
of his life, and Los Angeles, where he had been killed.

On Friday, July 22, in the ghostly stillness between three
and four A.M., police had been summoned to the Kyle mansion
in Bel-Air, California. There, on the dining-room floor, they discovered the entrepreneur's nude corpse. According to police, a
bullet had entered the back and ripped through the right side
of the chest. Alongside the body was a .357 Magnum.

The cause of death was immediately apparent. . . . The explanation for it was not.

The previous September, Henry Kyle had undertaken what
his friends referred to as "one of his fun projects"—the revi-
talization of a flagging film-syndication company. This endeavor
had caused Kyle to temporarily shift his base of operations from
Dallas to Los Angeles. The Texan had already spent considerable time in California, mostly to oversee his real-estate investments there. In 1968 Kyle had met David Charnay, the haughty,
white-pompadoured chairman of the board of Four Star International. This movie-syndication company was originally created in the fifties as a vehicle for producing films by actors David

Niven, Charles Boyer, Dick Powell, and Ida Lupino, the four stars from whom it took its name.

Two years later, Kyle accepted a seat on Four Star's board of directors, and in the autumn of 1982, Charnay allowed his starstruck protégé to purchase his 30 percent of the stock in the company. Henry Kyle thereby obtained a majority interest and with it, the impressive titles of Chief Executive Officer and President.

By this time Four Star was no longer in active production. Whatever profits it made were derived from syndication rights to a dozen or so canceled television series and some old feature films. Some industry observers tittered that the Texan's investment was as passé as the four stars who had founded the company. But such gossip did not deter Kyle, who promptly moved into movie legend Sam Goldwyn's former suite of offices and spent nearly a million dollars for a once-grand mansion in Bel-Air. It was to be his "showplace" to entertain colleagues in the movie business.

Built in 1928 of white stucco with a terra-cotta roof, the sprawling house was named Granada. A Mediterranean-Gothic marvel, it featured stately columns and balustrades and was crowned on each end with a massive turret.

The mansion's facade was on busy Sunset Boulevard, while the driveway and side entrance (distinguished by an elaborate courtyard complete with fountains) led to Stone Canyon Road, one of Bel-Air's most exclusive addresses. To Henry Harrison Kyle, who started life as a poor boy from the hills of Tennessee, the Stone Canyon location doubtless meant that he had arrived.

Clara Bow, the "It" girl from twenties films, was said to have owned the house. The fact that her name never appeared on the deed records did little to discourage the rumor. Indeed, when Kyle bought the house, he was told that the portrait hanging above the fireplace in the dining room was of Clara Bow.

Others claimed the portrait was of Mrs. Eloi F. Newman, a wealthy dowager whose husband had purchased the estate in 1965. The Newmans, originally from Texas, lived at the house quietly for many years until Mr. Newman died. Shortly thereafter, his elderly widow married her black chauffeur, an aspiring singer named Alton Albright. Mrs. Albright went through much of her late husband's fortune trying to help his former driver break into the music business. Several years and several hundred demo records later, Alton Albright's singing career fizzled, along with his unlikely marriage. The former Mrs. Newman died a few months after the divorce. Albright subsequently challenged her will and hoped thereby to acquire title to the mansion.

Henry Kyle purchased 110 Stone Canyon at Mrs. Newman-Albright's estate sale in May 1983. At that time Granada had been unoccupied and untended for over three years, the duration of Albright's will contest. The shrubbery had become so densely overgrown that most passersby were not even aware that it concealed the grandiose house. Yellowed newspapers lay on coffee tables and on bedroom dressers, the previous owner's clothes still hung in the closets, and everywhere there were boxes of 45s. On the Damilla label, they featured Alton Albright singing such non-hits as "My Little Black Book" and "I'm a Dreamer."

Such was the musty tableau that awaited Granada's new resident, who moved in on May 30, 1983, his sixtieth birthday. The date was an eerie choice: Both Kyle's father and his half brother had died of cancer before the age of sixty. Kyle believed he too might not live to see sixty-one.

During the course of spring, 1983, Kyle was joined at the mansion by his two sons, Henry Harrison Kyle, Jr., twenty, known as Ricky, and Scott Edwards Kyle, nineteen. They were the offspring of Kyle's marriage to Charlotte Edwards, a vivacious Georgia belle whom he had divorced in 1966. The boys were on-again, off-again college students—apparently neither was as desperate to succeed as their father had been. Kyle senior's fanatic drive extended also to physical fitness, as evidenced by the arrival at Granada in late June of Bobby Green, a tennis pro who had lived at Kyle's Dallas mansion since 1980. There he had been on twenty-four-hour call to the millionaire.

By July 22, the date Kyle was killed, only a few changes at the mansion showed that it was newly inhabited. Some of the boxes and furniture belonging to the previous owner had been sold at an estate auction; the rest was simply covered over with white sheets. The massive vegetation that had shrouded the house had been removed, but the plumbing and electricity were still not up to par. No structural work had been undertaken, despite the presence of a live-in carpenter named Rusty Dunn. Kyle had met Dunn too in Dallas, where he invited him to California to coordinate the renovation of Granada.

The new owner had not entirely neglected security, however.

Walking through the master bedroom in early July with his realtor, Kyle paused to pat the Smith & Wesson lying conspicuously on a nightstand next to his bed. "Ya know," he drawled, "I'm a big boy, and I'm an ex-marine, and I don't feel comfortable in this big house unless I have 'my friend' here with me. . . ."

Kyle also took the precaution of installing new locks on the entrances on Stone Canyon and Sunset. But he carelessly ignored the fact that the French doors in the dining room did not close properly, much less lock. They had to be propped closed with a chair. In a neighborhood where elaborate burglar-alarm systems, guard dogs, and electronic gates are the norm, the ridiculously run-down mansion, stripped of its protective disguise of foliage, was an invitation to a crime.

According to the initial statement Ricky Kyle made to the police, the tragic events of July 22 began at approximately 3:45 A.M., when he awoke to find towering over his bed his nude father, .357 Magnum in hand. Kyle senior said he heard suspicious noises outside the house. Ricky threw on a warm-up suit and followed his father to investigate.

The two men made their way silently from Rick's bedroom, just off the kitchen on the first floor, through the dark house to the loggia, which faced the courtyard on Stone Canyon Road. According to Ricky, his father burst through the door and stormed the courtyard. He searched in and around the cars parked in the circular drive but found nothing out of the ordinary. He then motioned to Rick to check the front of the house with him.

They reentered the mansion and approached the dining room. As they inched their way toward the French doors, which faced Sunset Boulevard, they both noticed that one door was ajar. According to Rick, he was three feet or so behind his father as they walked toward the open door.

Suddenly, Rick told police, his father turned toward him in slow motion. He heard a shot and saw Henry Kyle's figure brilliantly illuminated for an instant. He heard his father cry, "Oh, my God, no!" and saw his right arm come up to return fire. It wasn't until then, Rick related, that he "felt the presence" of someone else in the room. At that instant he ran for his life. Somewhere in the exchange of gunfire, he began to feel a dull pain in his arm, as if he'd been punched. He almost made it to the breakfast room when he heard two more shots, followed by breaking glass. "I was terrified," Rick told police a day later. "I thought I was dead. I thought Dad was dead."

He was half right.

When LAPD patrol officers arrived at 110 Stone Canyon at 4:02 A.M. in response to a call on their police radio, the house was dark and silent. Its owner lay dead, facedown on the dining-room floor.

Upstairs, the four other inhabitants of the mansion were huddled together in the darkness of what had once been the music room; Ricky Kyle was nursing a gunshot wound to his right elbow. He was attended by his brother, Scott; Rusty Dunn; and tennis pro Bobby Green, all of whom had been in second-floor bedrooms during the shooting.

By 8:00 A.M., the house and grounds were crawling with detectives, and there was some confusion as to who would handle the case. Around midmorning, Lieutenant Robert W. Grogan was officially designated lead investigator. In reality, he had assumed the role at 6:00 A.M., when he had arrived at the mansion and, in his words, "taken charge" of the crime scene.

Grogan is tall, balding, and moustachioed. With broad shoulders and barrel chest, he is a big bear hug of a man to whom taking charge comes naturally. Originally from Boston, he is a veteran of twenty-four years in the Los Angeles police force, seven of them in Robbery-Homicide. Grogan is no stranger to sensational crimes. He counts among his successes the Hillside Strangler investigation.

It is almost impossible not to like Grogan; he is the sort of man's man who can put his arm around a woman he's just met, call her "hon," and she'll seem to enjoy it. Appropriately enough, he is thoroughly enamored of Hollywood, and moonlighted for several years as a consultant for the television police series *T. J. Hooker*.

The day after the shooting, Grogan stated publicly that he was "still trying to put the pieces together"—meaning that details of the investigation were to remain confidential. This made for a curious sensationalism in the newspaper coverage of the case. Grogan, with his flair for the dramatic, would tell reporters in one breath that there were no suspects in the killing, then blurt out that "ten thousand people had a reason to shoot Henry Kyle."

This statement was picked up by the wire services, which ran the headline "TEN THOUSAND PEOPLE" HAD CAUSE TO KILL TEXAS MILLIONAIRE. The story underneath was embellished by several other of Grogan's colorful observations, portraying Kyle as a "ruthless businessman" with "many enemies."

The case made wonderful fodder for the tabloids. The *Midnight Globe* gave the Kyle killing full-page coverage beneath the headline WHO SHOT THIS J.R.? The comparison, inspired by Grogan's comments, made for a strange coincidence when it was discovered that actor Larry Hagman (who plays J. R. Ewing on the television series *Dallas*) was renting Kyle's Dallas mansion at the time of the shooting.

Despite his attention-getting commentary, Grogan was careful to allow few hard facts about the investigation to reach reporters. By the time of Henry Kyle's funeral, five days after the shooting, newspaper readers knew only that Kyle had been shot in the back at a range of four to six inches; his son Rick was wounded in the elbow during the fray and hospitalized briefly; a .357 Magnum was found next to Kyle's body; and in an upstairs bedroom a second gun was found, its owner and possible connection to the crime undisclosed. Finally, despite Grogan's "ten thousand people" with motives, no suspects had been named. A prowler was believed to be responsible.

2

AT KYLE'S FUNERAL, THE MORN-
ing of July 26, there was much speculation about the crime.
Those who came to pay tribute said they were in a state more of
shock than bereavement. Retired Major General Ralph Spanjer,
a devoted friend of Kyle's from their years together as marine
fighter pilots, referred to the mood at the funeral as "an excitement of something special or different . . . a kind of a tension."
Another guest said that everyone half expected Henry Kyle to
leap out of his coffin and yell "Surprise!" So vivid had been
Kyle's personality, so indelible the impression he had left on
people, that the mourners were having a difficult time accepting
the fact of his death, not to mention the way it had occurred.

"Henry was one of the few totally fearless people I ever
knew," Spanjer was heard to remark. "In flying, in World War
Two, in Korea . . . in just about anything." Spanjer shook his
head slowly, with disbelief.

The general's misgivings were echoed by nearly everyone at
the funeral. They could not believe that Kyle could have been
shot to death by a prowler in his own dining room. His circle of
male admirers seemed to take it as a personal affront.

These buddies were the kind of men who are pleased to be
called "macho." They gathered in small clusters at the funeral
parlor to debate Grogan's contention that a "business enemy"
had done Kyle in. Art Preston, an associate of Kyle's in the
"ole bidness" in Houston, insisted that Henry Kyle could have
been bested only in a surprise attack. "If somebody blind-sides

17

you . . ." he said hotly, "what the hell! You could get Wyatt Earp that way!"

Former Green Bay Packer Jerry Kramer, who had worked with Preston and Kyle on several coal-mining deals, was a bit more circumspect: "It's a puzzle," he said, turning over the facts in his mind. "I can't figure out what went on." He recalled that the two men had once taken their sons on a family holiday to Kentucky, where they stopped at a swimming hole. Kramer and the boys took turns swinging from a rope tied to an oak tree and flinging themselves, feetfirst, onto a floating inner tube. Kyle stood watching on the bank for perhaps twenty minutes. Then he walked over to the tree. "Henry was in his fifties then," Kramer recounted. "And he grabbed the rope and swung out. He let go, then he did a jackknife, and went head-first through the center of the tube. He didn't even touch the sides."

No, thought Kramer after pausing for reflection, this was not the ending he had envisioned for Henry Kyle. "It's surprising that a man with that coordination—that eye-hand ability and quickness—would get killed."

Henry Kyle's friends did have a point. Lawrence Cogan, the L.A. coroner who had examined Kyle's body for autopsy, proclaimed the millionaire to be a "remarkable" specimen. Detective Grogan noted admiringly that the sixty-year-old Kyle "had the body of a forty-year-old" at the time of his death. Even the investor's enemies conceded he was a "crack shot." How was it possible that a mere burglar could get the better of Henry Kyle?

Surrounded by his father's admirers, Ricky Kyle entered the funeral home in a daze. His brother, Scott, had arrived earlier. Though neither could boast their father's incredible physique, both boys possessed the same fine Aryan features that had made Kyle a much sought-after dinner companion. The two brothers, however, were as different as night and day.

Tall and blond, with winning ways, Scotty was often described as a "miniature Henry Kyle." "He walks, talks, acts and looks just like his daddy," one Kyle associate was fond of saying. Rick had dark hair, which he owed to his mother's side of the family, and was, at five feet ten, a full six inches shorter than his father had been. Yet it was Rick, who, in the words of one family friend, "wouldn't play any damn role for anybody"—the true Kyle legacy.

Rick was the focus of much attention at the funeral. As he made his way through the crowd to the chapel where his father's body lay, his manner was polite yet strangely detached. He avoided the other mourners' eyes, and the questions they held.

With Scott, Rick paused at the casket to say a final farewell to their father. Rick felt General Spanjer's arm rest on his shoulder in a gesture of fatherly support. As a fourteen-year-old, Rick had elected to attend the military academy where the retired general served as headmaster, and Spanjer's "deep and different bond" with his father was the stuff of family legend.

Recognizing this, he and Scott had invited the general to accompany them for the short, private memorial before the service. "If I can help you in any way, son, just let me know," the general said kindly.

When Spanjer leaned over the casket, he was distressed to see that his old buddy was not in uniform. Without hesitation, he removed the Marine Corps wings from the lapels of his own dress uniform and handed them to Rick, who pinned the insignia on his father. Then the boys cried. In that instant, General Spanjer later said, he knew they "understood the greatness of their dad."

But such moments of poignant dignity were to be the exception that day. Before long the guests' attention was diverted by a wholly unexpected development.

At first, Vicki Yang's presence at the funeral did not cause much of a stir. The diminutive, impeccably attired Oriental quietly took her place among the other mourners.

During a series of negotiations over an apartment project in Denton, Texas, in the spring of 1977, Yang had formed an unlikely business alliance with Henry Kyle. This had led to an even more improbable romance, which, however, was not classified information on the day of Kyle's funeral. A number of the entrepreneur's friends had met Vicki Yang, and it came as no surprise to them that she attended the funeral.

But as she circulated among the other mourners, Vicki produced a certificate recording that she and Henry had been married in a "confidential" ceremony in San Diego the previous November. No witnesses had been required, no blood tests had been administered, and the records were sealed to the public.

At first, her disclosure seemed like a bad joke, especially as she urged the other guests to examine the document for its authenticity.

Within minutes, the fur was flying.

"That's bull!" hissed Carolyn Shamis, a chic Dallas realtor who, in her eighteen-year acquaintance with Kyle had been variously his lover and real-estate agent. "Henry was single! Henry was *always* single." Vicki Yang's news enraged Shamis: "If Henry had wanted to announce that he was married, he wouldn't have cared if he'd married a dog!" she snickered. "If that's what he'd wanted to do, he'd put it in the papers. He'd *tell* everybody!"

Shamis, the owner of the agency that held the listing on Kyle's North Dallas mansion, had had ample opportunity to observe her friend's living arrangements, since the house had bounced on and off the market during the five years Kyle had owned it. "Vicki stayed at the house periodically," she grudgingly acknowledged. "A lot of people did that."

Carolyn Shamis might easily have been listed among them. Even though she officially stopped dating the millionaire the year they met, Kyle continued to invite her to stay at the mansion "whenever the mood struck him." In fact, though she was loath to admit it, Shamis had several things in common with Vicki Yang. Both were realtors; both were petite, comely brunettes; and both had "worshiped" Henry Kyle.

Unlike Vicki Yang, Shamis looked the part of the quintessential Dallas woman: carefully coiffed, expensively dressed, impressively bejeweled, and tastefully made up. Underneath her Max Factor exterior, however, the owner of Carolyn Shamis, Inc., was strictly business. Shamis herself denied a sexual relationship with Kyle. "I wasn't a romantic person with Henry," she liked to say. "You know, if I wanted to be romantic I could have been. It was just one of those things. You could or you couldn't. Better *not* to be."

Still, after she heard Vicki Yang's news, Shamis sniffed: "Henry asked me to go to Cannes with him in the month of May to see the U.S.A. Film Festival. So I would think he was single. He invited me to L.A. right before all this. I mean, he asked me *out*!"

Shamis found a sympathetic ear in her friend Helen Boehrns,

yet another real-estate agent associated with Henry Kyle. Boehrns had met Kyle in 1975 at the Preston Towers, where she had worked as a manicurist. They began dating shortly thereafter, and continued seeing each other up to and after Kyle's alleged marriage to Vicki in November 1982. According to Boehrns, Kyle never mentioned either the marriage or Vicki to her.

While Carolyn Shamis and Helen Boehrns compared notes, across the room a middle-aged woman named Barbara Bishop was having a similar conversation. Bishop, a Kansas wheat farmer, was regarded by Kyle's friends as a strong-willed woman with ''all kinds of goddam money'' and a fancy for Cadillacs. She had surfaced in Kyle's life in 1978.

Bishop and Kyle had met, appropriately enough, on an airplane. In Bishop, Kyle found a woman who could match his domineering temperament—and financial statements. Somewhere in the course of the relationship, the talk turned from money to marriage . . . and back to money again. The result was a prenuptial agreement, but the actual marriage never happened. This, however, did not appear to affect their friendship, and Bishop continued to give Kyle such presents as Cadillac El Dorados.

As she cast a wary eye on the crowd at Kyle's funeral, Barbara Bishop could not resist commenting. ''I told Henry we should have been married,'' she said ruefully. ''I told him to marry me. . . .''

In another corner of the funeral parlor, a tall, stylish blonde in her forties was talking in hushed tones. Her name was Ann Meidel. An interior designer from Palm Springs, she was also taken aback by the turn of events at the funeral.

Meidel was well known and well liked; she was regarded by Kyle's circle as a ''lovely person.'' As with Vicki Yang and Barbara Bishop, her fate had collided with the millionaire's in 1978.

Meidel's twenty-two-year-old son, Greg, was employed by Kyle. He introduced his mother to his boss one day as he drove them both to the airport. A few days later Ann Meidel received a telephone call from Saudi Arabia. Henry Kyle was on the line, and he asked her to redecorate his Dallas mansion. If Meidel suspected that her son's boss had ulterior motives, one look at his house convinced her otherwise. To her experienced eye, 9909 Preston Road was in need of a ''major overhaul''—the only work in progress was the construction of a tennis court in the backyard.

Meidel accepted the commission, and in July she took up residence in a guest room at Kyle's mansion. By September she and the millionaire had begun dating. Later that fall Meidel moved into the master suite. "She worked on that house night and day," recalled Ralph Spanjer. "It was a work of art. Everytime I stayed there they'd be tearing out a wall or something."

Sometime while Meidel was living at 9909 Preston Road, she accompanied Henry Kyle on a business trip to Cuernavaca, Mexico. When they returned, Meidel told Carolyn Shamis she and Kyle had been married. She began to receive mail at the house addressed to "Mrs. Henry Kyle," and would introduce herself as "Ann Kyle," even in the tycoon's presence. Kyle never contradicted her, nor did he deny the marriage; in fact, he never mentioned it at all. After this had gone on for about a year, Carolyn Shamis began to wonder—and worry. "I didn't know what Ann was doing," Shamis said later. "If she thought she could sue him. . . ."

One day at the house, Shamis confronted the millionaire. "Henry, what is going on? Are you married or aren't you?" she asked. Kyle just laughed. "Don't worry about it," he replied.

By the summer of 1980 Ann Meidel had moved back to Palm Springs and the whole affair blew over, just as Kyle had hinted to Carolyn Shamis it would.

At the funeral, after hearing Vicki Yang say she had secretly married Kyle, Meidel blurted out: "Well, *I* married him, too!"

Why, one might reasonably ask, were women so fascinated with Henry Kyle? No less an authority than Zsa Zsa Gabor, who dated the millionaire "quite a bit" in the mid-seventies, rated Henry Kyle a nine on a scale of one to ten. "He was competition for any man," she said of the suitor who gave her a diamond brooch and would send a hundred red roses to precede him each time he called at her Bel-Air hideaway.

In Hollywood, where most heroes are manufactured for the silver screen, Kyle was the genuine article. He was handsome—six feet four inches of barrel-chested splendor. He sported a luxurious mane of silver hair and had the sort of features described in women's novels as "ruggedly handsome."

"He was stunning," gushed his L.A. realtor Marjorie Helper, who sold him Granada. "The man was gorgeous. He was bright, fun, and a total gentleman."

Like his archetype, John Wayne, Kyle seemed to project an image of virile masculinity. "This is the type of man every woman wants," Gabor said simply. "A man who treats you like a woman. He reminded me of my first husband, Conrad Hilton. When he wanted something, he got it. Very no-nonsense man. Very Germanic." Yet Gabor was quick to point out that Kyle was no crude Texan. "He was an elegant, one-hundred-percent gentleman," she declared. "You could have taken him to the Queen of England's dinner party and he would have known how to behave." Indeed, his male friends invariably explained Kyle's behavior toward women with such adjectives as "gentlemanly," "unfailingly polite," and "well-mannered."

"To say that he was a male chauvinist would be the understatement of the century," said Los Angeles businessman Dick Traweek. "He went way overboard with respect for femininity—standing when a lady came to the table, and the whole Southern mentality. He was the personification of that."

Kyle's women were generally as glamorous and ostentatious as the Bentley in which he picked them up for dates. Though Carolyn Shamis staunchly denied that his head was turned by celebrities, the millionaire's choice of female companions suggests otherwise.

For a time, Kyle kept company with actress Pat Suzuki, best known for her performance in *Flower Drum Song*—in which she sang, appropriately enough, "I Enjoy Being a Girl." He also spent a celebrated evening with Natalie Wood. "Henry met Natalie at a party," recounted producer Harry Blum. "He walked over and said, 'You look miserable. Do you wanna go out to dinner and get out of here?'" According to Blum, "She said yes, and they went away together for the weekend."

Allan Conwill, a distinguished New York attorney who had known Kyle since Ricky was born, stood in awe of his old friend's success with women. "I was with him with a number of different ones," he extolled. "And they all seemed to like him. You know, a lot of men would like to *think* they're the greatest hot shots in the world. Well, few are. *I* would like to have had Henry's talents with women . . . if I hadn't been happily married for more than thirty years.''

There was one woman at the funeral everyone agreed actually *had* married Henry Kyle: Charlotte Edwards Kyle Whatley. She had met the Texan in 1959, when he was an aspiring real-estate investor and she was, by his proud description, ''the prettiest girl in town.'' Charlotte Whatley was then Charlotte Edwards, a dark-haired, bright-eyed nineteen-year-old college student with a Georgia peach of a smile. Henry Kyle first laid eyes on this vision of genteel womanhood one summer afternoon at the Castleview Country Club in Atlanta. He decided then and there that she was the girl for him. Charlotte hadn't even noticed the tall, thirty-six-year-old blond whose penetrating eyes had scrutinized her every move. The next day, she received a telephone call from Castleview's maître d'hôtel, who asked her to return to the club to go over a few last-minute details for a fund-raiser she was organizing. When she arrived, Henry Kyle was there instead of the maître d'.

Charlotte was impressed, and more than a little flattered. She was a mortician's daughter, raised in a small town in south Georgia. Men with Henry Kyle's unique brand of charm didn't walk into her life every day. An intense three-month courtship followed, and Charlotte Edwards was swept off her feet and married Kyle.

Two years later, Charlotte produced an heir: a ''beautiful child'' whom they named Henry Harrison Kyle, Jr. When Charlotte became pregnant again the following year, Kyle decided to move his wife and infant son to Mexico, where he was developing real-estate projects. ''We had Scott in Mexico City so we could buy land,'' Charlotte later said matter-of-factly. And, before he was a year old, Scott Edwards Kyle, as a Mexican citizen, had a house in his name in Acapulco, Mexico. Scotty's older brother, Henry junior, could speak Spanish before he could speak English. His Mexican playmates called him Enrique, which was shortened to Ricky, a nickname that stuck when the family left Mexico two years later.

By the mid-sixties, the marriage was deteriorating. Charlotte explained it this way: ''Henry was very domineering. Had to make the rules. And I'm a very independent person—was raised that way—and it just went against the grain. I cannot *stand* to be told what to do!''

The two divorced in 1966, and Charlotte returned to Georgia with the boys. She remarried some months later. Nevertheless, she remained on friendly terms with her ex-husband. "He'd call me after I was married and ask me, 'When are you gonna quit playing house?'" Charlotte reminisced after Kyle's death. "He just couldn't understand it. He didn't believe I'd give up that life: everything he could *give* me; every place he could *take* me. All those years," she reflected. "He held me. He'd never let go of me."

When she flew to Dallas to watch them bury her former husband, Charlotte Edwards Kyle Whatley was still a striking woman. At forty-three, she maintained a figure seldom seen on girls half her age, and she dressed to accentuate it. Her thick black hair was cut becomingly short, and her complexion was olive with a year-round Georgia tan that made her clear blue eyes sparkle.

At the funeral, when she was confronted with Vicki Yang's "confidential" marriage license, Charlotte remained unconvinced. "I know he would have told me," she insisted. "And he would have told the boys. Surely. But he didn't. He never did. He always denied it."

The other guests continued to wonder as well. Why had Vicki kept the marriage a secret for more than eight months? And why did she choose to reveal it for the first time at the funeral by waving a marriage certificate? The most obvious motive—money—did not seem to apply in Vicki's case.

Vicki had been born Vicki Heng-Fan into one of Taiwan's wealthiest families. She had married a Taiwanese man named John Yang and given birth to two children. However, in 1976, the year she turned thirty, Vicki's life took an unexpected turn. She decided to leave her husband and children and come to the United States to invest in real estate.

With her family money, Vicki did not seem to need a legacy from Henry Kyle—nor did she say she expected one. In a private moment with Charlotte, Vicki reassured the mother of Kyle's two sons that she wanted nothing from their father's estate: "I know it all belongs to the children," she said between outbursts of tears. "I know Henry meant it to be that way." Later, Charlotte expressed her doubts. "Y'all just wait," she told friends. "Just wait. When she gets over all this cryin' and carryin' on, there'll be a different situation."

In an interview with *Dallas Life* magazine a few months later,

25

Vicki told a reporter that the only reason she had announced the marriage that day was because she "wanted Henry's friends to know that he had had someone"; that she "couldn't stand the thought of letting him go as a solitary ghost." But this explanation did little to dispel the bizarre impression she had made at the funeral.

Another surprise guest at the funeral was Paula Holtzclaw. She was one of the first to learn that Kyle had been killed, when she received a predawn phone call at her home outside Atlanta on Friday, July 22, 1983. For two days the thirty-four-year-old housewife agonized over whether to bring her husband, their two small children, and her mother with her to the funeral—or simply to face the ordeal alone. After weighing the pros and cons, she decided that she should bring the children, but that her mother need not come. In retrospect, it was a wise decision. Considering the presence of Vicki and many other women with claims—real or imaginary—to Henry Kyle, Paula's mother, Rheba Rice, would have inspired intense curiosity. Rheba was the first, largely unknown, Mrs. Henry Kyle. Paula, their only child and Kyle's firstborn, knew that her own existence would come as a complete shock to most of her father's mourners. She did not relish the idea of causing a spectacle merely by appearing.

Paula's first recollection of her father was when he flew to Georgia to spend a few days with her dying grandfather. Paula was then in the fourth grade, and she didn't hear from him again for another three years. Then he called her mother's house "out of the blue" on Thanksgiving, 1961. "It shocked me," Paula said later. "He was doing business in Atlanta. I don't know why. He asked me if my mother was there and said, 'Who is this?' And I wasn't supposed to tell—you know how kids aren't supposed to say who they are on the phone?—and then he said, 'This is Henry Kyle and I wondered if you were Paula.'"

After this awkward encounter Kyle was able to see his daughter somewhat more frequently. He often visited in Atlanta then to oversee the development of several real-estate projects he had put together after his marriage to Charlotte Edwards in 1959. Strangely, he never introduced his daughter to his new wife. Paula found out about Charlotte by accident—she was visiting Kyle's farm in southern Georgia and saw bills addressed to Mrs. Henry Kyle. In 1965, the year she was sixteen, Paula met her half brothers, Ricky and Scott, for the first time. "The day stands out in my mind," she recalled. "I had just had adjustments on my braces and I was miserable."

Paula did not see her half brothers again until 1980. She went on to marry her high-school sweetheart, have two kids, and settle into a "quiet, boring, church-on-Sunday" existence in rural Georgia. "I never made a big to-do about my father," she said. "There are people, friends of mine, who never even knew my father had money, and certainly not about the movie-star thing."

When Paula remembers the last time she was together with her father, she cannot help but feel a twinge of sadness and regret. At the breakfast table at Paula's home in Georgia, Kyle had suddenly and uncharacteristically turned to his daughter and asked, with tears in his eyes, "Do you love me?" Paula was taken aback by this display of emotion and nodded yes. "I just needed to know," Kyle said solemnly. Then he took his daughter's hand and squeezed it, without further explaining.

The arrangements for Kyle's funeral largely fell on Paula's shoulders, since Rick and Scott were still too dazed by the shooting to offer much assistance. As she discussed the plans for the services with Charlotte and a few others, the name "Jackie Phillips" crept into the conversation in such a way that Paula became curious and asked who she was. It was only then that she discovered she had a twenty-eight-year-old half sister. Jackie, Paula learned, lived in Dallas and was the daughter of a former Texas beauty queen named Jackie Garrison, whom Kyle had married after he divorced Paula's mother and before he married Charlotte Edwards. Jackie Phillips had known Rick and Scott for several years, and Kyle had evidently told her about Paula.

In a strange way Paula was not surprised by the news. And it was somehow perversely appropriate that the funeral director was the first to point out Jackie to Paula. No one thought to extend the same courtesy to Jackie, who also had been overlooked when calls had been made to announce the particulars of the funeral—Jackie found out about them from the newspaper.

Jackie blustered over to her half brother Scott to ask if Paula had arrived yet. A woman by his side said blankly, "I'm Paula," as she looked into her half sister's eyes.

Like her father, but for different reasons, Jackie Phillips was usually the center of attention. At five feet eight, and one hundred fifteen pounds, Jackie had the lithe figure and angular proportions of a fashion model, which she had once been. Her face was oval and framed by thick light-blonde hair, which tumbled past her shoulders. Her ivory complexion was set off by a full, sensuous mouth—her most prominent feature, which she outlined with vivid red lipstick. Her piercing, green cat's eyes were a memento from her father, and like a cat, Jackie exuded a nervous energy that made her seem ready to pounce at any moment.

By nature intensely emotional, Jackie displayed at the funeral an outpouring of grief that contrasted sharply with her half sister's carefully subdued manner; for most of the day, Jackie clung pitifully to her boyfriend's arm, and dissolved into tears at the slightest provocation.

After Jackie's introduction to Paula, the news of the identities of the two young women spread through the funeral home like wildfire. The fact that Kyle had been married before he married Charlotte, and had two grown daughters, was like a bolt from the blue for the great majority of guests. "You could have blown me away!" exclaimed Jerry Kramer. "I knew Henry for over twenty years and only knew about the two boys." The few trusted friends who knew Jackie and Paula existed seldom, if ever, discussed the girls with the millionaire, by his unspoken directive. His sons were Kyle's obsession.

Charlotte Whatley understood the other mourners' bewilderment. Even she had not learned of Kyle's other marriages right away. On the eve of her own marriage to Kyle, "he told me about Jackie's mothuh and Jackie," Charlotte said later, in her languid Georgia drawl. "And the only reason he told me about them is because they'd lived in Dallas and he figured I'd probably hear about 'em, anyway. He said he didn't even know where Jackie was."

About a year later, Charlotte came across a photograph of a ten-year-old girl in Kyle's wallet. Since little Jackie was then under five, Charlotte asked her husband whose picture he was carrying in his billfold. Under the circumstances, he had little choice but to tell his wife that the child was Paula and that he had been married to her mother, Rheba Rice. Once again, he offered few details. It was as if they didn't exist.

* * *

Shortly after noon, the funeral party adjourned to Kyle's mansion on Preston Road, a few miles northeast of the Sparkman-Hillcrest Funeral Home.

Anyone familiar with Henry Kyle's admiration for Texas billionaire H. L. Hunt could see at a glance why he had been attracted to the property. The house—a big, white Southern colonial—was modeled after Hunt's famous Dallas mansion, itself a reproduction of Mount Vernon, George Washington's estate on the Potomac. Spread over eleven thousand square feet, the mansion featured fifty-six rooms; an elaborate indoor fountain, which served as the house's centerpiece; a Hollywood-style screening room; and exercise facilities that included a sauna, a steam room, and Nautilus equipment. On the grounds were a tennis court, a private lake and swimming pool, and also separate living quarters for the tennis pro, Bobby Green.

Despite impressive evidence to the contrary, Ann Meidel felt that her four years of interior-design work had been a waste. "Henry couldn't care less about this house," she said, somewhat bitterly.

When the guests arrived at the mansion for the reception, the liquor, in the words of one participant, "started flowing freely." The mourners congregated in small cliques. Some gossiped openly about Kyle's ostensible widow, past wives, and long-lost daughters, while others talked in low, conspiratorial tones with Bobby Green and carpenter Rusty Dunn—probing for details about what had happened on the night of the shooting.

Scott was teary-eyed and obviously distressed as he mingled with the other mourners. Ricky, on the other hand, kept his feelings to himself, and spent most of the afternoon at Charlotte's side. In the midst of all the hubbub, only one or two of the other guests saw him slip away from the reception with his sister Jackie and her boyfriend. "Everybody was trying to figure out who everybody was," Kyle's daughter Paula said later. "We were all interested in everybody else's position."

Later in the day, after the reception broke up, Jerry Kramer, producer Harry Blum, and several other friends of Kyle's gathered together to "sit around and tell 'Henry stories'" as a tribute to the man they had worshiped as a hero. "We started talking about Henry Kyle and what he had meant to us," remembered Bob Levinson, an East Coast executive on the board of Andrex Industries. Kyle had teasingly dubbed him the "New York Jewboy." "Then we all told what we knew about him, and learned things from each other. That's when we realized we didn't know Henry at all. Even though we considered ourselves close friends of his, after his death we found out he was an enigma.''

At one o'clock in the morning, Four Star board chairman David Charnay invited a select few of Kyle's closest cronies to his suite at the Anatole Hotel. ''Don't tell anyone you're coming,'' he said to each cryptically. When all had arrived that night, Charnay addressed the group.

''I guess I thought Henry Kyle was the finest man I ever knew,'' he began, somewhat theatrically. After spending a few minutes eulogizing his colleague, Charnay got to the point. ''Coming down the stairs naked with a gun . . .'' he said huffily, ''. . . that's just not Henry Kyle. Something's not right,'' he concluded. ''And I think we ought to get to the bottom of it.''

Listening to Charnay, George Shore, a business friend of Kyle's, could scarcely suppress a snicker. ''When he said, 'That's not Henry Kyle, comin' down the stairs naked with a gun,' '' Shore later recounted, ''I said to myself, 'Oh, yes, it is.' There's just one thing he missed: He'd be scratchin' his balls! *That* was Henry Kyle. He didn't give a shit.''

There was, however, one important point on which all present agreed. Henry Kyle's killer was on the loose, and they intended to act as a self-appointed star chamber to see justice was done—with or without the cooperation of the Los Angeles Police Department.

''I propose we secretly raise half a million dollars to find and convict Henry's killer,'' Charnay declared to the group.

3

DETECTIVE GROGAN OF THE LAPD
also took a personal interest in getting a murder conviction for
the Kyle shooting. His reasons were less obvious but equally
compelling.

Grogan's fascination with the case began the moment he
stepped into the dining room and sized up the situation. Here
was a crime at least as interesting as any for which he had served
as a consultant on *T. J. Hooker*. In addition, Kyle was a victim
with whom the manly detective could readily identify. Like Kyle,
Grogan was six feet four inches tall, with the same type of athletic, highly developed physique.

Grogan quickly came to understand that the millionaire had
been a hard-driving, competitive man's man in a world peopled
by celebrities, ex-jocks, and glamorous women. Grogan also had
an eye for a pretty girl, a fact that was well known in police
circles, as was his avid interest in football. It was only natural
that he would feel an affinity for Henry Kyle. Later in the investigation, he would say that he understood the victim "better
than anyone."

From the outset, Grogan made it clear to the millionaire's
macho friends that he was in charge of the case. When Kyle's
friends George Shore and later Jim Benford, both unaware of
what had happened, phoned the house the morning Kyle was
killed, Grogan answered the telephone. The detective immediately began pumping them for information. "Hey, wait a minute!" Benford finally said testily. "Why are you givin' *me* the

31

goddam third degree?!'' As the investigation progressed, though, Benford, Shore, and Kyle's other admirers came to admire Grogan. "I was impressed with the man," Benford later affirmed. To all outward appearances, Grogan initially conducted a routine, albeit high-profile, burglary-homicide investigation: Police photographers were called in to take pictures of the victim and the crime scene, while the coroner, criminologists, ballistics experts, print men, and six patrol officers swarmed over the house to attend to their respective tasks.

Around 8:00 A.M. on that first day, Grogan and Lieutenant Ron Lewis, an earlier arrival, requested the assistance of two other officers from the investigative division. After the arrival of sergeants Rick Jaques and Dave Crews, Grogan instructed the four principal detectives on the case to divvy up the rooms in the mansion and to look for any evidence that might be "pertinent and relevant.'' The search continued throughout most of the day. At ten o'clock, Detective Jaques visited Rick Kyle at his hospital bed in the UCLA Medical Center, where he was being prepared for surgery for the gunshot wound to his right elbow. While Jaques elicited Rick's eyewitness account of the shootings, Grogan discreetly questioned Vicki Yang, who was in California and whose status as Kyle's "secret wife" had already been ascertained. Later in the morning, the two detectives met at the West L.A. homicide office, where they tape-recorded interviews with the other residents of Granada: tennis pro Bobby Green, carpenter Rusty Dunn, and Scott Kyle. Late in the afternoon, Sergeant Rockwood questioned neighbors along Stone Canyon and Sunset Boulevard.

By 11:00 P.M. Friday, the police had released the crime scene, which they described to the press as a "potential burglary.''

In reality, he was later to say, Bob Grogan determined that Kyle's death was a premeditated murder ten minutes after he walked into the house. In addition, he was convinced he knew who had done it.

After viewing the body sprawled on the floor near the French doors, the detective scanned the dining room for any possible clues to the homicide. His eyes fell on an open briefcase, located at one end of the twelve-foot-long dining-room table. The briefcase belonged to Henry Kyle and contained business papers—various documents pertaining to Four Star, a passport, and a financial statement indicating Kyle's net worth to be $22,401,730.

Of greater interest to Grogan was the top document, a copy of the millionaire's last will and testament, dated June 13, 1978. It was typewritten on several pages of letter-sized paper. After closely examining the will, Grogan decided to keep its discovery a secret. He believed he had found both the motive and the murderer in the shooting of Henry Kyle, although he was not ready to make public his supposition or the reasons for it.

In a statement to the *Los Angeles Times* on July 23, the Special Crimes Division indicated it was operating on the assumption that an "intruder" had shot Henry and Ricky Kyle. Beyond that, the statement merely confirmed the discovery of Kyle's .357 Magnum and a second handgun located in "another room." "At this point we're still putting together the sequence leading to the murder," the police said obliquely.

Five days later, Henry Kyle's 1978 will was submitted for probate in Dallas. Arland Ward, a fellow Texan who had acted as the millionaire's accountant since 1973, was appointed independent executor and filed the necessary papers. According to the terms of the will, Kyle's personal effects were to be divided equally between Rick and Scott. The remainder of the assets in his multimillion-dollar estate had been bequeathed to a "family trust" established in his sons' behalf—with two exceptions: Paula Holtzclaw was to receive an inheritance of $100,000 from her father; her half sister, Jackie, was left $10,000. Vicki Yang's name was not mentioned, nor were the names of any other beneficiaries.

As the will was being offered for probate, Bob Grogan was behind the scenes following a hot lead, another piece of evidence he had slyly elected to keep secret.

Two weeks later, Grogan was sufficiently confident to leak a few well-chosen insinuations to the press. These cast the millionaire's death in a radically different light, and formed the basis of a feature story on Henry Kyle in the August 7 Sunday *Los Angeles Times*.

The *Times* quoted Grogan as saying that he was "investigating the possibility of a conspiracy to kill Henry Kyle." The detective offered few details to support his dramatic thesis, but explained he intended to present evidence to the district attorney's office later in the week.

He did, however, make public his discovery of the copy of the 1978 will in Kyle's briefcase, and hinted at its possible relevance to the case. "Henry Kyle was proposing significant changes in his will that legally were never filed," he said suggestively; according to Grogan, the millionaire had made substantial alterations to the document in pencil. He refused to elaborate on the changes, other than to suggest that Vicki Yang, whose "confidential" marriage to Kyle was now a matter of public record, "was not penciled in."

Grogan did confirm that Ricky Kyle had been administered a paraffin test to determine if he had fired a gun, but he would not disclose the results. When asked by reporters about the two guns found on the premises, the detective would neither confirm nor deny they had been fired, much less designate either one as the murder weapon. Even the coroner's report was ordered sealed.

However, Grogan could not resist once again embroidering his scant information with a few colorful and provocative comments. In his banter with the press, he waxed eloquent about the millionaire's perfectionist personality, and pointed out that Kyle frequently warned both his sons and Jackie that he would cut them out of his will if they did not live up to his high standards. "He was constantly threatening that he would take them out of the will," the detective told the *Times*. "He was constantly saying that to friends."

None of Kyle's children could be reached for comment. According to the *Times*, all but Paula Holtzclaw had hired Dallas criminal defense attorneys in the fifteen days since the shootings.

Grogan also cast suspicion on Vicki Yang. He characterized her wedding to the real-estate entrepreneur as a "marriage of convenience," orchestrated by Kyle to help defray the costs of a 1981 bankruptcy of one of his companies, and to enable him to purchase a controlling interest in Four Star International from David Charnay. "He was infatuated with Hollywood," the detective speculated. "He had a lot of big plans for Four Star." According to Grogan, Vicki's family was "one of the wealthiest in Taiwan," with holdings in radio and television stations and cement factories. "He got a commitment of $6 million from her and the family," the detective told the *Times*. In exchange, he continued, Kyle took out a million-dollar life-insurance policy, whose sole beneficiary was Vicki Yang.

4

HENRY KYLE BEGAN LIFE IN A
three-room, dirt-floor shack in the hills of Tennessee on May 30,
1923, the day Ernest (pronounced like Ernst, the German name
from which it was derived) and Della Kyle became the proud
parents of their only child together. Della Kyle, a kind,
straightforward "woman of the soil," had a son, Eugene, by an
earlier marriage. He was a quiet, slightly built youngster of six
when his mother had her second child. Della and Ernest called
the new baby Henry Harrison, but he came to be known as H.H.

A blond, all-American-looking kid, H.H. spent many an
afternoon at Stomp Creek, a fishing hole not far from his home.
Later, he loved to tell people about Stomp Creek. "We don't
know if it exists or if it was only in Henry's mind," Jerry Kramer once said with a laugh. "I never could find Stomp Creek. I
always accused him of making it up."

In reality, the millionaire's childhood was characterized by
relentless, grinding poverty. Charlotte Whatley found his childhood home inexpressibly depressing. "I couldn't believe that
Henry came from that sort of area. You'd never believe he could
come from those people." Most of the residents of Roane County
were either coal miners or farmers who could barely eke out an
existence. Many depended on hunting and fishing to survive.
Kyle's family was no different. His father, a big, strapping man
left partially disabled by World War I, found work where he
could as a sharecropper, grocer, and as an occasional peace officer, deputy, and jailer for the local sheriff.

As an adult, Henry Kyle seldom talked about his father, who died in 1959. He once described Ernest Kyle as a "strict taskmaster" and admitted he'd "experienced a razor strap" at his father's hand from boyhood to a "fairly advanced age."

In 1936, the year H.H. was twelve, Ernest contracted tuberculosis and was sent to a sanatorium in Asheville, North Carolina. Before he left, he passed the disease on to his son. For the next two years, H.H. was confined to the back bedroom of the three-room shack. He could do little but stare out the one small window and wonder whether he would live or die. Largely by sheer determination, Kyle believed, he conquered the disease. The experience changed the direction of his life. "I decided when I was laying flat on my back that if I ever got up I'd never live like that," he told his daughter Paula, ". . . and I'd never get down again."

The transformation was immediate and dramatic. As a freshman at Roane County High School, H.H. was tall, broadshouldered, and handsome, with curly blond hair—"big enough to eat hay," one friend said. He was popular, made excellent grades, and was the star of the football team.

He got a job lighting fires for Kingston shopkeepers and earned enough money to support himself and his parents until he graduated from high school in the spring of 1941. He scarcely had his diploma in hand before he left Kingston for good. He enrolled in summer classes at a state university several hours from Roane County. He called himself "Hank" Kyle, a new name for a new life.

In 1942, the summer after his freshman year in college, Hank felt it was not only his duty but an honor to enlist. It was, he was later to say, the best thing that ever happened to him.

In the Marine Corps, Hank Kyle felt he truly had found his place. In a marine uniform, everyone looked the same, regardless of who his daddy was or how he talked. Opportunity presented itself early and fortuitously, when, as a private, Kyle was selected to take part in a special marine training program for fighter pilots at the Corpus Christi Naval Air Station. "We were all standing in formation one day when our sergeant said he needed some volunteers," he was later to say. "I had no idea what I'd be training to do, but he said we'd be makin' more money and it was dangerous, so I stepped forward." (This story may be apocryphal. Kyle once told George Shore that his selection was random, he happened to be the "third marine on the left.")

As an aviator, Kyle was an ace; in battle, he was intrepid. "I've only met two or three totally fearless people," retired Major General Ralph Spanjer once said of his forty years with the marines, ". . . and Hank Kyle was one of them."

By the end of World War II, Kyle had earned a Distinguished Flying Cross, the marines' highest honor, for heroism in the battle of Okinawa. He would earn a second during his voluntary enlistment in the Korean War, during which he was shot down behind enemy lines. His friend Allan Conwill said of the incident, "I remember him telling me that when they crashlanded (the engine was shot out), neither of them was hurt. They got out, and the gunner carried everything in sight along with him. But Henry told him to take it off. He told him to take no weapons, because they were going to have to move fast. That's what they did."

Over the years, the story of Kyle's Korean War experience was glorified in the retelling, by his friends if not by himself. Peter Rachtman recounted that Kyle had wandered through the steaming jungle for twenty-six days.

Kyle loved the corps passionately. Even later, as a private citizen, he approached life as a professional marine, adhering to the values of hard work, discipline, and respect for authority. The President of the United States was always the "Commander-in-Chief" to Kyle, whose most impassioned conversational topics were the national defense and the state of U.S. military preparedness.

When he retired as a colonel after the Korean War, Kyle headed the Dallas reserve squad. A great source of pride was a course he taught at the war college in Washington, D.C.; a great regret was that he never made general, despite, in Spanjer's words, the "astronomical" odds against it for a marine in reserve status.

When Hank Kyle returned to Roane County at the close of World War II, he was given a hero's welcome, complete with parades and a "Henry Kyle Day." Kingston's native son had no intention of resting on his laurels as a war hero, however. He was eager to complete his college education, and this time around he resolved to do it right.

Hank went to the library and gathered together every book

he could find on the major universities of the United States. Based on his ensuing survey, he selected Southern Methodist University in Dallas, Texas. At first glance, it seems a curious choice. SMU, sneeringly referred to as "Smyoo" by students at the less expensive, Texas state-supported universities, is the favorite choice of moneyed Texans, particularly Dallasites. They tend to view it as an exclusive club in which membership is passed down from one generation to the next. "You really shouldn't go to SMU unless your parents are rich," Jim Benford would later offer as a piece of Texas wisdom. "But hell, Henry's didn't even have outdoor plumbing till after the war!"

Actually, that was the very reasoning that had led Hank to choose the school; according to his research, SMU had one of the wealthiest student bodies of any college campus in the country. Why take classes with coal miners' daughters when you could be hobnobbing with corporate presidents' sons? Thanks to the G.I. Bill, SMU's stiff tuition was within his reach.

By his second year, Hank had accumulated enough credits to earn his bachelor's degree in business administration. He decided to enter law school, where he planned "to do extremely well and make a lot of money." When Hank started his third year at SMU Law School, his friend and fraternity brother Tom Rippey asked him to handle his business affairs, since Rippey was going off to join the marines. It was the break Kyle had been hoping for.

While still in college, Rippey had inherited a substantial sum of money, and Kyle would now help him invest it. From their first "joint" enterprise—an oil-treating plant in the small town of Kilgore, Texas—Hank was hooked. Years later, he would compare the excitement he got from making deals to a schoolboy's thrill at winning a state championship. To Kyle, business was sport, a competition, where good deals were "winners"; profit was "hitting a home run."

When Tom went overseas, Hank took over the day-to-day operations of the oil-treatment plant and still maintained his regular course load of law classes. He excelled at both. On June 3, 1950, he received his Bachelor of Business Law degree from Southern Methodist University.

Although he wasn't born in Texas, Henry Harrison Kyle was born to be a Texan. His raw ambition, his rugged physique, his exaggerated drawl, and the cowboy boots that would become his trademark were all stereotypically Texan.

When Kyle put out his shingle as a newly licensed attorney in 1950, his goal was nothing less than to "amass an empire." "Henry admired people who made a lot of money," Tom Rippey would later say of him, "but he didn't pattern himself after anybody. Henry was Henry. That was the whole deal. He thought he was smarter than everyone."

At first, Hank had to accept any law business that came his way. Wayne Freeland, a classmate from SMU who worked down the street in the promotion department at *Time*, would later say laughingly that Kyle's practice consisted of "busting traffic tickets, representing drunks, and bailing whores out of jail."

To help support his struggling law practice, Kyle opened an insurance business on the side. "He worked his fanny off," Freeland recalled. "Everybody around him was makin' it and he wasn't." In time, Kyle's fortunes started to improve, mostly due to a loan from Tom Rippey. Hank used the money to purchase a couple of modest houses as investment property in a newly developed section of Dallas. Before long his law practice was taking a backseat to his other ventures. "Henry hated practicing law," one colleague would later say. "He couldn't sit still long enough to write a contract. He was too impatient."

In 1951, Irwin Scott, another acquaintance from SMU, who had a degree in geology, approached Kyle with a proposition to enter the uranium business. For his part, Kyle would buy up uranium leases and quickly sell them for a profit. For the next five years, he and Scott (the "Scotty" after whom he would name his second son) maintained a loose, amicable, occasionally profitable partnership. This was supplemented, in Kyle's case, by a few miscellaneous real-estate ventures—a small apartment house here, a share in a restaurant there. "He liked flexibility and latitude," observed a marine buddy who worked with him during this period. "He liked his money loose."

By the mid-fifties, operating in this fashion, Hank was on his way. In 1955, he purchased his first new car—a shiny Cadillac convertible, the time-honored status symbol of Texas rich. Around the same time, he began to introduce himself as "Henry" Kyle.

In 1957, the year he turned thirty-four, Henry and a couple of his former fraternity brothers hit upon the formula that would put him on the road to his first million: a new concept in the development of country clubs. They proposed building much larger clubs, with capacities for a thousand or more members, in lieu of the small, exclusive country clubs that were then the norm. This new set-up, they reasoned, would allow the developer to generate enough income from membership dues to support the venture. At the same time he could use the property on the periphery to build homes, thereby adding profit to profit. The idea seemed like pure gold to Henry, who persuaded his old standby Tom Rippey to back him. The result was the Castleview Country Club in Atlanta, Kyle's first "important money."

The following year, Kyle met a young man named Don Tanner, who was as easygoing as Henry was intense. "We got along right away," Tanner said of his first encounter with Kyle. Within two years Kyle and Tanner had put the finishing touches on a country club in Kansas City. It would serve as the flagship venture in a fifteen-year association consisting of, in Tanner's words, "twelve straight winners."

There were investments in Mexican golf courses, nightclubs (including the famed Whiskey-à-Go-Go in Atlanta), health clubs, and a "crazy idea" Henry dreamed up with Tanner and Tanner's friend George Shore to open a ski resort in Kansas City by using manufactured snow. Kyle had read in *Reader's Digest* about the snow-making process, and he flew to Gatlinburg, Tennessee, to see a resort that featured the artificial snow, returning to Kansas City with great enthusiasm. "Hell, let's do it!" he prodded Tanner and Shore. "We had a machine that combined air and water and turned it into crystal," Shore said later, chuckling at the memory of Henry's harebrained scheme. "Right in the middle of Kansas City, Missouri! It was absolutely insane!" Incredibly, the three turned a profit their first year, then bailed out just as the novelty wore off.

In addition to his far-flung ventures with Don Tanner during the sixties and early seventies, Kyle invested heavily in construction companies, shopping centers, condominiums, and such restaurants as Don the Beachcomber, in addition to his new investments in Hollywood. In 1961 he spent the year working as a lawyer-investigator for the SEC so he could learn its inner workings.

"What he enjoyed more than anything in the world was business," said a Texas friend, of Henry Kyle. "Putting together deals; structuring the management of a concern; working stockholders; things like that. He enjoyed the complexities of big business probably more than anybody I've ever seen."

Much of Kyle's success could be attributed to his sheer industry. He worked, quite simply, day and night. He wrote his own contracts, kept his own books ("He worked all weekend on his taxes," Tom Rippey remembered. "If *he* did it, it was done right.") and generally acted as his own secretary—a practical necessity, since amazingly, he did not use an office after he gave up his first cramped quarters in the Mercantile Bank Building. In Dallas, he would occasionally use his stockbroker's small office. When the broker went out of business in 1969, Kyle decided on impulse to take over the suite and everything in it. Thus he acquired the first secretary of his career.

The Jetco affair was, in Jim Benford's description, a "long story." The oil pipeline equipment company was started by a blacksmith in 1943. When the blacksmith's heirs needed more money to finance the company, they sold it to Kyle "for nothin'." Its new owner had big plans for Jetco. Within six months, Kyle had expanded the company significantly. He could talk ditches, drills, and trenches with the crustiest oil men. He would show up at the Jetco offices every day and kept track of the company down to the last metal tooth.

Kyle loved wheeling and dealing on behalf of his pet company with business trips to Saudi Arabia and the Middle East. In the late 1970s, he negotiated a dream deal with the Shah of Iran, who agreed to purchase an enormous order of heavy equipment from Jetco. Returning to the States, Kyle was euphoric, filled with new expectations for the company. He hoped soon to have enough clout in the oil community to win a seat on the board of Allied Bancshares of Texas, a dream Kyle had nursed since his SMU days.

Unfortunately, world oil prices went down, and Jetco became hopelessly mired in the confusion created by the Iranian revolution. When the Ayatollah came to power, his government refused to pay for the equipment that the Shah had ordered. Thus Kyle was left several hundred thousand dollars short. The resulting bankruptcy in 1981 was, in Benford's words, "quite a personal thing" for Henry Kyle. The man hated to lose.

By the terms of the bankruptcy action, Jetco's assets were sold to a Forth Worth company called Pengo Industries. In exchange, Kyle agreed to purchase 238,000 shares of stock in the new company. Shortly after that transaction, Pengo's stock took a dramatic plunge, causing Kyle to lose more than a million dollars on paper. As a final, humiliating blow, he learned that the stock was unregistered, which meant he could not sell it on the open market. "He was going to sue me," said Harold Owen, Pengo's chairman of the board. "He said, 'Surely you must have known.' But I told him the whole industry was going down."

Jim Benford later suggested that the Jetco affair was more a personal defeat for Kyle than a business catastrophe. Still, Kyle told Vicki Yang that it "could wipe him out."

"From the beginning to the end, I never knew what his financial statement was," she told a Dallas newspaper. She adamantly denied Grogan's contention that Henry had gotten a "commitment" of six million dollars from her family as a dowry. Whatever its significance, clearly the Jetco affair was crucial in Kyle's life, and it was during this time that he "married" Vicki Yang.

Vicki said she first met Kyle in 1978, when he was in Denton, Texas, to sign the papers on an apartment project she had purchased from him. "He was very down-to-earth for a rich man." Vicki was then thirty-two and had been separated from her husband and two small children for almost two years. "I just thought there's got to be something more in life than just sitting around," she said, explaining her decision to leave Taiwan. Kyle was then fifty-five. "He was youthful," she was quick to point out. "You see people with your feelings, your heart; you don't see them with your eyes. He was more like a man in his thirties than in his fifties."

When they had completed their business, Kyle invited his attractive new associate to spend a few days in Texas as his guest. "I don't want to be here for your convenience," she replied. "If you really want to see me, you can come to San Diego." Both intrigued and challenged, Kyle telephoned Vicki as soon as she got back to her home in California, and again a few days later. In the second call, he informed her he was flying out to see her. "Then I became nervous," she told her Dallas interviewers. "I want you so badly," Kyle told her when he arrived in San Diego. "That's why I flew thousands of miles to be here. But I don't want you unless you love me."

In the coming months, Kyle regularly visited Vicki's San Diego condominium for weekends she described as "idyllic":

They watched sunsets and walked along the beach, while Henry told her about his humble origins. Because Vicki was still married to John Yang, who was in Taiwan with her son and daughter, she told Henry she couldn't fall in love with him. "Yes, you will!" he supposedly responded with determination.

"In time you will. I'll spoil you rotten."

As Vicki explained it, she tried to "slow him down"; to convince Kyle there was more to life than business.

"He said I brought him inner peace," she recalled.

Charlotte Whatley took a more jaded view. "I can see why he adored havin' Vicki around . . . for a while. She waited on him hand and foot, and the man is the king, and he liked that. She would rub his feet for hours and hours and hours. She was the little servant."

New York attorney Allan Conwill took a moderate position. "I do know he was extremely fond of Vicki," he said carefully. "They enjoyed each other's company. Henry was something of a health buff," he added significantly, "and she was, too."

The fact that Vicki shared Kyle's interest in nutrition made their friendship easier to comprehend for some. Tales of the millionaire's fanatic interests in health food and fitness were legion. As a young man, he had banished such processed foods as white bread from his diet and he refused to let his daughter Paula use sugar in her tea. "He would get up," she remembered, "—and this was way back in the early sixties, before jogging was a part of our vernacular—and run around golf courses. He did all that before it was popular."

"Henry believed in a disciplined mind and a disciplined body," observed Jerry Kramer. "The relationship between Henry and I was a bit of a macho thing," Kramer admitted. "He was always tellin' me how good he was, and how he could beat me at this and that."

In his quest for physical and mental perfection, Kyle "didn't do much of *anything* to enjoy himself!" another friend, Jim Benford, noted wryly.

Vicki gave Kyle books on Eastern philosophy, she said, thereby hoping to encourage a sense of spirituality and contentment to offset his extraordinary drive. "He was really driven all the time," his daughter Paula said of him. "Always fighting. He was just learning as he got older to stop and smell the roses—that he didn't have to fight all the time."

Vicki characterized her five-year relationship with Henry as an ongoing struggle for her—in order to avoid detection by her parents, particularly her father, who would not approve because Kyle was Caucasian. She told a reporter with *Dallas Life* that her father was "already upset with her for having left her family and her native country."

By Vicki's account, she and Kyle discussed marriage often in the course of their romance, but it was she, not Henry, who balked. "My parents would be unalterably opposed to a marriage on racial grounds," she told the *Times-Herald*.

Conspicuously missing from Vicki's rendition of her courtship with Henry, of course, were the other women concurrently in his life. "All the beautiful and glamorous women did not fulfill what he really needed inside," she explained. "He kept looking and searching. I think there were so many marriages because he didn't really know what he wanted."

The turning point in their relationship came in 1982, the year Vicki's twelve-year-old son and ten-year-old daughter arrived in the United States from Taiwan, and the year after the bankruptcy of Jetco. According to Vicki, her children's decision to stay in the United States forced her to choose between marrying Henry and leaving him. "I didn't want the kids to think their mother lived with a man for years without being married," she said.

According to Vicki, Henry's decision to purchase Granada and the move to California came about because she "preferred California to Texas." She described his takeover of Four Star as a "semiretirement," and said that Henry had promised her he would cut back on his schedule and work at home. During their brief marriage, she urged him to "return to society some of the bounty it granted him." They spoke of endowing an orphanage.

This tale of romantic bliss elicited skepticism from many of Kyle's friends, especially in the light of Vicki's unorthodox behavior after the funeral. One of the first to encounter Vicki then was Charlotte Whatley, who had flown to Los Angeles from Georgia to be with her sons, Rick and Scott. Instead, she found herself consoling Vicki.

"I kept tellin' her—I said, 'Vicki, this is very hard on all of us. Very hard,' I said. 'Especially on the kids. You know, I got a boy in the hospital—layin' in the hospital, right now.' And I said, 'He saw his father *killed*.' And I said, 'We don't need this. We don't need this.'

"But she said, 'I feel so *close* to you. And I love you, because Henry loved you so much, and I feel like you are a part of him.' And I thought, 'Oh, let's get the violins out!' "

Even the redoubtable Charlotte was taken aback, however, when Vicki added, in all earnestness, "If Henry comes to you, tell him I need to talk to him. I *know* he's gonna come to you. If he does, I've *got* to talk to him. . . ."

Whatley later confided to a reporter: "She believes that the spirit stays in the body for fifty-six hours, or somethin' like that, and that we should all go down to the morgue and talk to him . . . before his spirit left. She begged us! You know, I'm a very strong person, and I went in there, just to be nice. And I told her, I said, 'Vicki, there is no sense in all this. There's no sense in it. We don't *do* these kind of things. . . .' She's Buddhist, and at first I was a little bit concerned, because she's the type that believes that when you die, you come back as an *animal* or somethin'!"

Many of Kyle's friends were appalled when they learned Vicki had taken "one last photograph" of Kyle at the L.A. County morgue and had insisted on sleeping next to his coffin at the Dallas funeral parlor. "She was really disturbed" was Jim Benford's assessment. "Hell, she called me up one night . . . and she was just crazy with grief!"

Such characterizations of Vicki were further perpetuated by her decision after the funeral to spend two weeks of "meditation and prayer" at a Buddhist monastery outside San Francisco, in order to determine "what she had done wrong." ("She invited *me* to go!" Charlotte Whatley fairly whooped.)

Vicki came to be labeled "Henry Kyle's Yoko Ono" by some members of the Dallas press.

But Marj Helper, the Los Angeles realtor who had sold Kyle the house at 110 Stone Canyon, insisted: "You've never seen two people more in love. Henry was crazy mad about Vicki."

On the other hand, Charlotte Whatley vehemently stated: "I'll never buy that marriage. That was the whole deal, goin' to California, was to get rid of her. Get her to *move out*. She had moved into the house in Dallas, and that was the way to get her out. He never intended to leave Dallas."

"I don't buy the fact that Henry was infatuated with Hollywood at all," Kyle's friend Allan Conwill stated flatly. "He told me he always planned to return to Dallas and use Dallas as his headquarters. He thought Four Star was a great investment and a fine opportunity, but he wasn't about to give up Dallas . . . and I think I would have known.''

The fact that Vicki had a confidential marriage license to substantiate her status as Henry Kyle's widow did little to dissuade the skeptics, particularly Charlotte. She considered the document as worthless as the apparently bogus Mexican license her former husband had used to "marry" Ann Meidel, and possibly one or two others. "Ann doesn't believe Henry was married to Vicki, either," Charlotte said. "*Nobody* does. None of the attorneys, none of Henry's closest friends. Nobody. He never told any of them that he was married to her. And I do believe he would have told a few. *Some* of them. I'm sure he would have.''

Tom Rippey didn't even try to figure it out. Over the years, Tom was one of the few to have seen the complete succession of Kyle wives and girlfriends. According to Rippey, Kyle told him in the fall of 1982: "Y'know, Tom, I've been thinkin' about this a lot, and I decided that there's one thing I've learned in my life." "What's that?" his friend asked. "I should never be married.''

5

By MID-AUGUST 1983, A LITTLE less than a week after he had leaked his conspiracy theory to the *Los Angeles Times*, Lieutenant Bob Grogan was satisfied that he had tied up the loose ends of his investigation and was ready to let the other shoe drop.

He went to see Deputy District Attorney Lewis Watnick. Watnick, a wiry, bookish-looking man of fifty-five, had thinning gray-brown hair, horn-rimmed glasses, and a modest moustache. He listened to Grogan's dramatic, booming voice, with its trace of a Boston accent, and by the end of the presentation he was as certain as Grogan that he could get an indictment.

With his soft, gravelly, occasionally inaudible voice and low-key manner, Lew Watnick hardly seemed the type to want to take on a front-page homicide. But Watnick indeed decided to handle the plum case himself rather than assign it to one of the junior DAs.

On Thursday, August 18, Watnick asked the Los Angeles County Grand Jury to officially investigate the murder of Henry Harrison Kyle. To the press he said cryptically: "It's not like a case where we have a targeted defendant. We just want to let the grand jurors know what we have and let them give us direction." He told reporters who asked about the conspiracy theory that he had no plans to subpoena any members of Kyle's immediate family, and that no date had been set for the grand jury inquiry.

Within a few weeks, it became clear that Watnick, like his

47

chief investigator, was not being entirely candid with the press. Hours after he had made his statement to the *Times*, the assistant DA requested that Henry Kyle's younger daughter, Jackie Phillips, and her boyfriend, Dallas heir Henry Miller III appear in Los Angeles at 9:00 A.M. on August 30 to testify before a secret session of the county grand jury.

As he took the stand as the state's first witness that Tuesday morning, Robert Grogan wore self-assurance like a new Sunday suit. Now he could reveal the prize piece of evidence he'd been holding back, the evidence he was confident would put his suspect behind bars.

Grogan wasted no time in getting to the point. First, he described for the twenty-three grand jurors the heavy sooting ("or tattooing, which we would call it") that surrounded the fatal gunshot wound on Henry Kyle's upper torso—"indicating to me," he said with authority, "that [it] was fired extremely close to the body." Then he went on to identify the six-shot, .357-caliber Smith & Wesson (bearing no fingerprints) that had been found in the dining room next to Kyle's corpse. The revolver, he noted, had belonged to the millionaire for a "long time." Another gun, a .38-caliber two-inch blue-steel Smith & Wesson, had been located elsewhere in the house, and was owned by "one of the residents." It was dismissed as inconsequential.

Finally, the detective produced a police photograph of the east side of the mansion at 110 Stone Canyon. It showed a fence that ran between Granada and the house next door to the east on Sunset Boulevard. There, he told grand jurors, in the ivy, a police recruit had discovered the gun that had been used to kill Henry Kyle: a .38-caliber two-inch blue-steel Rohm revolver with brown grips. The Rohm, which also revealed no fingerprints, was recovered the day of the shootings. The media had not been informed of the discovery, Grogan explained to the grand jury, so that he could investigate the ownership of the gun without alerting the killer.

Grogan and his team of detectives had traced the suspected murder weapon to its original point of manufacture in Rohm, Germany. From there, they learned, it had been shipped to Preston Firearms in Dallas, Texas, in April 1968, where it was sold wholesale to another dealer, then purchased by Joe L. Massie, a prominent Dallasite. Massie held on to the weapon until 1969, when he gave it to his stepson, William Barnes III, also of Dallas. Sometime the following year, Barnes presented the gun to *his* son, William IV, known as Quint, who in 1983 was an anesthesiology intern in his thirties.

Grogan had flown to Dallas to question Quint Barnes, who told him that his father had given him the Rohm in 1970 for personal protection. Barnes had kept the gun in his car until late August 1982, when he noticed that it was missing. There was one other significant detail: From June 1982 through February 1983, Quint Barnes had dated a Dallas model named Jackie Lynn Phillips.

Phillips, as the grand jurors already knew, was sitting in the courtroom with her current boyfriend, Henry Miller III. Both were awaiting their turns to testify in the proceedings. Their testimony, Bob Grogan knew, would turn the case into a sensation.

Before Watnick brought Grogan's two star witnesses from Dallas to the stand, he trotted out Deputy Medical Examiner Joseph Lawrence Cogan, the pathologist who had performed the autopsy on Kyle. Until now, the official cause of death had itself been something of a mystery, since the coroner's report had been ordered sealed by Grogan the day after the slaying. Cogan told the grand jury that Henry Kyle expired from a gunshot wound caused by a bullet that had entered his back and exited through his chest. Based on the amount of tattooing and powder marks around the entrance wound, he estimated that the shot was fired at a range of one to five inches from the millionaire's back. As the bullet tore through Kyle's body, it pierced the millionaire's lungs, and left behind what Cogan referred to as an "enormous" amount of gunshot residue.

Watnick's next, eagerly awaited witness was Henry S. Miller III, a name found (minus the "III") on FOR SALE signs on front lawns across the country. The Henry S. Miller Company, which Henry's father owned, was the third-largest real-estate organization in the world. Thus thirty-six-year-old Henry III was the son of one of Dallas's richest and most prominent families, the kind to which Henry Kyle had aspired for most of his life.

After directing the tall, blond Miller to the stand, Watnick identified his witness to the assembled jurors as Jackie Phillips's "fiancé." Then, without further preliminaries, he focused on a single afternoon in Miller's life, the afternoon of Henry Kyle's funeral.

On that day, Miller told the grand jurors, he had attended

the services for Kyle in Dallas in the company of Jackie. Afterward, he said, the two of them went on to the reception at 9909 Preston Road, where Miller "expressed sympathies and that kind of thing" to Jackie's brother Rick. Around midafternoon, Miller continued, Rick approached him and Jackie and said, "I've got to talk to both of you. I really need to get away from here. When can you leave and take me with you?"

Soon thereafter, the three left the reception and drove to Miller's house on Rowland Street, where, according to Miller, Ricky suddenly blurted, "I have to tell both of you. I shot him." Turning to Jackie, he repeated, "I shot our father."

"Did he tell you the circumstances?" Watnick queried.

"He said that he and Scotty, his brother, had planned it for quite some time," Miller responded evenly, "and that he woke his father in the middle of the night and said that he heard a prowler or intruder, and his father kept a gun by his bed. And his father got his gun, and they patrolled the house, went outside, looked around, and were satisfied that there was no one else on the grounds. And that when Mr. Kyle lowered his gun, or was not so ready for an intruder, that he shot him and hit him once and missed, I guess, on the second shot. And that Mr. Kyle on his way down got off three or four rounds and shot him through the elbow."

"Did Rick say what he did then?" Watnick continued.

"Yes," Miller told the DA. "He said that he ran outside the house around by the barbecue pit and threw the gun across some shrubs or something into the neighbor's yard, and asked Jackie and I to go and retrieve the murder weapon. He drew a map on my stationery and handed it to me."

Watnick produced a piece of blue stationery with a torn corner, on which someone had drawn a crude map with two parallel lines to indicate SUNSET [Boulevard] facing a rectangle marked HENRY'S HOUSE. A longer, skinny rectangle was labeled simply HOUSE (the neighbor to the east on Sunset Boulevard), a square signified CAR COVER, a round grid denoted BBQ, and a long line of XXXXs represented the "shrubs" to which Miller had referred in his testimony. A star on the neighbor's side of the shrubbery indicated where Ricky had supposedly said he'd thrown the gun.

After identifying the map as the one Rick drew for him, Miller explained the torn corner: "Well, it was my stationery

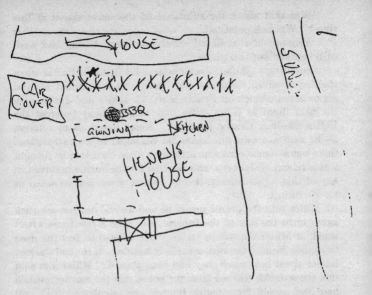

and had my name at the top and I didn't want it on there. I personally tore it off." Fingering the map, he added, "I was very tempted to throw this away, too."

Continuing his account of Rick's alleged confession, Miller stated: "[Rick] said that [the gun] was given to him by his brother, Scotty, and that Scotty told him that the gun was untraceable because it had been shipped from Germany—in pieces, or something like this. It didn't make much sense. . . . He said that he was wearing Playtex rubber gloves so that he would not leave fingerprints."

"Let me go back," Watnick interrupted. "Was this about the substance of the conversation, if you can recall?"

"Um, yes," Miller said carefully. "I mean, Jackie and I hugged him and we kind of cried together and we said we couldn't condone it but we understood, because of all of—because he had been a very, very abused child. I mean very abused."

"Was there anything said about possibly going back to California to retrieve the gun at that time?" the DA asked.

"He asked us to," Miller replied. "And we wouldn't have any part of that."

"Was that about the substance of the conversation at this time?" Watnick persisted.

"Yes, except that he said that, you know, Scotty had basically worked out this plan. . . ."

According to Miller, Jackie was at his house in Dallas when she first received word that her father had been killed, around six or seven o'clock on Friday, July 22. Miller and Jackie took the next flight to L.A., where they visited Ricky twice at the UCLA Medical Center Hospital. "Ricky asked us to retrieve a—he said a brown briefcase that belonged to his father, that there was a—some card with someone's name on it that he thought was a friend of Jackie's, and he didn't want Jackie involved in any of this, or something. It didn't make sense. But he asked us to. We didn't."

Miller told the grand jurors he and Jackie did not see Rick again until the day of the funeral, and then a few times afterward, at Miller's house in Dallas. "He seemed to feel the need to confide in us," the real-estate heir testified. "[He and Jackie] talked about how much they had been abused." Miller also said that when Jackie learned from the police that the murder weapon had been stolen from Quint Barnes, she telephoned Rick and said, "How dare you steal a gun from my friend and involve one of my very good friends in this sordid business?"

"Did Ricky say anything when she said this?" Watnick queried.

"He said that Scotty—he said that Scotty had stolen the gun from Quint Barnes and that he didn't know it prior to that time," Miller replied, then added, "Ricky also told us that Scott would admit it to the police that he had stolen the gun."

Asked to characterize Ricky Kyle's emotional state at his father's funeral, Miller said without hesitation: "Crying . . . I'm not qualified to describe whether or not there was remorse or what, but he was crying."

In his final question to Henry Miller, Watnick asked: "Did Ricky ever tell you during this conversation why he happened to pick this particular time?"

"Yes," Miller responded. "He said he couldn't—he said he just couldn't take it anymore, that he was afraid, desperately afraid, and he just couldn't take another beating."

As the state's next and last witness, Jackie Phillips followed her boyfriend to the stand, where all eyes followed her. Alternating between hysteria and a total collapse, the blond former model often lost her train of thought in midsentence. Recognizing his witness's shaky emotional state, the DA limited his queries to the bare essentials. He established, first, that she had known Quint Barnes for eighteen years; next, that she and Henry Miller had made their statements about Ricky to the police on August 10 at the home of Frank Wright, the Dallas attorney who represented both of them. Then he asked her what happened on the day of her father's funeral.

"Ricky asked me to take him with me when we left the reception. He just wanted to get away for a while," Jackie blurted. "He was injured at the time. He had been shot. And so his mother only gave us, well—"

"Where did the three of you go?" Watnick quickly interjected.

Jackie said the three of them spent most of the afternoon at Miller's house, until seven or eight that evening. "I had to have [Ricky] home early," she explained.

Going straight to the point, Watnick asked her to recite for the grand jury what Ricky told her about the shootings at Stone Canyon Road.

Jackie said haltingly, "That when my father was on his way back up the stairs, that they—he shot at him. Ricky shot at my father and my father shot at Ricky. He told the other people in the house, the carpenter and my father's tennis player whom he kept, that there was a prowler . . . and Scotty knew otherwise." Then Phillips burst into tears, sobbing, "I want to get it over with!"

Waiting a moment for his witness to regain her composure, Watnick framed his last question. "Did Rick or Scott ever talk in your presence about killing your father before he was killed?" he said finally.

"Yes," their sister testified. "Rick and Scott."

As soon as Jackie took her seat, Lew Watnick asked the grand jury to indict Ricky Kyle for the murder of his father, based on the fact that police had found the murder weapon in the "very area diagrammed" on the map. "It's what's called a 'key,'" he pronounced. "A piece of evidence that no one would know about except for the investigators or a perpetrator." Watnick said he would continue to look for "some other independent corroborating evidence to show a conspiracy and to establish a case against Scotty." Jackie's actions, he told the grand jurors, did not constitute a conspiracy. "Because of the family relationship," he stated, "it would seem very reasonable for somebody not to immediately come forward with a fact against a blood relative." To convict Scott, the DA needed to show some connection between Kyle's younger son and the crime other than Jackie's testimony, which was hearsay since Jackie testified that Rick *told* her Scotty planned it. This connection neither he nor Grogan had, thus far, been able to find.

At the close of the three-hour session, the grand jury issued a sealed indictment against Ricky Kyle on one count of first degree murder and a separate charge of using a handgun in the commission of a crime.

News of the secret grand-jury proceeding hit the papers the following Saturday, when "confidential sources who asked not to be named" informed the *L.A. Times*.

Rick had no comment for the newspapers, nor did Scott. Earlier in the week, a Los Angeles lawyer named Robert Talcott, working in conjunction with Dallas criminal defense attorney Mike Gibson as Rick's counsel, told reporters that an indictment against his client would come as a surprise since Ricky was a victim of the "same attack that led to his father's death."

On Wednesday, September 14, Henry Kyle's older son boarded a plane for Los Angeles. Upon landing, he went directly to the criminal courts building in downtown Los Angeles, where he was formally arraigned for his father's murder. He went to jail for two hours, until his attorneys could post a $100,000 bond (reduced from $500,000) and he was freed upon agreeing that he would not fight extradition from Texas, his legal residence. "We plan to enter a plea of not guilty," said Bob Talcott, as he shepherded his client through a throng of reporters.

6

FREED FROM THE GAG ORDER HE had imposed in the first days of the investigation, Bob Grogan was now happy to share his views on the case with journalists. "Absolutely, it was a crime of greed," he said emphatically. He revealed that the will found in Henry Kyle's briefcase *deleted Ricky's name* as one of two main beneficiaries in what was being reported as a $60 million estate. Responding to Jackie's and Henry Miller's allusions to abuse, Grogan said, "If the old man was beating the boys they could have left a long time ago. They didn't. In fact," he added confidently, "they followed him to California to live with him."

While Lew Watnick and Grogan savored their preliminary victory, Dallas attorney Frank Wright attempted to justify his client's apparent betrayal of her siblings. "Withholding physical evidence would have classified her as an accessory to the murder," Wright said of Jackie. "So at my instructions she turned the map over. She did not want to hurt her brothers, but I forced her to do so."

David Charnay, the fiery chairman of the board of Four Star, who had initiated the secret meeting to establish a reward to find Henry Kyle's killer, was among those who heard the detective present his theory about Rick and Scott. The white-haired movie executive got very upset once again and vowed not to rest until he saw Rick and Scott pay for what they had done. Charnay had already counseled Vicki Yang to fight the will.

Two weeks after the funeral, Vicki did indeed hire Dallas probate lawyer Edward B. Winn. On August 15, Winn filed an opposition to probate of the June 13, 1978, will of Henry Kyle "pending investigation of facts" on behalf of his client, whom he referred to in the petition as "Vicki Heng Kyle," the "surviving widow" of Henry Harrison Kyle. Elsewhere in the same instrument, Winn alleged that Kyle was a legal resident of Vicki's home state of California—not Texas, as the executor of the estate claimed in his application for probate, filed on July 25.

Vicki's lawsuit was exactly what Charlotte Whatley had predicted, despite Vicki's initial disclaimer that she had no interest in the estate. "When I thought it was burglary, I had no intention of contesting the will," Vicki explained to reporters. "When I found out the police department was heavily suspecting that the children had something to do with taking Henry's life, then I came to realize I should do something about it."

Three days after Rick's arraignment, on September 17, she went a step further and petitioned the Los Angeles Superior Court to name her as special administrator of Henry Kyle's California estate, and to decide the validity of the 1978 will naming Rick, Scott, Jackie, and Paula Holtzclaw as sole beneficiaries.

Vicki now admitted publicly that she needed money, saying that she had "let her own real-estate business slip" during the years she'd spent with Henry. Her investments, she stated, did not provide enough money for her to live on.

Vicki's will contest had scarcely been stamped by the clerk of the Dallas County Probate Court when all four of Henry Kyle's children responded with pleas in intervention. They challenged not only Vicki's opposition to the will but her status as their father's widow and her assertions that he was a California resident at the time of his death. Within days, depositions were popping like popcorn in and around Dallas, Mesquite, and Los Angeles, as lawyers questioned the witnesses to Henry Kyle's 1978 will, his colleagues at Four Star, friends and business associates, and Vicki herself.

But the darkest cloud hanging over the estate was not the plethora of wives and children; nor was it Vicki's claim, or the changes Kyle was contemplating to his will before he was killed. Rather, it concerned the criminal charges against Rick, and suspicions that he and Scotty had conspired to kill Henry Kyle before he wrote them out of his will.

If the boys were found guilty of Henry Kyle's murder, one assumed, their share of his estate would be divided among the other heirs—Jackie, Paula, and possibly Vicki. This added another dimension to the will contest pending in Dallas County Probate Court, and, quite possibly, to the alleged conspiracy to kill Henry Kyle. Was there more to Jackie's testimony than met the eye?

7

IF THERE WAS ONE THING RICKY
Kyle needed at this particular time in his life, it was a good
attorney. The week after the shootings at Stone Canyon, he had
hooked up with the best—Mike Gibson. Gibson was a blond, boyish-looking former assistant DA with a law degree from Henry
Kyle's old alma mater, SMU. He was a partner in the Dallas
criminal defense firm of Burleson, Pate & Gibson, widely acknowledged as the best criminal lawyers in Texas and nation-
ally known for defending Fort Worth billionaire T. Cullen Davis,
the richest man ever to stand trial for murder.

In that sensational trial, Gibson's firm and "Racehorse"
Haynes, the colorful Houston lawyer immortalized in *Blood and
Money*, had pulled off what seemed to be impossible: winning
an acquittal for their client in the face of eyewitness testimony
from three individuals. These witnesses identified Davis as the
man in black wearing a ski mask who broke into the Davis mansion at midnight on August 2, 1976, shot Davis's estranged wife,
Priscilla, and murdered her live-in lover and her twelve-year-
old daughter, Andrea. "If those guys could get *that* dude off,"
one observer noted after Gibson took on the Kyle case, "they
can do anything. . . ."

Although Rick's attorney was neither as flashy nor as glib
as Racehorse Haynes, his courtroom skills were no less formidable. "Mike's a surgeon, not an assassin," one Dallas litigator
said of the soft-spoken, impeccably polite Gibson. Once he had
a witness on the stand, Gibson might take hours to develop the

testimony, as he smoothly maneuvered his quarry through an intricate maze of details.

When Ricky returned to Dallas after the arraignment, Mike Gibson sat down with his newest client to discuss their strategy for the upcoming trial. His advice was simple and to the point: "Don't talk to the press. Don't discuss what happened with your friends. Above all, don't see or talk to Scotty. If you have to communicate with him, do it through Charlotte."

At this point the DA was trying to establish a case against Scotty and prove a conspiracy between Kyle's two sons. Under the circumstances, the lawyer reasoned, any contact between the two brothers could only help Watnick. Accordingly, Scotty disappeared from sight into an apartment somewhere in Austin, while his older brother chose to remain in Dallas in their father's condominium at the Preston Towers. Ricky enrolled in the fall semester of classes at North Texas State and tried to be anonymous in a city where his indictment was front-page news.

On October 4, Mike Gibson appeared in Los Angeles Superior Court to advise the judge presiding over the Kyle case that his client would plead not guilty to the charges brought against him. He said further that he fully expected Ricky Kyle to be vindicated.

As his second, equally interesting, order of business, the Dallas lawyer requested and was granted a preliminary hearing to allow him to question Jackie Phillips and Henry Miller III before the case went to trial. (He had not had an opportunity to cross-examine the state's two key witnesses against Rick during the secret grand-jury proceeding in August.)

As he walked out of the courtroom that morning, Gibson's Los Angeles co-counsel Bob Talcott paused long enough to drop a hint or two to reporters about the upcoming hearing; he intimated that it would show "other individuals" who had a "reason, motive and intent" to kill Henry Kyle. Talcott had to know this statement would lead to speculation about Jackie's and her boyfriend's testimony to the grand jury. "There will be a full explanation of Henry Kyle senior and his life-style and the person—or persons—who were capable of doing this thing," Mike Gibson added suggestively as he and Talcott made their way to the elevator. "Henry Kyle senior may be on trial at some point in the proceeding."

59

On November 10, with no new developments—at least publicly—Rick Kyle emerged from his three and a half month seclusion at the Preston Towers in Dallas to spend the morning of the day before his twentieth birthday in L.A. Superior Court.

Dressed in a sport coat and tie, Ricky was deferential and subdued as he entered his formal plea of not guilty to the charges of first-degree murder and using a handgun in the commission of a crime; he responded politely to the judge's brief, perfunctory questions. Five minutes later, as he and Mike Gibson made a quick exit, Rick held his head back purposefully and looked straight ahead with the fixed, expressionless stare he now routinely adopted to avoid the curious gaze of onlookers and reporters.

The Monday after Thanksgiving, lawyers for Henry Kyle's estate and civil attorneys for Jackie, Rick, Vicki Yang, Scott, and Paula Holtzclaw met secretly in Probate Judge Nikki De Shazo's private chambers in Dallas to announce that they had reached an out-of-court settlement. In as much time as it took Judge De Shazo to sign the order approving the settlement, Vicki was recognized as Henry Kyle's sole surviving spouse by all four of his children and the lawsuit she had instigated to challenge his 1978 will was unceremoniously dropped.

The quid pro quo of all this legal maneuvering was as highly classified as a Pentagon top-secret document. At the request of the participants, Judge De Shazo agreed to keep the settlement under seal in her chambers, where it could be seen only with a court order or by permission of the parties. This was an unusual practice for an estate proceeding. Such documents are generally considered public records, open to the scrutiny of anyone with the inclination to visit the civil courts building and request the file. To further ensure confidentiality, attorneys for the Kyle family drafted an unusual forfeiture clause, which would disinherit any heir who discussed the terms of the settlement with anyone other than each other or their legal counsels. The only clue to the distribution of the estate came from Ricky's civil attorney, Jack Pate. Pressed for comment as he strolled out of the closed-door hearing in Judge De Shazo's court, Pate intimated that Vicki had been given "some" income from Henry Kyle's holdings, and the rest was divided among Scott, Rick, Paula, and Jackie in proportions that "did not closely resemble'' those designated in the millionaire's 1978 will.

When news of the surprise agreement hit the Dallas papers the next day, speculation did not so much concern who got what as how and why. It seemed exceedingly strange, for example, that Jackie, Rick, and Scotty should agree on *anything,* when it was Jackie's grand-jury testimony against her brothers that led to Rick's indictment. If Jackie was lying, and Rick and Scott never told her they were planning to murder their father, it made little sense that the two boys would settle with her. If she was telling the truth, it made no sense that *she* would want to settle.

Similar considerations applied to Vicki Yang. She had filed her will contest in August because she suspected the children had "something to do with" her husband's death. Did her about-face mean she doubted her ability to prove her status as Mrs. Henry Kyle, or was there another reason for her compromise with his four children?

More curious still were Rick's and Scotty's motives in conceding a portion of their inheritances to *Vicki.* According to Texas lawyers, the explanation lies in Rick's indictment and Texas probate law.

As the chief suspects in their father's slaying, Rick and possibly Scott stood in danger of losing their inheritances by operation of law. However, in Texas, an heir suspected of killing his benefactor does not automatically forfeit the inheritance. For that to occur, an "interested party" to the estate must file a petition in probate court to request a mini-trial, complete with witnesses and evidence, to determine whether the suspect heir caused the death of the benefactor. If found innocent at this hearing the accused killer would not relinquish his inheritance, even if he were found guilty at his murder trial.

In the few cases where the issue has come up, Texas probate judges have generally allowed convicted killers to inherit from their victims if none of the heirs petition the court for a mini-trial. In one particularly notorious Houston case, a man who shot his parents inherited both their estates because his aunt and uncle—the other heirs—were too intimidated to request a hearing to disinherit him. "They just said, 'Let him have it,' '' the presiding judge, Pat Gregory, later explained. " 'We're afraid of the guy.' ''

So, perhaps, Rick and Scott decided to share their father's

estate with Vicki (and their half sisters) to avoid the possibility of being disinherited completely by the probate court.

From November 28, the day the agreement was sealed in Judge De Shazo's chambers, it was as if a curtain had dropped over the case.

Reporters trying to contact Scott in Austin, Rick and Jackie in Dallas, and Paula in Marietta, Georgia, found that all four of Henry Kyle's children had acquired unlisted telephone numbers. Jackie and Paula issued instructions to their attorneys that they would not talk to the press under any circumstances—Rick's and Scotty's respective counsels had already made that decision for them. Vicki Yang dropped out of sight completely, and her lawyer, Edward Winn, would not verify so much as the spelling of her maiden name to journalists calling his office. Charlie Schuerenberg and Gary Grimes, the lawyers representing the estate, refused even to take calls from the media pertaining to the Kyle affair.

"There's somethin' goin' on," Dallas realtor Carolyn Shamis was heard to remark to a friend. "*Got* to be. There's some reason this is all bein' kept so hush-hush. . . ."

8

MONDAY, JANUARY 9, 1984, WAS
the date selected by Los Angeles Superior Court Judge Robert
R. Devich for the preliminary hearing, which Mike Gibson had
requested in October.

This time around, Henry Kyle's older son was more than
adequately represented. Gibson chose two lawyers to assist him—
Steve Sumner and John Vandevelde. A third, Jack Pate, who
specialized in civil law matters, was also on hand merely to observe.

Steve Sumner, at six feet four and roughly two hundred
twenty pounds, had dark, wavy hair and an attractive face,
weathered from years in the sun. He did not resemble the typical Ivy-League lawyer—and, in fact, he was not one. A graduate
of North Texas State University in Denton, Sumner had come
to the legal profession by way of the baseball field, where he
had achieved success as a pitcher for the Chicago Cubs, Washington Senators, and Houston Astros. An injury to his pitching
arm forced him out of the game after five seasons.

After passing the bar in 1975, Sumner returned to his home-
town of Dallas, where he had the good fortune to be noticed by
Phil Burleson. He was signed on as the rookie lawyer in the
Cullen Davis murder case.

Sumner was responsible for most of the investigative work
behind Burleson's and Racehorse Haynes's courtroom razzle-
dazzle, and in the years following, Sumner had earned a reputation around Dallas as a criminal lawyer with a consistent

record for winning. His courtroom style was polite but aggressive. Whereas Gibson preferred subtle, intellectual manipulation, Sumner would make his points to a jury as a series of fast balls whizzing over home plate.

At the same time, however, he was generally regarded as an all-around good guy—the sort of trial lawyer who would spend a ten-minute recess making small talk with his opposing counsel. "I think my greatest strength is that I really like people" is Sumner's self-assessment. "I'm genuinely interested in what they have to say."

The third member of Ricky's defense team, John Vandevelde, was a handsome, sandy-haired Los Angeles trial lawyer with the two-man firm of Talcott & Vandevelde. Gibson had called him in as co-counsel to advise on matters of California law and procedure. Vandevelde tended to address his arguments to the court in an earnest, low-key fashion that relied on a thorough familiarity with the law.

Pitted against this formidable foursome, Lew Watnick seemed undercast as the prosecuting attorney. Judging by his attitude, however, Watnick was not in the least concerned about the competition, or his case. Within five minutes after the hearing commenced, he informed the court and a gallery of intrigued spectators that he had subpoenaed Scotty Kyle to appear as the first witness. Watnick hoped to force him to answer questions about Jackie's and Henry Miller's testimony that he had stolen Quint Barnes's gun and collaborated with Rick on a plan to shoot their father.

The nineteen-year-old who approached the stand a few seconds later resembled a candidate for the Young Entrepreneurs Club more than the popular conception of a criminal. Dressed in a conservative suit and tie, Scotty had Henry Kyle's handsome, regular features. He was tall, with a slender frame and light blond hair. As he took his seat in the witness box and focused attentively on the DA, he displayed none of the detachment, obliviousness even, that had characterized Ricky in his public appearances.

By day's end, this initial impression was all Watnick or anyone else in the courtroom had to go on. For nearly five hours, the extent of his testimony, Scott responded to every query posed to him by saying "I respectfully decline to answer the question because of my privilege against self-incrimination provided in the Fifth, Sixth and Fourteenth amendments to the United States Constitution and Article One, Seven(A) and Fifteen of the California Constitution.'' This defensive strategy left the district attorney's office at square one with its conspiracy case. In order to indict Scott as a co-conspirator, Watnick needed evidence to corroborate Jackie's and Henry Miller III's hearsay testimony. By pleading the Fifth Amendment against self-incrimination, Scott guaranteed that no such evidence would come from him.

At ten the next morning, Jackie and her fiancé were expected on the witness stand for cross-examination. Judge Devich's courtroom was buzzing with speculation. Would Mike Gibson indeed uncover ''other individuals'' with a motive to kill Henry Kyle, as he had hinted to the *Los Angeles Herald-Examiner* in October? Would the deal struck by the Kyle family to divide Henry's millions affect Gibson's cross-examination strategy . . . or Jackie's and Henry Miller's testimony concerning Rick's supposed confession?

Soon everyone had a pretty good idea of which way the wind was blowing. As his first witness, Gibson called Frank Wright, Jackie and her boyfriend's criminal lawyer. Wright's clients came almost exclusively from the elite of Dallas, and he himself was known for his white Rolls-Royce and expensive, European-tailored suits.

In the weeks since Henry Kyle's death, Wright had been quoted as saying that Jackie and Henry III had been ''forced'' by Lew Watnick to tell the grand jurors about Rick's confession and that the experience had been ''traumatic'' for Jackie. As Mike Gibson's brief cross-examination of the urbane criminal lawyer revealed, however, there was more to it than that.

Most significantly, it came out that Jackie herself had been a suspect until sometime in mid-August. After tracing the gun to Quint Barnes and discovering he had dated Jackie, Grogan paid a visit to Jackie in Dallas, just as the detective had testified in August. What Grogan *didn't* tell the grand jurors, however, was that he ''alluded'' to Jackie that *she* might be charged or indicted, along with Rick. It was sometime *after that*, Wright testified, that Jackie and Henry III retained his services, and mentioned for the first time that Ricky had confessed to them the afternoon of Henry Kyle's funeral.

Wright then contacted Detective Grogan to discuss ''how they would treat'' Jackie. By the end of that conversation he had reached an "understanding" with the two detectives that Jackie was "no longer a target," in exchange for her and Henry Miller's statements that Rick had confessed to the crime. On his advice, Wright said, Miller and Jackie also "divulged" the map showing where Ricky had supposedly thrown the gun.

As a final point of interest, Wright alluded—in response to a direct question from Gibson—to the fact that Jackie suffered from what he referred to as "chemical dependency difficulties," and Mike Gibson called a "drug problem."

Next, Kyle's younger daughter took her place on the witness stand.

While journalists scrutinized the lissome blonde fidgeting in her chair, Sumner began to plant seeds of doubt about her motives. First he established that his witness was twenty-eight years old; then he asked her occupation. "I am retired," Jackie responded coolly. "I was a fashion model for twelve years. As of a year and a half ago, I have been unemployed."

Before Rick's criminal lawyer could continue, Lew Watnick issued a strenuous objection to the entire line of questioning, and asked the judge to rule that Jackie's background was not relevant to the case. John Vandevelde, the defense team's by-the-book California lawyer, rose to present his argument: In essence, Jackie's background *was* the case.

"The whole relationship between Jackie and her father and Rick Kyle," he began, "her financial status, her need for money because of being unemployed, her need for money because of heavy drug dependency—the facts that will be elicited later in this proceeding or in any subsequent trial relating to her being in effect disinherited from her father's will—the fact that she was in a position to inherit a substantial amount of money if her brother Rick Kyle were to be unable to inherit money because of a criminal conviction relating to her father's death . . . all of that goes to her bias and motive to fabricate."

By the time the L.A. trial lawyer resumed his seat, he had persuaded Judge Devich to permit Sumner's cross-examination of Jackie.

Sumner seized the opportunity with fervor. For four hours, he fired an unrelenting volley of questions at Jackie. She responded with sporadic outbursts of tears, and flashes of indignation. By the time Jackie left the witness stand at the end of the afternoon, Sumner had pieced together a portrait of her shattered life and—not coincidentally—created the impression she was a witness of questionable credibility.

As she presented her story at the preliminary hearing, Jackie Phillips was born Jackie Kyle in Dallas on June 17, 1955. Her mother, Jackie Glenn Garrison, was Henry Kyle's third wife. She divorced Kyle and married a Dallasite named Bryan Phillips sometime in 1957. Phillips adopted Jackie, then two. Jackie met Henry Kyle for the first time when she was eleven. At that time he told her about her half brothers, Rick and Scotty, who were then living in Georgia.

Shortly thereafter, she told Sumner, her father began to "abuse" her. By Jackie's account on the witness stand, Henry Kyle threw her out of a moving car, and struck her. She also mentioned "delicate abuse," to indicate that she had been sexually molested as well. "My father abused me physically." When Sumner queried whether Henry Kyle would "fly off the handle" or had a "violent temper," his daughter responded affirmatively. To "protect" herself from her father, she said, she was sent to a boarding school in Arizona. This was paid for by Kyle—the only financial assistance, she said, he had ever provided for her schooling. "I was no longer around him, ever. . . ." she said bitterly.

After graduating from boarding school in 1974, Jackie moved to San Francisco, where she said she modeled for seven years. In 1980, when she was twenty-five, she moved back to Dallas and signed with the Kim Dawson Modeling Agency. For two years, she told Sumner, she did not see her father, by their mutual agreement. "Neither of us tried to communicate to each other," she explained. Kyle instructed her to keep out of his house at 9909 Preston Road, and ordered her to stay away from Rick and Scott, who were living with him by then. "He did not allow me to see any member of my family, including my grandmother," she stated. "Not only my brothers—any member."

The reason for the estrangement, Sumner's cross-examination revealed, was Jackie's "life-style." Jackie conceded on the witness stand that she was a "drug addict" with a history of cocaine abuse. She described her father as "something of a health bug," who was "very, very against narcotics. Through investigations of his own," she said mysteriously, he had discovered her cocaine addiction.

According to Jackie, a year before he was killed, Kyle called and asked to see her. "He wanted to tell me that he wanted me to change my life-style and he wanted to help me change my life-style and we simply talked." By her own admission, she was having "financial troubles" at the time. Prodded by Sumner, she acknowledged that her telephone had been cut off "numerous times," she had trouble paying bills, and she was in debt. Sometime afterward, she testified, her father bought her a condominium, and provided her with an allowance for two months so she could "get back on her feet." Did she ask Henry Kyle for financial support? "I never asked my father for anything," Jackie snapped. She also said she did not know what her bequest was in his will, and that her "mother told her" she'd been disinherited.

The following March—four months before Kyle was shot—Jackie entered the Orange County Care Unit, a drug-treatment center outside Los Angeles, where she was admitted for forty days of therapy for cocaine addiction. During her hospitalization, she stated, she received two phone calls from her father, and a check for $2,000 to help defray her $12,000 hospital bill. At Sumner's prompting, she also testified that Henry Miller III—whom she described as her "boyfriend of sorts"—had received treatment as a drug patient at the same clinic at the same time.

When she returned to Dallas from the rehabilitation center, Jackie said, she "still had problems with cocaine addiction." She confessed to being charged twice during that period with driving while intoxicated. "Trying to stop drugs I found myself changing chemicals to alcohol," she responded huffily to Sumner's insinuation that she had a drinking problem as well. "I am *not* an alcoholic."

Jackie said she had "never been" to Henry Kyle's house in Bel-Air until the weekend after he was killed, when she flew to L.A. to see Ricky. She was "not sure" whether she had visited California from mid-May to mid-July, between the time she was released from the Care Unit and the shootings occurred at Granada. Just before her father was murdered, she told Sumner, her relationship with Kyle was "better" than it had been. "[We were] not arguing, or he was very supportive of me at that time."

When asked about her relationship with Rick and Scott, Jackie testified that she had gotten to know both of her half brothers "well" after she had first met them in 1980, upon her return to

Dallas. When her father told her to stay away from them, she told Sumner, she continued to see Rick and Scott "behind his back." During the three and a half years she had been acquainted with her half brothers, she had developed a "better relationship" with Rick, whom she said she had seen "numerous, numerous . . . many times." Scotty she had seen "not as much," and "very, very rare[ly]" after she was released from the drug treatment center in April 1983.

On the subject of her half brother's alleged confession to her—the centerpiece of the prosecution's case against Rick—Jackie was a mass of confusion and contradiction.

In her first minutes on the stand, Sumner had asked her what Ricky told her happened the night Henry Kyle was shot. Jackie had paused, then said hesitantly: "That my father shot at him and he shot at him. They shot at each other. . . ."—which indicated that *Henry Kyle* had fired the first shot, not Ricky. This minor distinction could mean the difference for Rick between self-defense and first-degree murder.

During the afternoon session Jackie changed her story:

"Your response [this morning] was that they shot at each other, is that correct?" Sumner queried.

"Yes, sir."

"But you do now recall that Ricky told you that his father shot at him first?"

"I did not," Jackie said absently. "Ricky told me that when they were sure there were no prowlers in the home, he was standing in the hallway, the door hallway to the dining room. My father was on his way up the stairs, and he fired at him. My father turned on his way down, fired back, and Rick fired once more."

When Sumner asked Jackie at the preliminary hearing if Rick told her why he had shot his father, she said no, then added, "For abuse."

"Did he say that to you?" Sumner persisted.

"I *know* that is the reason," Jackie responded. Later in the day, she volunteered that Henry Kyle had sexually molested her, and that she had seen Rick physically abused. "Black eyes," she recited. "Abuse. I've never seen anything beyond that."

Jackie's testimony contradicted Henry Miller's—and her own—on another point as well. At the grand-jury proceeding in August, Miller had testified that Ricky told them he was wearing "Playtex rubber gloves" the night he shot Henry Kyle, so he wouldn't leave fingerprints on the gun. Now Jackie said that Rick told her and Miller he was wearing "a" glove and that he "didn't say what kind." After the lunch break, when Sumner brought up the topic again, she came up with a third version, saying she "didn't recall" whether Rick talked about gloves at all.

Part of the reason for such confusion, Sumner's cross-examination implied, was Jackie's condition at the time Rick supposedly confessed. Sumner first asked her whether she had taken any drugs the night before or the morning of Kyle's funeral. When she said she had not, he moved on to the reception. According to Jackie, she had "one drink" before she and Henry Miller left with Ricky sometime in the early afternoon. From there, she said, the three of them stopped at the Café Pacific, a Dallas restaurant and bar, where she had "three martinis." Then, Jackie testified, she, Miller, and Rick decided to go to Miller's house so they could "consume some narcotic substances." During the next three hours (roughly 5:00 to 8:00 P.M.), she testified, she, Miller, and Ricky free-based "no more than a gram or half-gram" of cocaine. It was then that Ricky supposedly confessed to shooting Henry Kyle, and drew the diagram on Miller's stationery.

"After receiving the diagram, what did you do?" Sumner asked Jackie.

"I kept hold of it" was Jackie's explanation. "I did nothing with it. I just kept hold of it."

"Did you later turn it over to somebody?" Sumner said suggestively.

"I turned it over to Frank Wright," she stammered, "when the detectives questioned me thinking I had anything to do with the weapon . . . I turned this to Frank Wright and Detective Grogan . . . and I was accused of stealing the weapon—Well, not accused," she corrected herself, "but they had believed that I had anything to do with stealing that weapon. . . ."

Before excusing her from the stand, Sumner questioned Jackie briefly about her trip to California July 22 to 24, the weekend after Kyle was killed. Henry Miller had earlier testified that he and Jackie had visited Rick in the hospital twice at that time.

Now Jackie told Sumner that she and Henry Miller also visited 110 Stone Canyon twice. The second time, Jackie testified, she and her boyfriend were let into the house by Rusty Dunn, the carpenter. While she was there, Jackie said, she asked Rusty and Miller to "leave her alone" in her father's bedroom for a few minutes. When Sumner asked her why, Jackie responded that she was in an "emotional state" over Kyle's death, and wanted to be alone in his room. The next day, Sunday, she telephoned Rick and "maybe" visited him once more at the hospital, after which she and Miller flew back to Dallas. She "might" have talked to Rick again by phone before the funeral in Dallas on Tuesday. If so, Sumner implied, Jackie would have had three to five conversations with her half brother after the shootings and before she said he confessed: ample opportunity for him to ask Jackie and Miller to recover the gun . . . or tell them he killed Kyle.

As at the indictment hearing, Henry S. Miller III was dressed in a conservative suit and wore his sandy-blond hair banker-short. During the half hour or so he was cross-examined by Mike Gibson, the real-estate heir again answered the questions put to him in a calm, forthright manner, and displayed none of the agitation or hysteria of his fiancée. Nevertheless, by the end of his brief interlude on the witness stand, he had raised several interesting points for the defense.

First, Miller repeated his grand-jury testimony that Rick had said he was wearing Playtex gloves the night he shot Henry Kyle—this conflicted with Jackie's statements earlier in the day that Rick either didn't mention gloves, or told them he was wearing one glove and didn't specify what kind.

Miller also mentioned in passing that Jackie had stayed at a ranch near San Francisco sometime in July 1983—the month her father was killed—making one wonder why she had told Steve Sumner she "wasn't sure" whether she had been in California from mid-May to mid-July.

Jackie had also testified that she "held on to" the diagram she said Rick drew on Miller's personalized stationery showing where he had thrown the gun; that she "did nothing with it." Miller told Gibson that he "crumpled up and discarded" the map after Ricky gave it to him. "I really didn't think there was much reason to save it," he testified. According to Miller, Jackie recovered the diagram from his trash can a "few days" later.

The most significant portion in Miller's testimony, however, concerned Rick's confession. At the grand-jury proceeding in August, Miller testified that Ricky said he and Scotty had planned their father's death for "quite some time"; that Ricky woke Kyle in the middle of the night to look for an intruder; and when they returned to the house "[and] Mr. Kyle lowered his gun, or was not so ready for an intruder, that he shot him and hit him once and missed, I guess, on the second shot. And that Mr. Kyle on his way down got off three or four rounds and shot him through the elbow."

Now, Miller said simply, "They fired at each other. I believe that Rick said he did fire first. . . ." he added tentatively. ". . . Bear in mind this was a very stressful emotional situation . . . he said he did it for all of us."

9

IF MIKE GIBSON'S INTENTION IN calling for a preliminary hearing was to stir things up, he met his goal.

The wild card was clearly Jackie. Her testimony and that of Henry Miller raised more questions than they answered.

Why, for instance, would Rick leave a piece of incriminating evidence—the map—with Jackie and Henry Miller if he had murdered his father? Why, if he was guilty, would he ask his sister and her boyfriend to retrieve the murder weapon instead of Scott—Scott was in California at the time of the shootings and, according to Jackie and Miller, had helped plan the crime and stolen the gun. And why would Rick wait until the Tuesday afternoon of the funeral, five days after Kyle was shot, to make this request—especially considering that Jackie and Miller were in Los Angeles at the hospital and had visited 110 Stone Canyon twice?

And what about the contradicting testimonies of Jackie and Henry Miller? The inconsistencies were so glaring as to suggest to some that confusion was *deliberately* being caused. Such speculation raised yet a new hypothesis: that Jackie might have plotted Henry Kyle's slaying *with her brothers,* either as retaliation for abuse, or to divide their father's estate.

Jackie's decision in November to join the settlement agreement with Rick and Scott had already inspired conjecture to this effect. If Jackie was in secret complicity with her brothers, the muddled account of Rick's confession offered by her and

Henry Miller might have been an Agatha Christie-like device to help acquit Rick for the murder so all three siblings could walk away with a piece of Henry Kyle's estate.

Including Jackie in the conspiracy theory would tie together a number of loose ends. First, it provided the obvious link between Quint Barnes's gun and the crime—Jackie could easily have stolen the revolver from her former boyfriend between June 1982 and February 1983, then passed it on to Rick or Scott. In addition, Jackie herself had already told the grand jurors she was present at preliminary discussions of the plot.

But Bob Grogan maintained, "I don't believe Jackie's involved in the conspiracy. She was more or less used by the boys. Jackie's a very weak individual. Rick and Scott are very sharp. She was maybe present during their discussions . . . but that's where her part ends. She wasn't actively involved. I don't think she would have condoned it. She was extremely pissed off that Rick killed him."

Lew Watnick defended his key witness with equal ardor. "Jackie didn't come forward initially because Rick told her not to," he said to one journalist. "Jackie wasn't in California [when Kyle was killed]," he added. "She had nothing to do with it." Watnick also glossed over John Vandevelde's insinuation that Jackie might have fabricated Rick's confession so she could inherit part of Henry Kyle's estate. "Jackie doesn't have the wherewithal and intelligence," he said complacently. "She's very emotional."

Some observers of the case suggested that Grogan and Watnick were taking the easy way out on a crime too convoluted to figure out—particularly when it came to Jackie's involvement. This allegation is supported by the fact that neither the DA nor Grogan had learned the terms of the secret settlement agreement two months after it was signed—despite the tantalizing prospect that the settlement contained clues to the ulterior motives of key participants in the case.

The only part of Jackie's story Watnick and Grogan *didn't* accept at face value was her testimony concerning Henry Kyle's abuse. "That's horseshit," Grogan said of Kyle's alleged brutality. "That's the defense's only justification—to show that Henry Kyle was a bastard and beat up his kids." The only reason Jackie mentioned it, the detective volunteered, was because she was "trying to tell the truth *and* protect her half brother."

"There was never any child or sex abuse," Lew Watnick

added in agreement. "I think maybe Jackie craved her father's love. She wanted to be approved by her father. She needed a father figure."

According to Jackie's testimony, it was in 1967, when she was eleven, that she first met her father and he started to physically and sexually abuse her. When she was fourteen, she told the court, Kyle paid for her tuition at a boarding school in Arizona because she had to "protect herself" from him.

Charlotte Whatley offered a different account of how Jackie was enrolled at boarding school. Whatley said that in 1969 Henry received a phone call out of the blue from Jackie's mother, Jackie Glenn Phillips, who said she "couldn't do anything with" Jackie, and "would he please take her." From what Henry told Charlotte at the time, he had not seen little Jackie since the divorce and "didn't even know where she was."

According to her school records, Jackie enrolled as a freshman at Highland Park, a public high school in an affluent section of Dallas, in 1969. The following summer, when she turned fourteen, she entered a boarding school in San Marcos, Texas, two hours west of Dallas. The current principal of San Marcos Academy could not be certain whether Jackie's record had reflected that she had been the victim of parental abuse, or that she was admitted because of drug or other behavioral problems. "She was maybe transferred here in hopes her grades would improve," he speculated.

The next fall, Jackie went back to Highland Park as a sophomore, then returned to San Marcos for the spring semester. According to the principal, her grades remained poor at both schools, although her only infractions at the academy were one unexcused absence and two tardies. In the autumn of 1971, the beginning of her junior year, she transferred again, this time to the Judson School in Paradise Valley, Arizona. This is the small, expensive college-preparatory academy whose purpose, Jackie claimed, was to distance her from her father.

According to Henry Wick, the director of the school from 1971 to 1974, Judson accepts only students who "want" to attend, which suggests that the school was Jackie's choice—for whatever reason. Wick also said the academy would not admit girls with drug dependencies, or those who had been in trouble with the law. In her three years at Judson, Jackie did not make a particularly vivid impression; ten years later, Wick remembered her as a "nice girl," "very pretty," with no outstanding problems. In the spring of 1974, she graduated in good standing, a year behind her former classmates at Highland Park.

After graduation, Jackie, who had done some modeling while she was in school, moved to San Francisco to sign with an agency full time. She did not tell her father. Within two years, her sexy, slightly pouty features and coltish figure enabled her to reach the top echelons of the modeling profession, and she was in particular demand for lingerie ads. At the apex of her career, in 1977, she was featured on the cover of *Oui* and several other magazines. She was earning enough money to buy herself a Mercedes and to join the fast-track crowd in San Francisco.

"That's how Henry found out what she was doin' after Judson," Charlotte Whatley remembered. "Somebody had a magazine, and he was flippin' through it, and saw her picture." By his friends' accounts, Kyle was "real proud" of Jackie during this interlude.

It was while she was in San Francisco in the mid- to late seventies, Charlotte and others said, that Jackie got hooked on cocaine, and her life really started to unravel. "She had a wonderful career—did a lot of magazine work—and she blew it," Whatley said caustically.

In 1979, reportedly because of her cocaine habit, Jackie left San Francisco and returned to Dallas. She was welcomed with anything but open arms by Henry Kyle, who had recently gotten custody of both his sons from Charlotte. The last thing he wanted was to introduce them to a half sister involved in drugs.

If opinions were slightly mixed among his friends about Kyle's relationship with his two boys, they were unanimous when it came to Jackie. He considered his younger daughter to be, in a word, "trouble."

"I knew about Jackie . . ." Allan Conwill said hesitantly. "Henry didn't volunteer any more, and that struck me as an area I shouldn't get involved in."

According to Charlotte, Kyle bought Jackie a condo in Dallas the year before his murder on the strict condition that she stay away from Rick and Scotty. "Henry despised the ground she walked on," his ex-wife stated. "He didn't want her to get *anything* from him. He wanted to make sure of that. He knew it would all go on drugs."

After moving back to Dallas, Jackie signed with the Kim Dawson Agency there.

Jackie earned less than one hundred dollars from modeling assignments through the Dawson Agency—supposedly her only source of income—between 1979 and her ''retirement'' in 1982. ''She was never around,'' Dawson explained. ''I'd try to arrange a booking for her and she'd never show, or never call back. She was always gone somewhere, and she was completely unreliable. I remember talking to her in my office one day and thinking, 'Here is a girl who needs a lot of help.' There was just something about her . . .''

Sheila Colombe, one of the women who booked assignments for Dawson's models, remembered, ''She always had a rich boyfriend and she ran with a pretty rough crowd.''

Henry Kyle's friends viewed Jackie with even more suspicion and angrily dismissed her claims of abuse at the hands of her father. ''It's totally unacceptable to me to think of Henry as a child molester. I think she's flat-out lying,'' said Jerry Kramer.

''I can't even keep my temper about that,'' New York lawyer Allan Conwill said heatedly, referring to the sex-abuse testimony. ''I think that's one of the most asinine and absurd things I've ever heard, and you can quote me. Henry Kyle would never molest a child. It's unthinkable. . . . From what I have read,'' he said suggestively, ''it strikes me that it would be very much in the interest of one child and potential heir to lay off all the evidence possible that the murder was committed by another child and potential heir, because that would increase the take for *that* heir. . . .''

Marj Helper, Kyle's earthy L.A. realtor and most ardent admirer, maintained that part of the reason Kyle moved to California was to get the boys out of Dallas and away from Jackie. ''He was not fond of her,'' Helper said crisply. ''She was an influence on the boys—not a good one.

''I think Jackie hated her father's guts,'' Helper added. ''She got even with Henry through the boys.''

Where Scotty fit into the conspiracy picture was also speculation. On the witness stand neither Jackie nor Henry Miller had referred to Scott's relationships with his father or Rick, and their statements about drug use and Kyle's physical abuse did not include Scott.

According to Grogan's interpretation of the crime—based in

part on Jackie's testimony that Scott planned the shooting and stole the gun—Scotty coolly orchestrated the murder from beginning to end; he formulated the plan to rouse Henry Kyle from bed with the ruse that a prowler was in the house and persuaded Rick to implement it, then allowed his brother to take the rap alone.

"I don't see that," Jerry Kramer commented on the detective's conspiracy theory. "It's confusing to me. I didn't see Scott as devious. He was definitely Henry's favorite, no question about that . . . to a disproportionate degree."

Carolyn Shamis, who spent time with Scott and Henry while Ricky was away at school, was adamant in her defense of Kyle's younger son. "There are all these implications that Scott's had a part in this," she said hotly in the spring of 1984. "I absolutely—if that is true, they're gonna have to really teach me something. I would be shocked."

In addition to such testimonials, there was also the fact that Scott, unlike Rick, had not been crossed out of Henry Kyle's 1978 will. This fact seemed to remove any obvious motive for killing his father and supported the view that he was getting along with Kyle immediately before the shooting. Moreover, there was no evidence to indicate that Scott was taking drugs, his father's bête noire.

It is difficult to find out much about Scott Kyle's adolescence, especially once he moved from Georgia to Texas.

Scott became a boarding student at the exclusive Selwyn School in Denton from the fall of 1979 until the spring semester of his senior year in 1981. Then he mysteriously transferred to a public high school, Hillcrest in Dallas. One Selwyn staff member described Scott as a "mystery figure," but refused to say any more about him, or comment on why he had transferred from the school for his last semester. "Nobody will talk to you," she advised inquirers. "You're running up against family. The students here have a feeling about each other that's unusual." Asked for a character evaluation, she would say only, "He is a nice boy."

Since the shooting, Scott had not come forward to confess to taking Quint Barnes's gun, as Rick had supposedly told Jackie he would. Grogan and Watnick could find no evidence other than Jackie's hearsay testimony to link him to the crime.

Whatever role Jackie and Scott might have played in Henry

Kyle's death, the actual evidence pointed only to Rick. It was his name that was crossed out of Kyle's will; he was with his father when he was shot; Jackie and Henry Miller testified that Rick had confessed to the murder; and the murder weapon was found in the very spot they said Rick had diagrammed on the map.

PART
TWO

PART
TWO

10

On October 22, 1984, fifteen months to the day after Henry Kyle was shot to death, the State of California's charges against Ricky finally reached the head of the Los Angeles criminal courts docket. This was heralded by an article on the front page of the *L.A. Times* with the two-and-a-half-inch headline MURDER TRIAL—A FAMILY DIVIDED WILL BE THE STARS.

However, the proceedings were decidedly undramatic that first Monday in Department 123 on the twelfth floor of the Criminal Courts Building in downtown L.A., where the Kyle case was being heard by Judge Robert R. Devich. Ricky's defense lawyers and Lew Watnick sat at separate ends of a long counsel table facing Judge Devich's bench. They began by scrutinizing prospective jurors, a process Watnick had earlier told newspaper reporters would last "a couple of days."

In actuality, it turned into a tedious, five-week question-and-answer marathon. Mike Gibson picked the jury members with the same care he displayed while questioning a witness on the stand. He and Steve Sumner even hired a consultant who specialized in interpreting body language and other indicators of psychology.

By the Thanksgiving holidays, the defense team and Lew Watnick had come to terms on a panel of twelve jurors and three alternates. Sumner said later he and Gibson were trying to assemble a jury of "gentle people." Six of the jurors chosen to hear Ricky's case were black women, all but one of whom—a

83

sweet-faced elderly lady who wore her hair in a bun and took her knitting to court—were in their twenties or thirties. Three of the four other women on the panel were middle-aged, middle-class Caucasians, primarily homemakers; the fourth was an attractive, stylish young mother who worked as a nurse. Of the five male jurors, there were a young Mexican-American and a serious-looking Oriental in his early forties. The three remaining men were Caucasian, including an engineer in his twenties; a middle-aged Western Union employee with a gray goatee who favored leisure suits; and a thirtyish California bartender in the midst of a divorce and custody suit.

Judge Devich scheduled opening arguments to begin at 10:00 A.M. the Monday after Thanksgiving.

A throng of observers assembled for the opening day, including TV cameramen, photographers, and reporters from such media as *USA Today*, both wire services, CNN, local L.A. television stations, and several Dallas newspapers. All eyes were fixed on the long counsel table in front of the bench, where sat Ricky Kyle, dressed in a beige corduroy jacket, white shirt, and tie. He appeared more relaxed and a few pounds heavier than when he had entered his not guilty plea a year earlier. He sat in the chair to the far right end of the table. To his left were the three criminal defense attorneys and Jack Pate, Gibson's civil-law partner. Clad in nearly identical expensive dark-blue suits, and huddling with their client, the four lawyers called to mind a row of defensive linemen waiting to pounce on the opposing quarterback.

On the opposite end of the counsel table, accompanied by his sole associate, John Moulin, sat Lew Watnick. He wore a slightly tattered suit, in the same nondescript shade of brown as his horn-rimmed glasses, thinning hair, and moustache. If everything about Ricky's defense team reflected their reputation as the Cadillacs of criminal defense work, Lew Watnick came across like a used Chevy. Instead of carrying a briefcase, he wheeled his papers into court in a supermarket shopping cart—"part of his 'humble servant of the people' act," Steve Sumner noted dryly. In Sumner's view, Watnick's shabby appearance was calculated to get the jury's sympathy.

Judge Devich appeared in a swirl of black robes from a door behind the bench. Rick's four attorneys immediately rose from their seats as the clamor in the courtroom gave way to abrupt silence. Walking over to his chair, Devich motioned to Gibson and his colleagues to take their seats. He explained with a smile that it wasn't necessary to stand when he entered the courtroom—such informality was an indication of his low-key style.

Robert R. Devich was tall and distinguished-looking. A former cop and one-time prosecutor, he had an easy, avuncular air. Since his recent appointment to the downtown bench, he had come to be known among prosecutors and defense attorneys as soft-spoken and genial, except on the rare occasions when he was pushed too far.

Devich announced to both sides that Mrs. Stewart, one of the defense's original choices for the jury, had come down with the flu over the Thanksgiving holidays. This development could postpone the trial until she recuperated. He suggested to Watnick and Gibson that they replace her with an alternate. Immediately Gibson rose to object, arguing to Devich that a substitution would be "too precipitous" for his client. In his first ruling, the judge denied Gibson's request: He wanted "no further delay" in the proceedings, which had already been deferred nearly seven months. Devich's clerk drew a name from the alternates, and selected Bruce Bauder, a thirtyish, sandy-haired bartender.

Moving forward, Devich advised the jury that the DA was about to make his opening argument on behalf of the State of California. But before turning the floor over to Watnick, the judge issued a sober reminder to them to make their final decision on Rick Kyle's innocence or guilt based on the evidence alone, not on statements by any of the lawyers.

Lew Watnick slowly stood up from his chair at the counsel table and turned to face the fourteen remaining members of the jury panel. As he uttered the first few words of his opening statement, many of those in the courtroom leaned forward in their seats to make out his gravelly half whisper. "What I'm telling you now is what the State of California will prove," he began. "A 'preview of coming attractions.' The trial will be a gigantic jigsaw puzzle to you . . . then you'll get a clear picture.

"We will prove beyond a reasonable doubt that Henry Kyle junior murdered—no, executed—Henry Kyle senior," he asserted, his raspy voice turning flat and emotionless. "It *was* an execution because the victim had no chance. It was a deliberate and premeditated murder to obtain money, and the estate, and to prevent any other distribution."

Watnick then went on to recite how the murder took place,

explaining to the jury that Henry Kyle was killed at 3:45 A.M. on Friday, July 22, 1983, by a bullet fired from a range of two to five inches. "It was closer to two inches, in all probability," he said. "As shown by powder burns or 'tattooing'—the residue from powder, which leaves a pattern around the wound." To prove it, he contended, he would call ballistics experts to the stand and show jurors photographs of the entrance and exit wounds. "There were other lacerations or injuries, also," Watnick revealed. "He didn't die immediately," the DA added. "He fired six shots from his gun. One struck the defendant in the right elbow as he was running out of the room."

Moving on to set the murder scene, Watnick told the jurors that Kyle, whom he called a "millionaire real-estate developer," was found nude at the base of the stairway at 110 Stone Canyon, which he described as a "large old mansion once owned by Clara Bow.

"Present in the house on the night the millionaire was killed were Henry Kyle junior; Scott Kyle; Rusty Dunn, a carpenter; and Bobby Green, a friend of the family, confidant of Henry Kyle senior, and tennis pro.

"Early in the evening before the murder," he went on, "Thursday, July twenty-first, Henry Kyle, Scott, and Rusty Dunn went to dinner in Westwood. Bobby Green remained at home. They returned around eight P.M., and Henry Kyle and Rusty discussed architectural plans, then Henry Kyle went to bed." Rick Kyle was not at home that evening, Watnick explained, because the previous afternoon he had driven Ellen Yang, the eleven-year-old daughter of "Vicki Kyle" (whom the DA identified as "the wife of the victim") to Vicki's San Diego condominium, where he spent the night and all day Thursday. Thursday evening, Watnick said, Rick, Vicki, and Ellen went to dinner in San Diego with two women named Ruby Rains and Michele True; afterward, Rick drove back to Los Angeles and arrived at Granada around 11:00 P.M.

The prosecutor described how the house's occupants were then situated: Scott Kyle and Bobby Green were sleeping in an upstairs bedroom on the Stone Canyon side of the house, one that shared a bathroom with the bedroom Rusty Dunn was using. Henry Kyle senior slept in the master-bedroom suite, located in a separate wing on the second floor. Kyle's suite, Watnick pointed out, had its own staircase leading to the dining room directly below on the first floor. The only person to sleep downstairs was Rick Kyle, who was in a bedroom next to the kitchen.

According to Watnick, Rusty Dunn was the first to go to bed after Henry Kyle. When Rick returned from San Diego at eleven, Scott and Bobby Green were in his first-floor bedroom watching TV. Both Scott and Bobby went upstairs to bed shortly afterward.

"Early in the morning," Bobby Green was awakened from his sleep by the sound of Scott flushing the toilet in the bathroom between his bedroom and Rusty Dunn's—an occurrence the DA described as "unusual." Five minutes later Scott went back to bed; then "shots were heard." Bobby, Scott, and Rusty all got out of bed, and Scott located a gun Bobby Green kept under his mattress. A few minutes later Scott and Rusty went downstairs together while Bobby Green called the police from the telephone in Rusty's bedroom. The time then, the DA observed, was about 3:45 A.M.

Because it was "quite dark" in the house, Scott and Rusty "couldn't see much" as they went downstairs. Once on the first floor, Rusty noticed a body on the dining-room floor. As they passed through, Rick came out of the kitchen, dressed in a blue warm-up suit. Rick told Rusty and Scott he had been shot in the arm and that "someone was in the house."

While waiting for the police, Rick—whom Watnick referred to as "the defendant"—told Rusty, Scott, and Bobby that he had been in bed asleep when his father, nude and carrying a gun, woke him up. He wanted Rick to help "investigate" because he had "heard something." Rick put on a warm-up suit and he and his father walked around the house, then came back inside. When they reached the dining room, Rick said, one of the French doors facing Sunset Boulevard was open and he and Henry walked over to the door. Rick was "near and to the left" of Henry. "Then the defendant heard a shot and Henry Kyle said, 'Oh, God, no!' and fired approximately three times," said Watnick, repeating Rick's explanation to Scott, Bobby, and Rusty. "The defendant told the three of them he ran toward the kitchen and felt something hit his right arm. He ran out the back door to the garage area, then he reentered the kitchen and saw Rusty and Scott in the stair area.

"He later told the same story, with minor variations, to investigators at the UCLA Medical Center," Watnick informed the jury. "One of the statements was taped."

Watnick next told how the Rohm .38-caliber revolver had been found, identified as the murder weapon, and traced to Quint Barnes. He said a holster matching the gun had been found in Ricky's bedroom. Then he revealed Rick's alleged confession to Jackie and Henry Miller: "Rick said, 'I killed Henry Kyle.'

"Scott gave him the gun and said it was untraceable because it was shipped in pieces from Germany," Watnick added. "It had been planned for a long time. Rick woke Henry Kyle, who took a gun with him. Both of them looked outside, and when they came back in, Henry Kyle put his gun to his side, getting ready to go back upstairs. Rick shot him, then ran—that's when he was shot by Henry Kyle.

"Rick told Jackie and Henry Miller that he fired twice and wore a Playtex glove," Watnick continued, as the fourteen members of the jury panel listened in rapt attention. "He said he told a story about a prowler to Rusty and Bobby Green. Then he asked Jackie Phillips and Henry Miller to get the gun, and drew a map and diagram on Henry Miller's stationery showing them where it was. The location drawn," the prosecutor noted with triumph, "is exactly where it was found. . . ."

Watnick continued: "Jackie Phillips said when she visited Rick at UCLA, he whispered that she should get Henry Kyle's briefcase because there was 'incriminating evidence' in it. The police found it first," he said with a trace of satisfaction. "Inside, there was a financial statement of Henry Kyle, showing his net worth to be twenty million dollars, plus his stock in Four Star. There was also a copy of his will, leaving almost all to Rick and Scott. Rick's name was crossed out in pencil in one area."

After pausing a second to let the jury absorb what he was saying, Watnick injected, "The murder of Henry Kyle was not spur-of-the-moment. The motive was simply greed and money. Henry Kyle had many conflicts with his sons—particularly Rick, because Henry Kyle was a health nut. He played tennis every day. He hated drugs and drinking and smoking, and wanted his sons to excel. He had conflicts about school, drugs, and drinking with Rick."

Kyle, Watnick told the jury, was making "radical changes" in his life just before he was killed. "He bought Four Star, and the house at Stone Canyon, and spent millions on renovation," he noted. "He planned to sell the Preston [Road] house and move to California. He recently married Vicki Yang, whom he'd known four years. He was starting an entirely new life with her in L.A."

Vicki, Watnick said, went to Taiwan on June 10, 1983, to visit her family for forty days. Just before she left, he pointed out, gesturing toward the defense table, Rick arrived at Stone Canyon "unexpectedly. He drove up in a Mazda," the DA said. "He had been living in Denton and allegedly attending North Texas State. He hadn't been in regular contact with Henry Kyle for a long time." Scott, he noted, was not in California yet. "In the prior year," Watnick told the jury, "most of the communication between Rick and Henry Kyle was through Scott. Henry Kyle didn't even have Rick's phone number or address in Denton."

When Rick arrived, the DA remarked, Henry Kyle was "feeling pretty good" because Rick had told him he had been accepted at Stanford and made the dean's list at North Texas State. "He wrote a letter to Henry Kyle on about May thirtieth, Henry Kyle's birthday, to say how well he was doing and how much he loved his father."

As Watnick picked up a piece of slightly crumpled notebook paper, Rick Kyle bowed his head and stared at the floor.

"'Dear Dad . . .'" the DA began, reading the letter in a cynical, mocking tone of voice, "'. . . Maybe my grades will brighten your day. It would be impossible for me to explain to you how hard I worked to achieve this kind of report card. I also took the Scholastic Achievement Test and made a remarkable score of 620 verbal and 600 math. My GPA score was 3.4. I applied a couple of months ago to Stanford, and they have accepted the scores on my transcript. . . . I should receive a letter of acceptance in about a week or two. I also applied at Columbia, Northwestern and Berkeley, however Stanford is my choice because of the prestige and location. Of course all this work will have been in vain without your help to continue.

"'I know I have crossed you. My intentions were not dishonest—only the process in which I used the tape recorder. . . . I have been inconsistent to you and I'm sorry. I wanted to accept a sense of responsibility and independence to relieve some of your tension, however it appears I have only added to your frustrations. It's the first time I have taken some control over my life. I am going to make mistakes. . . . I wish you are as happy about my accomplishments as I am. I hope to see you soon. I love you very much. Rick. P.S. "Always do right—this will gratify some people and astonish the rest." Mark Twain. A nice philosophy for me to adopt.' "

Putting down the letter, Watnick cast a reproachful glance at Rick, who was still sitting with his head bowed, apparently in embarrassment. Then the DA turned to face the jury panel. An expression of disgust was etched on his narrow features. "Rick Kyle actually dropped out of North Texas on May thirty-first, 1982," he said in a grating, flat monotone. "He was failing. His acceptance at Stanford was a gigantic lie."

At that moment, as if on cue, Judge Devich announced the lunch break. He told the jurors, who were clearly absorbed by what Watnick was telling them, to be back in their seats by 1 :30 that afternoon.

As the reporters, cameramen, and spectators gathered their belongings and pushed their way out the doors toward the elevators down the hall, they gossiped openly about Rick's deception of his father, and the other incriminating allegations.

By 1 :25, Ricky and his four counsel had already taken their places. They talked calmly among themselves and did not seem to be unduly concerned by the morning's disclosures. At the other end of the counsel table, Lew Watnick exuded a confident, nonchalant air. He glanced at the scribbled notes on his yellow legal pad from time to time, and turned around to observe the last of the reporters and onlookers straggling into the courtroom.

A few minutes later, the bailiff called the court to order and Judge Devich motioned Watnick to proceed with his opening argument. Watnick promised the jury they would be hearing from Rusty Dunn and Bobby Green, both of whom had heard Rick say he would kill his father.

In addition, he said, Henry Miller III and Jackie Phillips would be testifying for the prosecution. This announcement caused a ripple of surprise among the journalists, who had been wondering for weeks whether Jackie would show up for the trial.

But the greatest surprise in Watnick's opening statement came a few seconds later, when he told jurors he would be calling to the stand a witness named Louis Douglas Halley, whom he identified as Rick Kyle's brother-in-law.

Halley, Watnick explained, was the brother of Kelly Moore,

a girlfriend whom Rick had invited to stay with him at Granada, when his father was out of town. Kelly and Rick, it was revealed, were married in September 1984, during the time between Rick's indictment and his murder trial. The month before—August 1984—Kelly gave birth to their son, Justin.

The DA claimed that Louis Douglas Halley would testify that Rick discussed with him how he shot his father. "He told Halley he hated Vicki, and that he killed Kyle when Vicki was not there," Watnick said, clenching his teeth. "He and Scott planned the murder in the summer of '82. They were afraid Kyle would find out they'd falsified their grades."

On Thursday, July 21, he continued, repeating Halley's account of Rick's statements, Scott went downstairs sometime before midnight and said to Rick, "This is the night." Rick told Halley he hid the gun in his sweat suit while he and his father looked for prowlers, the DA asserted. They never went outside the house.

When Kyle turned his back, Watnick said, "the defendant shot him. Then Kyle shot the defendant. The defendant was scared and ran out of the house. The fact that he'd been shot by Kyle ruined his plans."

Rick, Watnick said, told Halley he wore surgical gloves "so he wouldn't leave fingerprints," and that he "threw them in the trash.

"It was Scott's idea," Watnick said of the murder plot.

"It's really a simple question," Watnick said in conclusion, facing the fourteen men and women in the jury box, listening intently to his raspy, slightly sneering delivery. "Did Rick Kyle murder his father, and was it premeditated? There's only one verdict you can return. . . ."

A moment later Judge Devich announced a ten-minute afternoon recess and the jury filed out of the courtroom. When they were safely out of earshot, the courtroom resounded with statements hostile to Rick: "So he was indicted in August of 1983 and the kid's just been cruisin' around ever since?" one middle-aged reporter for *USA Today* said incredulously. "Jesus!"

Around 3:45, Gibson, the blond, boyish-looking criminal lawyer representing Rick, rose to address the court. He said merely that he would reserve his opening statement until the prosecution completed its case—a common defense strategy in California criminal proceedings. It was greeted, nonetheless, by a palpable wave of disappointment in the courtroom.

The *L.A. Times* speculated that Ricky's lawyers' strategy could be inferred from points they had made at the preliminary hearing in January.

"They are expected to hit hard on [Jackie] Phillips', [Henry] Miller's and Ricky Kyle's use of alcohol and drugs on the night the confession was allegedly made," the newspaper predicted in its account of the first day of the murder trial. The article also pointed out that Gibson and his colleagues had contended already in pretrial motions that Jackie and her boyfriend "were so intoxicated as to be incompetent to testify."

11

THE NEXT MORNING, WHEN MIKE
Gibson, Steve Sumner, John Vandevelde, and Jack Pate walked
into court together with Rick, they had nothing to say about the
Times's predictions. In every other respect, however, they were
open, direct, and in Steve Sumner's case, downright Texas-
friendly to those who approached them. In fact, Sumner's folk-
siness had won over Judge Devich's bailiff, court reporter, and
court coordinator. They teased him regularly about his physical
resemblance to the deceased. "They want us to reenact the
shooting for the jury right here in the courtroom, exactly as it
happened, with me as Henry Kyle," Sumner remarked. "The
thing is," he said, grinning, "Kyle was nude at the time—and
old Watnick keeps making such a big deal of the fact that he
was standing 'erect' when he faced the French doors . . . hell,
I'm not sure I can take that kind of pressure!"

The combination of Sumner's charm, Mike Gibson's smooth
professionalism, and John Vandevelde's earnestness was bound
to impress the courtroom audience—a much smaller audience on
this second day. The cameras and microphones that recorded the
opening day were now nowhere to be seen, and the journalists
in attendance dwindled to a half dozen or so: the *Los Angeles
Times* reporter who had been covering the story from the beginning, along with two or three journalists from Texas papers and
a UPI representative. They were joined by a trio of scruffy-
looking men, middle-aged and older, one of whom carried a sack
lunch. They were the "court-watchers"—retired or otherwise

unoccupied residents of Los Angeles who spent their days in the Criminal Courts Building. "We only attend if there's more than a million at stake," one court-watcher explained, and took great pride in the fact that he had been in court "every day" for John De Lorean's drug conspiracy trial and Carol Burnett's lawsuit against the *National Enquirer*.

Also in attendance was Bob Grogan, who strode confidently into the courtroom and took a seat directly behind Lew Watnick. Grogan's manner suggested that he was going to thoroughly enjoy the upcoming spectacle.

Once everyone was in place, Judge Devich said a cheery good morning to the jury panel, and they repeated the greeting back to him in unison, as if they were students in school. Then Devich asked Lew Watnick to call his witness. The reporters turned around in their seats, expecting to get their first look at Rusty Dunn. But instead the DA announced Joseph L. Cogan, the pathologist who conducted Henry Kyle's autopsy.

Cogan was short, slight of build, and had thinning, unkempt hair, a lock or two of which dangled defiantly on his forehead. When he spoke, it was with a slight stammer, and he frequently pushed his wire-rimmed glasses back up against his nose. Somehow he looked exactly as one might expect of a man who spent most of his waking hours with corpses.

Watnick handed the coroner a stack of papers to identify. After glancing at them for a few seconds, Cogan testified that they were his autopsy report and notes—the documents Bob Grogan had sealed from the press throughout the murder investigation.

Referring Cogan to his official report, Watnick asked the coroner to tell the jury the exact cause of Henry Kyle's death.

"A gunshot wound to the chest," the pathologist replied matter-of-factly.

Reaching under the counsel table, the DA picked up a life-size mannequin of a nude male torso, with a steel rod resembling a giant arrow protruding dramatically from under the left armpit at the back and from the upper right chest. As the jury looked on with obvious interest, he explained that the mannequin was a facsimile of Henry Kyle's corpse—the steel rod represented the path of the fatal bullet, based on Cogan's autopsy findings.

Gesturing at the steel rod, Cogan explained to the jurors,

who   :areful notes, that the fatal bullet had entered Kyle's
back on the left side and had come out through the right half
of his chest. It had left behind gunshot residue and tattooing
around the entrance wound—this was simulated on the mannequin by a black ring. On its way through the body, Cogan said,
the bullet had punctured Kyle's heart and lungs. The pathologist also referred to a ''second wound,'' which he described as
a ''near-miss''—meaning the bullet grazed Kyle without actually penetrating. It had caused stippling, or discoloration of
the skin, on his ''left neck, shoulder and face.''

While Cogan was talking, Watnick walked up to the front of
the courtroom and placed a large white posterboard on the wall
behind the witness. To this he had attached several photographs
in vivid color of Henry Kyle's nude corpse taken from three or
four different angles, all from the waist up.

Officially, his purpose in displaying the pictures was to show
the jury firsthand the gunshot wounds and abrasions to Kyle's
body. His unofficial purpose was shock value.

Seeing the gruesome photographs of his father's corpse, Rick,
who had been looking directly at the coroner, turned his head
away for the first time.

Meanwhile, Cogan continued to answer Watnick's queries
about his autopsy report. Based on the size of the entrance
wound—approximately a quarter of an inch in circumference—
he ''rough-estimated'' that the bullet that killed Kyle came from
a .38-caliber revolver. He was certain more than one bullet was
fired at the victim because the stippling from the ''near-miss''
shot was ''entirely separate'' from the stippling on the chest.

''Generally speaking,'' the coroner observed, ''the closer the
barrel is to the body, the tighter the charring and the larger the
pattern.'' In his opinion, whoever shot Henry Kyle fired at a
range of two to five inches—nearly point-blank. Several of the
jurors' mouths dropped slightly at hearing this.

''I would qualify that with a lot of hedging,'' Cogan added,
''because at the time I did the autopsy I didn't know the kind
of weapon that was used.''

''But you still stick with it?''

''Yes, but it's a rough estimate. It's better to test-shoot it.''

Asked if Kyle died immediately after being shot, Cogan responded, ''Not necessarily.'' Although the bullet that had punctured Kyle's lungs and heart had caused a fatal wound, the length

of time to death depended on "several factors," including the victim's general stamina and physical makeup and the availability of medical help. Henry Kyle, he estimated, had lived "minutes" after he was shot. "Possibly as long as fifteen to twenty minutes," he added. "That's an upper estimate."

After allowing the jury a few seconds to absorb the significance of what the coroner was saying—that Kyle was alive long enough for him to have fired six shots at Rick, including the one that caused the gunshot wound to his elbow—Watnick asked Cogan to describe Kyle's physical condition.

"He was in remarkably good shape," the pathologist answered, "very muscular," with few signs of coronary-artery disease. It was likely that Kyle would have lived longer than most people with a similar wound.

Once he had established that point, Watnick asked the coroner to describe Kyle's other wounds. As Rick now watched with intense interest, Cogan went through the graphic police photographs one by one and painstakingly identified "approximately five" lacerations on the head.

The "first wound," a small gash at the top of Kyle's skull, was described by the coroner as a two-inch oval contusion or abrasion. Next to it were two other "small oval areas," which could represent separate injuries. A second photograph revealed what Cogan diagnosed as a "fresh" one-and-a-half-inch hemorrhage over the back of the head. The most severe head injuries, in Cogan's opinion, were two contusions behind and above Kyle's right ear. These were plainly visible in another of the autopsy pictures. Both had caused "profuse bleeding." There was also a two-inch-by-one-and-a-half-inch contusion above Kyle's left eye, over the forehead.

The pathologist stated that in his opinion, none of these lacerations to Kyle's head and face would have been lethal by themselves. Neither would they have "necessarily" caused him to be unconscious.

When asked by Watnick if Kyle's head injuries could have been caused by a fall, the coroner replied, "I don't think so. I would think they were caused by some kind of force and trauma."

Watnick picked up a handgun he identified for the jury as a .38-caliber revolver—the same size as the weapon Cogan had testified caused Kyle's fatal gunshot wound, and the same size as the one police had found in the bushes next door to 110 Stone Canyon.

"Were the lacerations on the victim's head consistent with the use of this gun?" the DA demanded, holding the weapon up in the air for the jury to see.

"That could account for *some* of the injuries to the head," the coroner said carefully, "if the short barrel hit the top of the victim's head with the gun upside down or with the butt of the weapon. The wounds at the top of the head are most consistent with the use of a gun."

Where, Watnick wanted to know, would Kyle's attacker have been standing in order to produce the sort of head injuries Kyle suffered?

"It's difficult to say," Cogan responded. "Especially with regard to the wounds on top of the head."

"How about the other wounds at the back of the head?" the DA persisted.

"Those might suggest that the assailant was behind the victim," Cogan replied in his slow, methodical way, giving the answer Watnick was obviously after.

After pointing out the autopsy also revealed a minor wound to Kyle's knee, Watnick passed the witness to Mike Gibson, thereby giving the jury, reporters, and court-watchers their first chance to see Ricky's highly touted criminal lawyer in action.

As it happened, Gibson could hardly have been presented with a better witness with whom to showcase his impressive cross-examination skills. Gibson had actually spent his college years preparing to be a dentist. In his second year of dental school he decided, as his partner Steve Sumner put it, that "he didn't want to spend the rest of his life looking down people's mouths," and switched to law instead. But his training did not go to waste—whenever Gibson has a doctor on the stand, he can question him or her convincingly on minute details of even the most technical issues.

Gibson introduced himself to the coroner with affable good manners. He immediately called the jury's attention to the fact that the mannequin Cogan had been using to clarify Henry Kyle's gunshot wounds was not made to scale—with respect either to Kyle's body or to his injuries. Then he asked the pathologist to define a "contact wound."

Cogan explained that it was an injury caused by a weapon in "close physical contact with the skin." Gibson noted that Kyle's fatal injury to the left back side did not have any of the characteristics of a contact wound (a small point of entry and no visible powder marks on the skin), meaning, if he was correct, that the murder weapon was not in "close physical contact" with Kyle when he was shot.

"It was a wound in close proximity," Cogan confirmed, looking slightly uncomfortable at Gibson's close questioning, "not a contact wound."

Gibson asked Cogan to name the "most significant vessel" damaged of Kyle's internal organs.

"The pulmonary artery and vein," the coroner responded immediately, comparing it to a "rubber hose" going through the midline of the body.

"What was the size of Kyle's pulmonary artery at the time of the autopsy?" Gibson inquired.

When Cogan replied that he hadn't measured the size of Kyle's artery, Gibson looked at him with disbelief, then asked, "Did you make any *diagrams* or *notes* about the damage to the artery at the time you conducted the autopsy?"

"No," Cogan answered sheepishly. "The average diameter of a male artery is approximately two centimeters, or three quarters of an inch."

"What was the size of the laceration?" Gibson demanded.

"One-quarter to one-half inch," the coroner responded. "I don't recall exactly." Then he added defensively, "That's an estimate based on experience and other observations in autopsy. The projectile's size was about a quarter of an inch, and the laceration roughly corresponds to the size of the laceration in the skin."

"[But] the bullet tumbles, and therefore can cause damage not corresponding to its size," Gibson pointed out. "Could the injury to the pulmonary artery have been as large as one-half inch?"

When Cogan stuck with his "one-quarter-to-one-half-inch" estimate, Gibson asked if a three-quarter-inch vessel, lacerated by a half-inch wound, would be severed.

"I can't say," Cogan responded. "The larger the hole, the more blood can come out. I don't know how large the hole was, other than my one-quarter-to-one-half-inch guess."

"Was the pulmonary vein damaged?" Gibson inquired.

When Cogan said yes, Gibson responded, "Then two major vessels were damaged," a note of satisfaction in his voice. "Some of the largest vessels in the body. Was the pericardial sac also damaged?"

"Yes," the coroner replied, and then explained to the jury that the pericardial sac was a "fibrous, loose-fitting structure that surrounds the heart."

When he had established via the coroner that the injury to the pulmonary system was the "major cause" of Henry Kyle's death, Gibson asked, "How long would someone live after the damage you just described?"

"You could only guess," Cogan said hesitantly, as he fiddled with his wire-rimmed glasses. "Blood will start oozing within seconds."

"What effect would the blood loss have?" Gibson wanted to know.

"That would depend on one's strength and mobility, to a certain extent," the coroner answered. "I would guess Kyle was alive fifteen to twenty minutes."

"What if you didn't have immediate medical attention?" Gibson persisted.

"You'd be in a declining state to the point of death" was Cogan's reply.

At Gibson's prompting, the pathologist also testified that it would be impossible to determine a person's position in a room based on the path of a bullet, or "angulation," because, in Cogan's words, "the angles of the shot and the body could be variable and produce the same result."

"So you don't know if Henry Kyle was erect, prone, or what?" Gibson said with satisfaction.

"That's correct," the pathologist replied.

For the remainder of the afternoon, Gibson continued to probe into the coroner's autopsy findings with excruciating thoroughness. At 4:30, Judge Devich dismissed the weary jury.

"He's a nitpicker," Watnick said of Gibson at the end of the day. "He likes to cross-examine." Scowling slightly, he added, "If that's the way he wants to play it . . ."

12

THE NEXT MORNING, A BRIGHT AND sunny Wednesday, the crowds and TV cameras were back in full force—a sure sign, court-watchers said knowledgeably, that someone in the DA's office had tipped off reporters to expect an important witness. Ricky had loosened up considerably since Monday morning. Instead of sitting stiffly in his seat and gazing into space, he strolled in and out of the courtroom while waiting for the jury, nodded hello to the *L.A. Times* reporter, and complimented John Vandevelde on his jacket.

His own wardrobe, the defense team would later acknowledge, had been carefully selected by Steve Sumner off the racks of a men's shop near the UCLA campus. "As soon as we got here," Sumner chuckled, "I took one look at Ricky's clothes and took him straight to Westwood and bought him some sport coats and ties to wear in court. The idea was to make him look like an average college kid."

On this Wednesday, Rick was outfitted in a camel's hair jacket, button-down shirt, and sporty but conservative tie.

During the morning session Gibson put the finishing touches on his cross-examination of the L. A. County coroner. He used the same exacting, highly technical line of questioning as he had the day before. The most significant point was his suggestion that Kyle's head wounds had been caused by a struggle.

Gibson's last questions to Cogan concerned his autopsy, specifically, whether he decided not to measure Kyle's blood because of anything Bob Grogan or John Rockwood had said to him at the time. (Measuring Kyle's blood might have shown his wounds to be more serious than Cogan was now proposing.)

"My measurements of blood were not related to information given to me by Rockwood or Grogan," Cogan stated.

"Did you rely on what they told you when you were performing the autopsy?" Gibson persisted.

"I did rely somewhat on that," the coroner conceded.

As the spectators breathed a sign of relief, both Gibson and Watnick indicated they had no further questions for Dr. Cogan, who stepped down from the stand gratefully.

After the lunch break the DA stood up and announced the name "Rusty Dunn." In his first public appearance, Henry Kyle's carpenter walked up the aisle, past the counsel tables, to the witness stand.

Dunn was in his mid-thirties, but looked ten years younger. He seemed a friendly, likable sort, with sandy brown hair, a solid build, and attractive, wholesome features—the kind of guy who might appear in a beer commercial. He wore blue jeans and cowboy boots, a corduroy jacket, and an argyle sweater vest over an open-necked shirt.

He said his name, "Carroll C. Dunn," in a bright, personable voice, as the TV cameras focused on him from the rear of the courtroom. When Watnick inquired about his occupation, Dunn replied, "Cabinetmaker." He explained that he had lived in Henry Kyle's house on Stone Canyon from Memorial Day, 1983, until August 15, 1983.

Dunn said he had met Henry Kyle in the fall of 1982, when Kyle had hired him to do cabinetwork for his Dallas mansion. In late January 1983, he said, Kyle asked him about doing some work at Granada. In April, Dunn flew to L.A. to meet Kyle to "see whether he could do the job."

"What was the condition of the house at that time?" Watnick asked.

"There was water and rodent damage," Dunn responded. "The doors and windows were nailed shut—similar to the condition it was [later] in July."

After inspecting the house with Kyle in April, Dunn was hired as the "superintendent" of carpentry and cabinetwork. "I stayed with a friend and made measurements," the carpenter went on to say. "Then I went back to Texas."

On May 15, he said, he "came back to L.A.," and noted with

exasperation that Kyle had "no plans" ready for the house, so Dunn "visited his wife in Lake Tahoe."

Around Memorial Day, he returned for a third time to "push the plans through," and moved in.

"Was anyone living there at the time?" Watnick asked him.

"Mr. Kyle resided there," Dunn answered politely. "He left periodically for business trips to New York or Texas."

There was still "little happening" with the renovation of the house. "I helped with the measurements and with the estate sale," he said, frustration evident in his voice. "I just maintained the place." Eventually, because there was no work for him to do, he was forced to set up a cabinet shop at Granada, "with Henry Kyle's consent." (". . . I paid the electricity," Dunn added.)

"When did you meet Rick Kyle?" Watnick asked next.

"I met him briefly in the fall of '82 during the Preston Road work, and then in L.A. in the summer of 1983."

According to Dunn, Rick called up one day and asked him to tell Kyle he was coming to California. Rick showed up at the house the second week in June in a "Mazda sports car."

That night and for several nights afterward, Dunn testified, Rick slept "adjacent to the garage." About a week later, he "rearranged" a room downstairs to use as his bedroom.

"Mr. Kyle," Dunn noted, was "in and out" of the house throughout the summer. "He was in New York one week, and he was in Dallas prior to the incident."

Dunn testified that he was working on a job in Sherman Oaks while Rick was staying at the house. Watnick asked sarcastically, "What was Rick doing?"

"Organizing belongings for an estate sale," the carpenter answered, "at Mr. Kyle's request."

"How did Henry Kyle feel about Rick smoking or drinking at Stone Canyon?" the DA queried.

"Mr. Kyle didn't appreciate Rick smoking in the house," Dunn said carefully. "He didn't like him drinking at all."

"What did he say?" Watnick pushed.

Hesitating a moment, then imitating Kyle with a gruff, belligerent tone of voice, Dunn responded, " 'If you're going to live in *my* house you're going to live the way *I* want you to. If you want to drink, you can go back and live with your relatives in Georgia.' "

Dunn said Kyle kept bourbon and vodka in the house for guests, but Rick drank it.

"What did you tell him when he did that?" Watnick asked.

"I said, 'You have to clean up before your old man gets here or he'll chew your ass out.'"

Usually, the carpenter observed, Rick didn't do anything about it, so *he* had to "clean up quickly" before Kyle got home. Once, he said, Kyle "found out" after he saw cigarettes in the ashtrays.

"What did he say to Rick?" Watnick inquired.

"He proceeded to chew his ass out," Dunn answered. "'You'll live in my house the way I want you to live if you're going to Stanford. . . .'"

Changing the subject, Watnick asked the carpenter what sort of relationship he had with Rick. Dunn told him they "became friends." The DA questioned him about drug purchases.

"Rick asked me to get him some cocaine," he answered, as Rick scrutinized him from across the courtroom. Dunn testified that Rick asked him "four or five times," the first time "the second week he was there. I got it for him twice," the carpenter stated.

"How much did you purchase?" asked Watnick.

"It was a small amount," Dunn answered. "About a gram or a half gram." Rick paid for it, the carpenter noted—about a hundred dollars a gram—then shared it with him.

"How did you ingest it?" Watnick continued.

"We snorted it off a mirror," the carpenter replied, without apology.

Watnick later asked Dunn about a twenty-dollar loan he made to Rick in late June. The day after, the carpenter testified, Rick had a "wad of hundreds" on him.

"Where did he say he got the money?" Watnick inquired.

"He said he had a pot farm in Texas and that's where the money came from," Dunn said firmly, as reporters scribbled down his testimony furiously.

Without skipping a beat, Watnick asked about a chandelier Kyle discovered missing from the house during the same period of time.

"Mr. Kyle asked *me* where the chandelier was," Dunn said, clearly annoyed. "He said he knew it was an inside job, and that Rick and I did it. I asked Rick if he stole the lamp and he said no. About three weeks later, Mr. Kyle and Rick went for a walk and when they came back Rick said to me, 'Remember that lamp? I stole it.' "

"Did the defendant ever say anything to you about killing Henry Kyle?" the DA demanded.

"He told me at least six times he wanted to kill his father," Dunn responded, causing one of the regular court-watchers to let out a low whistle. "The first time was in the cabinet shop after an argument. He said, 'I gotta kill him.' Another time, he asked me, 'How should I kill my father?' We were drinking together in my room once and I said, 'I don't wanna talk about it, because if you do it, I'll know, and then you'll come get me.' "

"Was there anything that precipitated these statements?" Watnick coached.

"He'd refer to it if Mr. Kyle belittled him or chewed his ass," Dunn responded. "He'd say, 'I've gotta get rid of him. . . .' He once said if he got rid of his father he'd have people come out of the woodwork cheering."

The jurors sat in stunned silence. Watnick asked next about some conversations Rick had with him about building a restaurant in Barbados or on the Riviera. Rick told Dunn how "he and Scott were the sole recipients of Henry Kyle's will."

"He never referred to how much he owned," the carpenter added. "I knew his father was very wealthy."

"Did you see any blows between Henry Kyle and the defendant?"

"No," said Dunn. "Mr. Kyle argued and yelled at Rick about drinking and smoking."

In the closing minutes of Wednesday's testimony, Watnick asked Rusty Dunn to tell the jury about an incident that occurred at Granada shortly before the murder.

"I went to the bathroom, and wanted to read a *Penthouse*," the carpenter said obligingly, "and I found a pistol in Rick's room under the bed on the left side as you face the headboard, while I was looking for the magazine."

"Did it look like this?" Watnick asked, holding up the Rohm revolver with the brown handle police found in the bushes next door to Kyle's house.

"Yes," said Dunn.

"Tell us what happened a few days later, after the shootings," the DA directed.

"I visited Rick in the hospital," the carpenter answered, looking nervous for the first time since he took the stand, "and I asked him where the gun was."

"What did he say to you?"

"He said he didn't have a gun," Dunn said coldly, "'. . . And be careful what you say.'"

On Thursday morning all fourteen members of the jury panel watched with keen interest as the carpenter took the stand for a second time.

Fueled by the sensational impact of Wednesday's testimony, Watnick jumped into his questioning with a burst of energy.

According to the carpenter, Rick arrived at Stone Canyon with "all his clothes," and told Dunn he had "no money." "He got money from his dad. Mr. Kyle gave him money to buy supplies for the house."

"Did the defendant tell you *why* he came to California?" the DA prodded.

"He wanted to stay and get on the good side of his father so he could go to Stanford," Dunn answered. "He said he needed to make relations good with his father. They'd had previous bad circumstances and he wanted to make up for it. He wanted his own apartment and car. He said he wanted to major in journalism."

"Did he say he'd been *accepted* at Stanford?"

"Yes."

"What did the defendant tell you about his grades?" Watnick asked.

"He said he made the dean's list at North Texas State that spring. He said he was a journalism major, and that he studied a lot because he had previous bad marks."

"Did he ever tell you he failed?"

"No."

"What did he say about Scott?"

"He said Scott was the 'yes man,' the 'quiet man,'" Dunn stated. "He stood behind his father and did the things he said, he was being built in his father's image. Rick was the 'bad guy.' He said, 'The reason my father and I clash is because I'm like him.'"

"How did they clash?" asked the DA.

"Mr. Kyle would belittle him, knock him down verbally."

"What did he say?"

Pausing a second, Dunn said, " 'You're lazy,' 'Quit smoking'—Do you really want me to repeat what he said?"

"Yes," Watnick instructed.

Looking slightly embarrassed, Dunn said, "He'd call him a 'stupid son of a bitch,' 'lazy asshole.' "

"How many times did this occur?" the DA asked.

"Mr. Kyle verbally mentioned 'lazy' and 'son of a bitch' to Rick about twelve times."

"Did the defendant say anything back to him?"

"He never said anything to his face," Dunn said. "Once he came into my shop in the garage afterwards and gave a closed fist and said, 'Son of a bitch.' Another time, he and I were sunning on the deck and Mr. Kyle said, 'You lazy asshole. Get off your ass and do something.' When he left, Rick went to the edge of the deck and said, 'Just push him and create a heart attack. . . .' "

"Did he say anything else about killing Henry Kyle?"

"He said to me in the shop once, 'I gotta figure out the perfect murder.' "

Asked if Rick ever used swearwords to refer to his father, Dunn said, "He called him an asshole, prick, son of a bitch. It was always after an altercation between the two. A reaction to Mr. Kyle's verbal abuse. 'I'm gonna get nowhere with this guy . . . gotta get rid of him.' "

"How often did he say this?" asked Watnick.

"It came up several times in casual conversation. He said, 'I have to create a situation to get rid of him—a car accident or a heart attack.' "

According to Dunn, Rick "usually showed respect" to his father in his presence. "Mr. Kyle had a way of talking to people," he commented. "If he was very nice, something was wrong. If he said, 'You do nice work for an asshole,' it meant he liked you. He had a sort of John Wayne image."

"Was anyone else present when the defendant mentioned killing Henry Kyle to you?" Watnick inquired.

"No. It was always in my shop or in my bedroom in the evening."

"Where did the 'perfect murder' conversation occur?"

"It was a casual conversation in the shop."

"Did you take him seriously?"

"I didn't believe him," Dunn said offhandedly. "I kinda

put it off to a hotheaded kid pissed at his father. Rick had a real coolness about him . . . he never showed anger.''

Dunn also testified that Rick told him twice that he was ''growing pot near Denton'' with a partner, and that it was his ''means of income.'' ''He said he did coke back in Texas, and marijuana.''

''When did you find the gun under Rick's bed?'' the DA asked next.

''The day before the murder.''

''Did you tell the defendant?''

''No. Not until I saw him at the hospital,'' Dunn replied. ''He said, 'I guess we're goin' to Barbados,' '' the carpenter repeated, in a singsong voice. '' 'Be careful what you say.' ''

''What did he say when you mentioned the gun?''

''He said he didn't own a gun. . . . Then I got scared, because I suspected Rick of murdering Henry Kyle.''

For the next few minutes Dunn recounted the events preceding the shooting. Vicki returned from Taiwan on Wednesday, and when she got to the house, Rick's girlfriend, Kelly, was still there. Rusty told the jurors he was angry with Rick over that, and Rick in turn ''got mad and said, 'You'd better get ready, because the shit's comin' down!' ''

Kyle got home later that night, Dunn testified, and Vicki left for San Diego the next day. Thursday night, he, Kyle, and Scott went to a sushi restaurant for dinner. Bobby Green stayed home. At dinner, Rusty related, Kyle told them he was planning to take Scott to San Diego for the weekend.

The three of them returned home from the restaurant between 8:15 and 8:30 and Dunn and Kyle ''walked around the grounds.'' Kyle was ''tired'' and went to bed shortly afterward. Dunn said he went upstairs about the same time, and fell asleep in front of the TV.

Dunn then related his version of the shooting: that he had been awakened by ''four or five rounds'' in rapid order; that Scott and Bobby Green had rushed into his room; that he and Scott had gone downstairs to investigate and had found a body on the dining-room floor.

''I noticed a bullet hole in the window of the breakfast nook, so I went over to take a look. Then Rick came out of the kitchen behind my back. He was standing in the doorway in a blue warm-up.

''Rick said, 'Scotty, I've been shot. There's someone in the house.' I told everyone to go to my room. We left the door open to see the prowler, put the light on, and stayed low. Bobby Green was still calling the police.''

"How was the defendant behaving?" asked Watnick.

"He was cool," said Dunn. "Shocked; in pain. We put him on the floor.''

"Was he emotionally upset?''

"No," said Dunn. "Scott was pretty frantic.''

"What did the defendant say happened?''

"He said Mr. Kyle woke him up and said my dog was outside barking, and there was a prowler on the premises,'' Dunn answered. "They surveyed the grounds, then they came in the courtyard entry. Rick said he was behind Mr. Kyle as they were walking to the French doors. Mr. Kyle said, 'Oh, shit!,' there was an exchange of gunfire, and Rick ran outside behind the garage.''

"Did he say where he saw the prowler?''

"He said he saw him in the dark to the right behind the fireplace. The prowler was there, and the confrontation was there. He said he was two to three feet behind his father.

"Ten minutes later, the police came. The four of us were in my room. Rick relayed the information. Scott was frantic, in tears, saying, 'Where's my Daddy? Where's my Daddy?' Rick said, 'I don't know where Dad is.' I had to comfort Scott.''

Mike Gibson made careful notes throughout Dunn's testimony. After the lunch break he introduced himself politely, as usual.

Then, like Watnick, he began by asking the witness about his background and his association with Henry Kyle. Whereas the DA had covered the subject in ten minutes or so, Gibson took almost an hour.

Dunn testified that he grew up in California and first worked as a professional ski patrolman. When he was twenty-one, he switched to carpentry. Ann Meidel introduced him to Henry Kyle in October 1982. At the time he was doing some carpentry work for Meidel in Houston, and Kyle needed someone to install an oak cabinet in the guest bath at 9909 Preston Road.

Dunn accepted the job, which took three days. He spent the first night at a hotel, and slept at Kyle's mansion the second. There he was introduced to "Vicki Yang," Scott, and Bobby Green, who played tennis at the house all three days. Rick Kyle arrived late in the afternoon during his second day on the job. Dunn was told he was a student at North Texas State doing weekend Marine Corps reserve duty. Rick and Kyle "seemed to be fine" together, the carpenter testified. Rick didn't smoke or drink in Dunn's presence, his defense attorney pointed out.

Several weeks later, Dunn testified, he telephoned Kyle to ask if he would be interested in backing him on a furniture-design venture. "He liked the idea; he wanted me to expand on it." In January 1983, Kyle invited Dunn and his wife to dinner. "He said that he bought a production company and a house in Beverly Hills and would I like to help," the carpenter said. "He wanted me to be the superintendent, coordinate the job. Mr. Kyle was going to tell me when to go out there." If the renovation was successful, Kyle told him he "might back" his furniture-design project.

According to the carpenter, he first visited Stone Canyon on April 1. The previous tenants' clothes were still in the closets and their furniture was covered with white sheets. "It was a mess. The electricity and plumbing were not up to scale, there was a leaky roof and rodent damage." In May, when he moved in with Kyle, "no improvements" had been made. "One bathroom didn't work at all. There was no water pressure. Everything needed a thorough cleaning." In Dunn's opinion, the house was "not habitable, even into July . . . no significant improvements were made."

Asked about the grounds, Dunn said, "You could barely make out the house from Sunset. There were a lot of tall bushes. The vegetation provided some protection on the Stone Canyon side from people milling around—it was hard to get in. You could barely see the fence for the trees."

"Was there a security problem when the vegetation was removed in May?" Gibson asked.

Two days after Rick arrived, Dunn replied, his car was stolen out of the driveway in front of the garage. "They found the car and impounded it. He never saw it again."

Rick, Dunn said, arrived the first week in June, followed by Bobby Green a week later. Green took an upstairs bedroom, and Rick stayed in one of the two rooms adjoining the kitchen downstairs. When Scott arrived the third week in June, he stayed at first in Rick's first-floor bedroom, then moved upstairs.

"He moved back downstairs occasionally, though," Gibson

interjected, more in the form of an answer than a question. "Henry Kyle insisted he sleep downstairs. . . . And he was afraid to sleep downstairs in that dark room, wasn't he?"

When the carpenter said he didn't know, Gibson seemed surprised, then asked, "There was no security system in the house, was there?"

"No," Dunn answered.

"Did Henry Kyle lay down rules for protection in the home?"

"Yes."

"Didn't Henry Kyle instruct you to always have a gun at night if the door was open?"

"No," replied Dunn.

"Didn't he give you a shotgun when you first showed up and say, 'Use this if there's a prowler'?" Gibson asked impatiently.

"Yes."

"Didn't you once go after a prowler without a gun and Henry Kyle told you, 'You stupid idiot. Use the gun next time'?"

"Yes," admitted Dunn.

"After that," Gibson continued, slightly irritated, "didn't he instruct all of you to keep a gun?"

"He said, 'In the future, arm yourself.' "

Kyle, Dunn testified, was "always armed." He kept his gun on the nightstand next to his bed, out of the holster, or under his pillow or bedcovers.

"Did he ever keep it in his briefcase?" Gibson asked.

"I never saw it," said Dunn.

"Eventually," Gibson noted, "there were all men in the house. What did Bobby Green do during the day?"

"He was waiting to go to law school," Dunn answered, then added, "Basically just hanging out. He wasn't around all day."

"Did he do any work around the house?"

"He maybe cleaned the dishes," Dunn said offhandedly.

Before leaving the subject of Bobby Green, Gibson made the point that Dunn saw him cleaning the dirt and leaves from the porch by the French doors that led to the dining room as Henry Kyle, Scott and the carpenter were leaving for dinner at the Horosushi restaurant at 7:00 on Thursday, July 22. Thus any footprints found on the porch after the shooting were made sometime during that same evening, Gibson demonstrated, suggesting the presence of a third person or prowler.

"Would you say there was a concern about burglars in the

house from May thirtieth to July twenty-second?" Gibson asked next. "That's a fair statement?"

"Yeah," said Dunn.

"In fact, you even fired a shot from your shotgun at Rick and [his girlfriend] Kelly when they were coming in one night the week Henry Kyle was out of town, didn't you?" Gibson said accusingly, as spectators exchanged shocked glances.

"I was out on the sundeck and Rick and Kelly were coming in the back," the carpenter answered defensively. "I discharged the gun once to scare them."

"There was a confrontation, wasn't there?"

"I told them, 'You could have been anybody,'" Dunn said hotly. "We'd made a big point about keeping the house secure. My concern was that I had a wad of money in my room."

"So you shot a one-gauge shotgun. . . . Scared them, didn't it?" Gibson said sarcastically.

When the hum in the spectator section quieted, the defense lawyer continued: "How were relations between Rick and his father?"

"There was frustration."

"Tell us about that," Gibson suggested.

"First there was the problem with the drinking," Dunn said. "Mr. Kyle left on business soon after Rick got there, and while he was gone Rick got into the bourbon and vodka. I told him to clean it up. He didn't, so I did, and the old man noticed."

"What did he say?"

"'If you wanna drink, go live with your fuckin' relatives in Georgia and get out of my life. If you wanna go to Stanford, clean up.'"

"You said yesterday that Henry Kyle ruled with an iron fist. What did you mean by that?"

"It was a figure of speech. He'd tell you how it would be. Accept the law, that was the law."

"How did he treat Rick?"

"He was demeaning to him—called him a 'lazy S.O.B.,' 'worthless asshole.' 'Get off your ass and do something.'"

"How often did he say these things?" Gibson pressed.

"Numerous times," said Dunn. "Whenever it came to a confrontation, that's what happened. He belittled and demeaned him, used slang language and rough words. That was his way of communicating."

"Did Rick ever cuss back or demean his father?"

"Not to his face."

"How would you describe Henry Kyle's behavior toward Rick?"

"Frustration. Anger. He was upset with his son. The way parents get mad at children."

"Did he ever threaten to throw Rick out of the house?" asked Gibson.

"Three or four times."

"Did Rick ever react to Henry Kyle face to face?" Gibson persisted. "Did he ever hit him?"

"No. He didn't make any physical advances. It was always a one-sided confrontation."

Later Gibson asked Dunn if Kyle gave Rick any spending money.

"Mr. Kyle gave Rick and Scott money for stuff around the house," the carpenter testified. "Whatever was left over, they could spend."

"Was it a lot of money?" Gibson inquired.

"Mr. Kyle was not overly generous with his son," said Dunn.

Judge Devich had decided before the Kyle case came to trial that he would set aside Fridays to hear the other cases on his criminal docket. So Dunn's testimony did not continue until the following Monday.

But the three-day break seemed only to enhance interest. The print and TV reporters returned Monday morning, along with a full complement of court-watchers dressed in outfits ranging from rags to leisure suits. They passed each other notes and food and gossiped in loud voices.

Dunn appeared relaxed and engaged in a friendly conversation with Mike Gibson—a sight that set tongues wagging, considering Dunn was a witness for the prosecution. When Judge Devich appeared, the two immediately resumed the formality of the attorney-witness relationship.

Gibson pointed out that there were four guns at Stone Canyon the Thursday before the shootings: one under Rick's bed, one in Kyle's room, another in Bobby Green and Scott's bedroom, and Rusty's shotgun. Then Gibson turned toward Dunn and said, as a rebuke: "Didn't you have several conversations with Carl Berestein, a neighbor's butler on Stone Canyon, before and after the incident, when you told him you were severely chastised by Henry Kyle for not having a gun one prior night?''

Looking startled, Dunn replied, ''I told Carl that Mr. Kyle told me to always have a gun if I was investigating something out of the ordinary—on the grounds or something.''

''Isn't it a fact,'' Gibson continued, ''that you told Carl Berestein Henry Kyle instructed all of you to keep a gun, and that Henry Kyle treated his children like a sergeant major?''

''I never said Henry Kyle verbally *and physically* abused his children,'' Dunn corrected.

''Tell us how Henry Kyle described your friends after the lamp was stolen,'' Gibson coaxed.

''He said, 'I don't want any of your clammy friends coming around here anymore,' '' Dunn responded bitterly.

''What about the time Henry Kyle dropped a flowerpot in front of you and Rick in the garage . . . didn't you say he was 'pissed off at everybody'?''

''I was mad at him,'' Dunn answered, a look of annoyance crossing his face, ''and I was upset about it. I didn't say anything.''

''Isn't it true he badgered you, too? Henry Kyle *told* you, 'Don't use my kids to help you.' And Ricky Kyle cleaned that flowerpot up, didn't he?''

''I'm not sure,'' said Dunn.

''He also damaged some of your prepared work, didn't he? Didn't you say, 'If he ever does that again, I'll knock his damn head off'?''

''Maybe out of frustration,'' the carpenter said, looking uncomfortable.

According to Dunn, Bobby Green spent a considerable amount of time at Stone Canyon washing his car, a Chrysler Imperial.

''That was his job, wasn't it?'' Gibson said sarcastically. ''His contribution.''

''He'd do some work,'' said Dunn, ''when Mr. Kyle was around.''

''Did Bobby Green listen on the phone when Henry Kyle wasn't around?''

''I don't know.''

''Didn't he tell Henry Kyle you were a drunk?''

''I don't know,'' Dunn repeated. ''He called me a sloth and a leech.''

"Wasn't Bobby Green Henry Kyle's snitch at the house?"
Gibson asked, with marked distaste.

"I had that feeling about Bobby Green."

"He'd try to get the boys in trouble, wouldn't he?" Gibson
pursued.

"I didn't trust Bobby Green," Dunn said carefully. "Because of his relationship with Mr. Kyle."

After the lunch break, Gibson asked Dunn whether Rick had
told him he had moved to California partly to "put back together his relationship with his father."

"Yes," Dunn replied. "He said they'd had bad circumstances, and their relationship had deteriorated."

"So it was his original intention to reform?" Gibson suggested.

"That's what he told me his intentions were."

"But the problems and confrontations grew?"

"They began fairly quickly after Rick arrived," said Dunn.
"Not all built up at the end."

"When did Rick begin making the comments you testified to
last week, about killing Henry Kyle?"

"Two or three weeks before the incident."

"So he didn't say anything like that in June?"

"Correct."

"Didn't you overhear a confrontation between Rick and his
father when Henry Kyle said, 'You'll follow the rules of the
house or I'll kick your ass, and you know I can do that'?"

"Yes," said Dunn.

"And that's when Ricky made his comments about 'I gotta
kill him'; is that right?"

"Yes."

"He never told you he planned to shoot his father, did he?"

"There was no plan scheduled, no. . . . . I didn't take them
seriously," said Dunn.

"And you told Detective Grogan that when you made your
statement to the police, didn't you?"

"Yes."

"And that's a true statement, isn't it?"

"Yes," Dunn responded.

Gibson showed the carpenter a photograph of the inside of
his trash can taken by police the morning after the shootings. It
showed a coffee cup and two shotgun shells.

"You fired the shotgun a second time, too, didn't you?"

"Yes," said Dunn sheepishly.

"When was that?"

"I fired it one night to scare Scott and Bobby Green."

During the fifteen-minute midafternoon break, a rumor suddenly spread like wildfire that Jackie Phillips was somewhere on the twelfth floor, and would be testifying next.

"She's here . . . I saw her," Steve Sumner whispered to one journalist as they passed in the hall. "We were expecting Bobby Green next."

But when the crush descended on Department 123 again at quarter past three, Jackie was nowhere to be seen. Instead, Dunn went on to his first two meetings with Jackie Phillips—at Granada the Saturday after the shooting and at the funeral. Dunn denied that Jackie was intoxicated at the funeral reception.

"You said at one point that Jackie Phillips was 'highly emotional' at the house and at the reception," Gibson continued. "You also said she was 'under control and calm.' How could she be both?"

"She wasn't very drunk," Dunn answered, "so she was in control. She was boisterous, so to say."

"What did she say or do when she saw [longtime Kyle employee] John Greer?"

"She was happy to see him and she hugged him."

"Wasn't she also mad at him 'cause he ran out of mixers, so she started drinking straight bourbon?" Gibson said sharply.

"I don't know."

"Weren't you talking to Jackie Phillips out in the hall just a few minutes ago?" the defense attorney accused, while the jurors looked at Dunn disapprovingly. "She asked you to call her tonight, didn't she?"

"Yes," answered Dunn.

Judge Devich asked the jury to leave the courtroom, indicating he had something he wanted to take up with counsel.

"I'm upset that Miss Phillips asked the witness to call her," he announced after the jurors had filed out of the room.

"He invited her to dinner," Watnick hurriedly tried to answer for Dunn, who was squirming nervously in his chair.

"I don't like the idea of two witnesses talking to each other before their testimony," Devich said sternly, eyeing Watnick reproachfully. He then told Dunn to cancel his dinner date. "It makes me wonder . . . and I don't like to wonder."

13

TUESDAY MORNING, A SEAT IN
Judge Devich's courtroom was the hottest ticket in town. Word
had leaked out that Jackie would be on the stand, and reporters
seemed to drop out of the sky, along with a small army of court-
watchers. The crowd elbowed and pushed their way into the
courtroom for a close-up view of the prosecution's star witness.

A little after 10:00 A.M., Phillips arrived on the arm of Bob
Grogan. He escorted her into the courtroom with the deference
accorded a visiting dignitary. Jackie looked stunning. She had
lost at least ten pounds since she had posed for the photographs
in her portfolio at the Kim Dawson Agency—she was almost
dangerously thin, but the natural beauty of her features was
still remarkable, as was her blond hair, worn shoulder length
and full, with lavish curls and bangs. She dressed in a simple
black suit, black stockings and pumps, and a prim white blouse
with a princess collar and bib front. Her only jewelry was a
single strand of pearls. "Why don't they just stick a lollipop in
her mouth and put on a big red bow?" Steve Sumner cackled
as she walked in with Grogan.

When Judge Devich took his seat on the bench a few minutes later, the tension in the room was electric. Watnick helped
Jackie to the witness stand, where she practically collapsed into
the chair.

Handing her a glass of water, the DA asked her to state her
name for the record.

"Jackie Lynn Phillips," she said weakly.

"Could you spell that, please?"

"J-a-c-k-i-e," she began. "P-h-i . . ." Looking confused, Phillips stammered: "l . . . l—"

"Ms. Phillips," Watnick interrupted in a soothing voice, "would you relax a little bit?"

On the verge of tears, her voice breaking, Phillips finished spelling her last name, with difficulty. She explained to the jury that her mother was also named Jackie Phillips, and that her parents were divorced when she was two. She said that she had lived with Henry Kyle "very little. He sent me to schools," she added brusquely. "I hadn't lived with him since high school."

"When did you first meet Rick Kyle?" Watnick asked suddenly.

"Three to four years ago," Phillips said, her voice barely audible. "He resided in Atlanta with his mother before that."

"Where did this meeting occur?"

"At Henry Kyle's home," she said, sticking out her lower lip.

"Did you become friendly?"

"*Very* friendly."

"How old were your half brothers at the time?"

"Ricky was sixteen, Scott was fourteen . . ." Phillips paused for an awkward moment. "Fifteen. Fifteen. They were both in private school."

"Did you see them often afterward?" Watnick continued.

"I saw Ricky on a number of occasions," Jackie answered, infusing the word "Ricky" with contempt.

"And this continued until when?" the DA asked.

"March of 1983."

"What happened then?" Watnick said straightforwardly.

"I went into a hospital here in California."

"When did you first hear of your father's death?" the DA changed the subject.

"Friday," Jackie said flatly. "Early evening."

"Who told you about it?"

"My fiancé at that time, Henry Miller. My mother called us."

"Where were you living at the time?"

"I lived in a condo on Holly Hill rent-free," Phillips said.

"Who provided the condo for you?"

"Henry Kyle," Jackie said defiantly.

117

"You had a Mercedes then, too," Watnick continued. "Who paid for that?"

"*I* bought it," she responded. "Henry Kyle paid for repairs and upkeep."

Describing what happened after the shooting, Jackie told the jury that she and Henry Miller (who she said was no longer her fiancé) flew to Los Angeles, where they stayed with her half brother Jim Phillips, at his home in Laurel Canyon. They saw Rick on Saturday morning "eleven-ish" at a hospital. "I don't remember the name," she said. When they arrived, Rick's arm was in a cast and sling.

"Did he appear to be rational?" Watnick asked.

"Yes. He was not in great pain," she added, looking over at Rick with an expression of derision.

"What happened next?" coaxed Watnick.

"I hugged him," Phillips said coldly. "Charlotte and an uncle of his were there—I don't remember his name. Charlotte left to make a phone call and Ricky asked me when I was going to see Henry's house and asked me to get a briefcase in Henry's room because there were names written in it that would hurt me—a first name, 'Tom.' "

After thirty to forty-five minutes in Rick's hospital room, Jackie testified, she and Henry Miller drove to Granada. "I'd never seen it or been there," she noted. "The front door was locked. No one was there."

"What happened when you got back to the house?" the DA said suggestively.

"I pushed open the [back] door and saw blood on the floor and started crying," Jackie said, her voice now strong and clear. "Naturally that was disturbing."

"Did you meet Rusty Dunn at the house?"

"Yes. He took us in."

"Why did you want to visit Stone Canyon?" Watnick asked solicitously.

"I just wanted to see the house," Phillips said, her voice breaking. "He took us on a tour—avoiding the room where my father was shot. I started to cry. Then I went to my father's bedroom for five or ten minutes."

"What did you do there?"

"I laid on the bed and cried," Phillips said, looking at her feet.

"Was that upsetting?"

"Yes," Phillips responded, sobbing into her hands.

"What were you feeling when you were in the bedroom?"

"Total confusion. Grief."

"Did you ever see a briefcase?" the DA asked finally.

"No."

At the time, Jackie testified, she thought a prowler had killed her father. "That's what my mother told me."

"Did you have any idea the defendant may have shot your father?" Watnick said forcefully.

"No."

Tuesday, the twenty-sixth, she and Henry Miller attended Henry Kyle's funeral at 11:00 A.M., then drove to his house.

"What were you feeling the day of the funeral?" Watnick continued.

"I was naturally upset," Phillips responded.

"How long were you at the reception?"

"About an hour."

"Did you have anything to drink?"

"I had one drink. Henry had one drink. I believe we both had only one."

Rick, Jackie said, attended the funeral with his arm in a sling. "Not much was said at the funeral. At the reception, he asked Henry and I to get him out of there for a little while."

"Was he upset?" Watnick asked.

"He was not emotional," Jackie said flatly. "He wasn't crying."

From the reception, she testified, Henry Miller drove her and Rick to the Café Pacific, located ten minutes from Kyle's house on Preston Road. "We had three martinis," she said, indicating that none of them was intoxicated. At the café, she and Henry and Ricky had a "discussion," then they continued on to Henry's condo on Rowland Street, where they arrived at three in the afternoon.

"Were any of you under the influence of anything?" Watnick stressed.

"No," answered Phillips.

"What happened at Henry Miller's home?"

At this question, Rick stared with steely resolve at his half sister.

"My brother proceeded to tell Henry and I how he had shot

my father," Jackie responded, her voice wavering slightly. "He said he woke Henry up around four in the morning with a gun, that Henry got his gun, and he told Henry there was a prowler in the house." Stopping to take a drink of her water, Phillips continued: "They went downstairs and searched the house all over, checking the doors. When they were satisfied that no one was in there, they stood at the door of the dining room and as my father turned . . . he fired and hit him in the back. And my father started letting off shots, also. And he told authorities a prowler was standing in the shadows."

"How many shots did the defendant fire?" Watnick quizzed.

"I don't know the exact answer. Several."

"How many shots did Henry Kyle fire?"

"I don't know," Jackie said, "but he was hit by one."

"Did the defendant tell you where he got the gun?"

"He didn't tell me then," Phillips said, then changed her mind, saying: "His brother Scott. Scott gave him the gun that night and said it was clean and untraceable. Rick said he wore Playtex gloves. I believe he said they had planned this."

"Did he tell you what he did with the gun?"

"He said he ran out into the back and threw it over the fence into a neighbor's yard. Then he drew a map and asked me to come to L.A. to try and find it for him."

"Where did he draw the map?"

"On Henry Miller's stationery."

"Is this the map?" asked Watnick, handing her a piece of blue stationery with the corner missing.

"Yes," answered Jackie. "Henry Miller was there and he tore his name off."

Watnick showed the jury another piece of blue stationery with the imprint FROM THE DESK OF HENRY S. MILLER III, to show where Miller's name had been printed on the earlier exhibit. Then he asked Jackie if she had been familiar with the area the defendant had diagrammed. Phillips testified that "the only time she'd ever been to Stone Canyon" was the week before, but that she did recognize the spot Ricky had drawn on the map.

"What did you do with the map?" Watnick queried.

"I gave it to attorney Frank Wright," Phillips said defensively. "I kept it. I was stunned."

"You and the defendant and Henry Miller were all using

cocaine that afternoon,'' the DA continued. ''Who brought it up?''

Seeing Phillips's blank expression, Watnick rephrased the question: ''Whose idea was it?''

''Oh,'' Jackie responded. ''I didn't understand the question. It was a mutual agreement.''

''How much cocaine did you use?''

''A half gram to a gram. A small quantity.''

''Did it affect your perception?''

''I got a little high,'' Phillips chuckled, as Mike Gibson stood up to raise an objection to the DA's question.

Waiting for the judge to rule on the objection, Jackie ostentatiously ran her hands through her hair and occasionally emitted long, expressive sighs, none of which was missed by the reporters.

When the judge overruled Gibson's objection a few minutes later, Watnick turned to Phillips again and asked if she was able to see and remember what was going on at Henry Miller's apartment.

''Yes,'' she replied, appearing bored.

''How did the defendant appear?''

''I remember him not using much because he was wounded. None of us used much.''

''Had you ever used cocaine with him before?''

''Many times.''

''On these prior occasions, how much cocaine did you use?''

''Much more quantity.''

''How much more?'' Watnick pressed.

Jackie snickered and said, ''Depends on how many days we were partying. A lot more.''

Watnick asked Jackie what the term ''free-basing'' cocaine meant.

''Removing what makes cocaine water-soluble and smoking it in a pipe,'' she said meticulously, going on to explain that she, Henry Miller, and Rick shared one pipe at Miller's house.

''How long were you there?'' Watnick queried.

''Not long. Rick's mother wanted him back because of his injury.''

''What was your reaction when the defendant told you about the murder?'' Watnick queried.

''Very confused. I did and said nothing.''

The Thursday after the funeral, Jackie testified, Detective Grogan questioned her about a Rohm revolver.

"Did you tell Grogan what the defendant confessed to you?" Watnick pushed.

"No."

"Why?"

"I was confused . . . and scared," said Phillips.

"You said you didn't want to implicate your brother?" Watnick said suggestively.

"I loved my brother," answered Phillips.

"I object," Steve Sumner said hotly, standing up suddenly and facing Watnick with a look of irritation. "He knows better than that. . . ."

The DA dropped this line of questioning altogether.

"Before July twenty-second," the DA continued, "were you very close to your brother?"

"I thought I was," Jackie said sarcastically, making a face.

"Did you see him often?"

"Until March of 1983."

"Did he visit you regularly?"

"Yes."

"Did he ever say anything to you about his inheritance from your father?"

"He told me he was always afraid of being cut out of the will, that Henry told him to do better or he'd be cut out. He told me that several times."

"Did the defendant ever say anything to you about *killing* his father?"

"Scott and Rick told me how when they were little boys they thought of poisoning him and different ways of killing him."

"Did you believe it?" asked Watnick.

"No," answered Phillips, adding caustically, "It's pretty hard to believe."

"Did the defendant ever say how he felt about his father?"

"He told me how much he hated him many times."

"How about Vicki?" Watnick pressed.

"He disliked Vicki very much. He called her very discriminory [sic] names."

"Like what?"

"A gook . . . because of her religious practices."

"How did he feel about Vicki and his father's money?" asked the DA.

"He was afraid she'd take the money out of his pocket," Jackie said bitterly. "Scott and Rick were afraid she was after his money."

Comparing notes during the lunch break, reporters couldn't figure out what to make of Phillips. Her obvious hostility toward both Rick and Scott was a new and puzzling development.

Ten months earlier, at the preliminary hearing, Jackie cried and said that she "didn't want to hurt her brother," and her criminal lawyer, Frank Wright, complained that she and Rick still got together and "hugged and kissed and cried."

Some thought her change in attitude suspicious. It didn't take Perry Mason to realize that if Jackie had been involved in a conspiracy with her brothers, she would have feigned hostility to throw the jury off the track.

One thing was certain: The inconsistencies in Phillips's testimony hadn't improved with time. In her first few hours on the witness stand, she had already contradicted herself on at least two key points: At the preliminary hearing she had testified that Henry Kyle was "standing in the stairwell" when Rick shot him; now she was saying her father and brother were "in the door to the dining room." She now cited "Playtex gloves" to the jury; previously she couldn't remember even whether there was "a" glove.

Another discrepancy arose in regard to Rusty Dunn's testimony: Jackie said that Rick told her Scott gave him the gun to kill their father on Thursday night, just before the shootings. If that was true, why did Rusty Dunn find the gun under Rick's bed on *Wednesday afternoon*?

Whether the jury believed her testimony was anybody's guess—the looks on their faces were impossible to read. She did, however, have their complete and undivided attention. Those who had been taking notes during Rusty Dunn's testimony put down their pens within five minutes after Jackie took the stand. All stared at her unabashedly while she fidgeted, fumed, and fretted her way through Watnick's questions.

The consensus among court-watchers was that if Jackie couldn't make it as a model, she had a career waiting for her in Hollywood.

This impression was reinforced during the lunch break, when she was spotted in the hall. She was laughing and joking as if she didn't have a care in the world. A few minutes later, she took her seat on the witness stand and immediately transformed herself with slumped shoulders, bowed head, and a sullen, disconsolate expression.

"What was your father's attitude about drugs?" the DA asked some way into the afternoon session.

"My father was very against drugs," Phillips said lazily, putting her hair on top of her head, her elbows sticking out beside her. "He was a physical-fitness addict."

"Didn't you play tennis or basketball with him?" Watnick continued.

"From time to time."

"What was his attitude before you went into the rehabilitation center?"

"He was disappointed with my drug use."

"Did he say anything to you about staying away from Rick and Scott?"

"He told me not to associate with them because he was having problems with them," Jackie answered, causing a few whispers among reporters who remembered her admission at the preliminary hearing that Kyle forbade her to see her brothers because of her "life-style."

"What kind of problems?" the DA asked, as if he were curious himself.

"In school," Phillips said sullenly. "Not taking care of personal property. It disturbed him."

"Was Mr. Kyle happy that you went to the rehabilitation center?"

"Very much so."

"Did you get a letter from him when you were there?" the DA asked suddenly, as both Mike Gibson and Steve Sumner looked up with interest.

"Yes."

"And you showed this letter to me yesterday," Watnick continued with a look of self-satisfaction. He handed the court reporter a piece of paper to mark as an exhibit for the prosecution. After Jackie identified the paper as a note from her father dated April 22, 1983, with which he had enclosed a check for two thousand dollars for her hospital expenses, the DA asked her to read the letter to the jury.

Holding the note with both hands and trembling slightly, Phillips began: " 'Take care,' " she read, her voice breaking with emotion as she reread the letter from her father. " 'Win race. Get a tan for Acapulco. Join me in the winner's circle. You can. You must. You will.' " Then Phillips sobbed quietly.

Waiting a moment for Jackie to regain her composure, Watnick asked her to recall what her father told her when he telephoned her from Dallas the day before he was killed.

"He said he was very proud of me and wanted me to straighten out my life," Phillips answered softly.

"What were your feelings toward the defendant before July of 1983?" Watnick asked next, looking in Rick Kyle's direction.

"I *thought* he loved me," said Jackie. "I loved him."

"What were your feelings *after* July of 1983?" Watnick pursued.

"Objection," Gibson interrupted. "Irrelevant."

When Judge Devich sustained Gibson's objection, Jackie seemed about to collapse. She asked the judge's permission to leave the courtroom for a few minutes.

While everyone looked on in mute fascination, Phillips stumbled out of her chair and staggered out of the courtroom toward the ladies' room.

She returned a few minutes later.

A little later, the defense began its cross-examination. Mike Gibson, Ricky's smooth, polite lead counsel handled the questioning—not Steve Sumner, his brasher partner, who had reduced Phillips to tears at the preliminary hearing in January. The switch surprised some journalists and disappointed Sumner, who made it no secret he was eager to "tear her apart" a second time.

Gibson, however, seemed to have dropped his nice-guy pose in favor of a somewhat more sarcastic approach.

He immediately zeroed in on Jackie's cocaine use, and asked her about her admission to the Orange County Care Unit in March 1983.

"I was seeking help for my addiction to the drug cocaine," Phillips responded.

"You're a drug addict, aren't you, Miss Phillips?" Gibson said tauntingly.

"I had a problem," Jackie answered haughtily.

"You did testify before that you were a drug *addict*, isn't that so?" Gibson persisted.

"I have a drug *problem*," said Phillips.

After establishing that her boyfriend Henry Miller "helped

make the arrangements" for Jackie's forty-day stay at the rehabilitation center, and pointing out that he was also a patient there, Gibson asked, "Was your father supportive of the help you were getting?"

"Yes," said Phillips.

"Did Henry Kyle agree to pay for your hospitalization?"

"No, sir. I did not ask him," Jackie said defensively.

"Did he ever volunteer prior to your admittance?"

"He was unaware of my admittance," Phillips said peevishly.

"Then you had no communication with him . . ." Gibson said, picking up on Jackie's last response.

"I did when I entered the Care Unit," Phillips replied, clutching a tissue in her right hand.

"And did he agree to pay for your hospital bill?" the defense attorney pushed.

"He offered financial aid to help pay."

Noting that Jackie's hospital bill was $11,000 and that Henry Kyle sent her a check for $2,000, Gibson asked who paid the remaining $9,000.

"Henry Miller," said Jackie.

"What kind of treatment did you receive?"

Staring blankly, Phillips said, "I saw doctors, there were educational classes, exercises. I really don't understand what you want."

"You were released mid-April," Gibson continued. "And your relationship with your father continued to improve through July?"

"The remaining part of his life, yes," Phillips said bitterly.

"He was proud of you and proud of how you were doing . . ." Gibson said, a note of incredulity in his voice.

"Correct," snapped Jackie.

"How many conversations did you have with him?"

"I spoke to him several times."

"How many?" the defense lawyer pushed.

"I could not give you an exact count—at least every other week. I reported my progress to him."

"Did you also report to him you'd had contact with Rick?" Gibson interjected accusingly.

"I had not had, after April," Phillips responded.

"How about before that?"

126

"My father knew that Rick and I were seeing each other," said Jackie, looking annoyed.

"Did *you* tell him?"

"No."

"Did you tell him you were continuing to use cocaine?"

"I did not discuss that with my father."

"So you weren't being candid and truthful with him, were you?" the defense attorney persisted. He was cut off by Watnick, who objected to the question.

When Judge Devich told Gibson to rephrase his question, he dropped it completely, and asked instead: "Did you tell your father about the fact you fell back into your drug habit?"

"I have slipped a few times."

"Right out of the hospital?"

"That can happen," Jackie said defensively.

"And it did happen, didn't it?" Gibson asked.

"Yes."

"How bad was your habit before you went into the hospital?" Gibson asked, a look of disapproval on his face.

"Bad enough to want to seek help," Jackie said flippantly.

"How bad was your habit?" Gibson repeated.

"I had a habit," Phillips responded grudgingly. "A bad cocaine habit."

Singling out the month of February 1983, the month before she was admitted to the Care Unit, Gibson asked how many days out of the twenty-eight she used cocaine.

"Half," she replied.

"How did you ingest it?"

"Free-base."

"Is that the most potent way?"

"I can't answer that medically," Phillips responded.

"What other ways can you take cocaine?" Gibson persisted.

"You can snort it or inject it."

"Have you ever tried either of those methods?"

"I've snorted it," Phillips said. "I haven't injected it."

"Is it true that free-basing causes a dependency and its effects are greater than snorting?"

"Yes."

"Did you go on binges, or what?" the defense attorney asked. "What was your experience?"

"In February I was up several days at a time," Phillips

127

answered, adding that she free-based cocaine with Ricky, Henry Miller (before he went into the hospital), and Scott Kyle (although not in the month of February).

"It depends on the amount of 'partying'?" Gibson said caustically, referring to Phillips's testimony from the day before. "How long can you free-base before you collapse?"

"It would depend on the circumstances," Jackie said wearily. "The quality of the cocaine, the amount, the number of people, et cetera."

"Were there ever any occasions when you and Henry Miller free-based together alone?"

"Henry was in the hospital the first of February," Phillips responded. "Before then we free-based alone together."

"How long after your release from the hospital did you first fall off the wagon and free-base cocaine?" Gibson inquired.

"Two to three weeks," said Jackie.

"So you were free of it for two weeks," the defense attorney said in conclusion, leaving that fact in the jury's mind and moving on to the subject of Phillips's upbringing.

Jackie told the jury that as a child she saw Kyle only "occasionally. On my birthday," she stammered. ". . . um . . . occasionally. Couple times a year."

"Did your opportunity to see your father increase after your modeling career?" Gibson asked.

"When I moved back to Dallas, about 1980," said Phillips.

"And you 'retired' from modeling when you were twenty-seven?" Gibson said sarcastically.

"I began modeling when I was twelve years old," Phillips said huffily. "And I retired when I was twenty-seven."

"When did your relationship with your father start to improve?" Gibson continued in the same skeptical vein.

"When he made moves to help me get away from people who had drugs," said Jackie.

"When was that?"

"1981 . . . As I improved, our relationship improved."

"Did you improve?" Gibson asked doubtfully.

"I've been trying," Jackie said haltingly. ". . . I *know* I'm improving."

For Wednesday morning, December 5, Phillips dressed in another dark suit, this one navy with a peplum jacket, worn over a simple white blouse. Her hair was pulled stylishly to one side and secured with a large white comb.

The tone for Wednesday's cross-examination was set immediately when Jackie responded to Gibson's initial, innocuous questions with abrupt, hostile snarls. Gibson asked her if she did any modeling after she returned to Texas in 1980.

"I continued to do some work in Dallas," she testified, adding breezily: "You could say I retired."

"You retired in 1980 . . . ?" Gibson repeated, looking at her mockingly.

"Yes."

"You've done no work of any kind since 1980—"

"No."

"—no income from *legitimate* sources?"

"I object," Watnick interrupted, in reference to Gibson's innuendo.

"Sustained," Judge Devich said, and instructed the court reporter to strike the defense attorney's last question from the record.

"How did you support yourself, Miss Phillips?" Gibson asked.

"I received financial support from my family and I have money of my own," Phillips said disdainfully.

"And . . . from friends?" Gibson asked suggestively.

"Objection," Watnick interjected, prompting the judge to once again strike the defense attorney's statement.

"And you say you met Ricky Kyle in 1981 or 1982?" Gibson continued.

"Specifically, I couldn't give the date," said Phillips. "Three and a half years ago."

"You said yesterday that Ricky was sixteen when you met him," Gibson interrupted. "That would make it 1978."

"Sir, I might have made a mistake when I met him," Jackie said.

"If he's twenty-two now—"

"Then subtract three and a half years," Phillips snapped.

At the time, Jackie testified, Ricky was attending military school in Harlingen, and Scott was living "between home and school."

"How long after your first meeting did you next see Ricky Kyle?" Gibson queried.

"Sometime . . . I believe it could have been six, eight months, I'm not sure," said Phillips, adding that it was a "long period of time" and "not an immediate relationship."

"When did you next see him?" Gibson continued.

"Just very sporadically at first we would see each other, does that answer your question?" Jackie said petulantly.

"No, ma'am, it does not," responded Gibson.

"I don't know," Phillips said impatiently. "I *don't know* the answer to your question!"

Ignoring Jackie's outburst, Gibson asked her about her conversations with Henry Kyle regarding Ricky and Scott.

"When did he first tell you not to be around them?"

"After I met them."

"Why?" Gibson quizzed. "Because of your cocaine problems and the friends you were living with?"

"That's half correct," Phillips said sullenly.

"Also because he didn't want them to be influenced by your conduct? . . . Yes or no, ma'am?" he pushed when Phillips failed to answer.

"Yes."

"You didn't follow his advice, did you?" Gibson taunted.

"Nor the boys," Phillips retorted, "my half brothers."

"The brother you said you love?" Gibson said sarcastically. Pausing a moment, he added, "Henry Kyle told you you couldn't stay in your condo if you saw the boys; that's true, isn't it?"

"That's not true," Jackie responded.

"Did you ever tell anyone that you wouldn't receive any help from Henry Kyle if you didn't stay away from them?"

"No."

"Isn't it true that you introduced Ricky—the brother you said you love so much—to cocaine?"

"I don't know," said Jackie.

"In fact you helped him free-base cocaine on your first meeting, didn't you?" pressed Gibson.

"No."

"You never told anyone you introduced him to free base?" Gibson asked disbelievingly.

"No," said Phillips; she and Ricky first free-based together "two years ago last summer" with a friend in a garage apartment.

130

"Who provided the cocaine?" Gibson said caustically.

"My friend and me."

"How many times after the first time did you and Ricky Kyle free-base cocaine together up to March of 1983?" the defense attorney inquired.

"Numerous occasions," said Jackie.

"How many?"

"Many times. I couldn't put a numeral on it."

"Try."

"Let's give it a rough three dozen," Phillips said, chuckling.

"How many times did you free-base with Scott?"

"Only a few times," said Jackie. "Five to six."

After lunch Gibson opened up the transcript of an interview Jackie had with Bob Grogan on July 29. Gibson asked Phillips to look at page 25 and read aloud a question by Grogan asking Jackie whether she provided coke for Rick. "You said, 'No, I didn't,' " the defense attorney read. "Then, 'I supplied cocaine for Ricky twice.' "

"Do you recall saying that?" Gibson asked.

"Yes," said Jackie, looking down at the transcript.

"In the transcript you said Rick wasn't involved," Gibson pointed out. "Do you admit you said that?"

"Yes," Phillips answered.

Turning to page 27, Gibson read a question by Grogan asking Jackie if she ever provided coke to Scotty. " 'Never' " was her answer. " 'Scott never used coke that you know of?' " Grogan continued, in the transcript. " 'Not that I know of,' " Jackie had answered.

"What is the truth today, Miss Phillips?" Gibson asked Jackie, putting down the interview with a look of disgust.

"I supplied cocaine for my brothers," Jackie said dully.

"How many times?" said Gibson.

"Many times."

Focusing on the day of Henry Kyle's funeral, Gibson established that Jackie and Henry Miller arrived between 10:30 and 11:00.

"You said yesterday that Ricky was 'not emotional.' Have you reviewed transcripts of your testimony at the preliminary hearing in Los Angeles in January?" Gibson asked.

"I did on Monday," said Phillips, who was being carefully scrutinized by the jurors.

Showing her Volume III, page 18, line 13, Gibson read, quoting Steve Sumner's query at the preliminary hearing: " 'Did you observe [Ricky]?' 'Yes.' 'Was he extremely emotional and upset?' 'Everyone was.' 'Including Rick?' 'Yes, sir.' "

"What is the truth today?" Gibson demanded.

"Ricky was not crying. There were no tears," said Phillips.

"Was he emotionally upset?"

"My answer is no tears," Jackie said coldly.

"Did you say no tears in January?" the defense attorney hammered.

"It doesn't say that I did."

After leaving the funeral home, Phillips testified, she and Henry Miller arrived at the reception at Preston Road around 1:00 P.M. Ricky was already there. She said she took no drugs that morning, and had nothing alcoholic to drink. At the reception, she testified, she had one drink, was not intoxicated, and had no difficulty talking or walking. She had a "casual conversation" with Ricky.

"What was his emotional state then?" Gibson inquired.

"It was the same," Phillips responded, with a half snicker.

"Was he under great strain?"

"No."

"He didn't appear emotionally upset?"

"No," Phillips said crossly. "I'm sorry, he didn't."

"That's your testimony today. . . ."

"That's right."

According to Phillips: As she and Henry Miller were leaving the reception, Ricky asked her to take him with them. The three of them left the house "between two and three" and drove to the Café Pacific in Henry's car. Once there they each had three martinis and nothing to eat. She did not recall seeing anyone there she knew, and they left after less than an hour, "around four-ish."

"Did you talk to Ricky about the shooting while you were at the Café Pacific?" Gibson asked.

"I don't recall a conversation there," said Jackie.

"Did Henry Miller bring it up?"

"No."

Picking up his copy of the transcript from the preliminary hearing in January, Ricky's defense attorney asked Jackie to look at Volume III, page 24, and read aloud her testimony that there was a conversation about the incident when she, Miller, and Ricky were at the Café Pacific.

"And you weren't under the influence of cocaine then?" Gibson interrogated.

"No," said Phillips, bristling.

"But you do not recall the conversation . . . whether it happened or not?"

"I do not remember the exact conversation at the Café Pacific, sir."

"You can't recall the conversation," Gibson taunted. "Even though you testified in January there was one. . . ."

After they left the Café Pacific, Jackie testified, she and Henry and Ricky went to Miller's apartment.

"You didn't stop at the San Francisco Rose on Greenville Avenue first to score cocaine?" Gibson interrupted.

"I could be mistaken, but I don't remember it," said Phillips.

"Do you remember trying to score cocaine before going to Henry Miller's house?"

"No."

"Do you remember *drinking* at the San Francisco Rose after leaving the Café Pacific?"

"I don't recall that."

"Have you ever been to the San Francisco Rose?"

"Numerous occasions."

"Is it close to the Café Pacific?"

"Yes."

"But you don't remember stopping to get cocaine there?"

"No," said Phillips, growing peevish. "I do not recall doing that. It was the day they buried my father."

"When you're emotionally upset you can't recall all the details, isn't that right, Miss Phillips?"

"Yes."

"That's why you're having trouble today, isn't that right? Is that a fair statement?" Gibson coaxed.

"That's a fair statement."

The three of them spent a "short time"—a half hour to an hour—at Miller's house on Rowland, Phillips testified.

"When Rick allegedly confessed?"

"Yes," said Jackie.

"Did you have cocaine at the house?"

"Yes."

"Did you leave to go get some?"

"I don't remember where we got it," Jackie answered. "I thought it was at the home already."

"You don't remember where you got it?"

"No. I know we had it."

"How much did you consume?"

"We did no more than a gram of cocaine."

"And you had that much in the house?" the defense attorney questioned.

"Yes."

"Where was it kept?"

Chortling, Phillips replied, "I'm sure on the living-room table. On the coffee table."

"You had cocaine just laying out on the coffee table in the living room—" Gibson said, looking at Jackie as if she were a disobedient child.

"We had a whole gram laying out. . . ." Phillips said sarcastically, with a snicker, causing a few of the jurors to laugh with her.

"Did that have to be changed to free base?"

"Yes. You have to cook it."

"Who did that?"

"I don't recall."

"Where was that done?"

"In the kitchen."

"How long does it take?"

"Five to ten minutes."

"Were you all in the kitchen at the time?"

"Probably," Phillips said, looking bored.

"You said you used a pipe to smoke it," Gibson pursued. "Where was that?"

"In the living room," said Jackie, growing more impatient. "We went back into the living room to use it."

"And then did you 'load' the pipe?"

"That's right."

"Tell us how you do that. . . ."

Looking at Gibson with an expression of utter disgust, Jackie paused, then said, "You suck on the end of it and you light it."

"And does each individual put his own portion in the pipe?" Ricky's lawyer continued, undeterred.

"Right."

"How much?"

"My Lord!" Phillips responded, with a snigger. "A normal size."

"What sort of reaction does free-basing cocaine cause in you?"

"It's a stimulant," Phillips said succinctly. "It makes you think faster. Makes you more alert, aware, quick. It accelerates you."

"How long did the effects last?"

"A couple of hours. A very brief time."

"How long does the reaction last from the first hit?"

"Fifteen to twenty minutes."

"So at a party, you have to constantly smoke to keep the high?"

"Right," said Phillips. "Ricky used some, too," she added.

"Wasn't he on some sort of medication?" asked Gibson.

"He was on something for infection," answered Jackie. "Maybe on pain pills. I don't recall exactly."

"Do you recall appearing at the preliminary hearing in this courtroom in January?"

"Yes."

"This was a very serious matter then and today," he pointed out, adding condescendingly: "Do you appreciate how serious this is?"

"Yes," Phillips said with hostility. "I appreciate how serious my father's death is."

"Do you appreciate how serious this is for this young man here?" Gibson countered, gesturing toward Ricky Kyle.

"Objection," Watnick said with annoyance.

"Overruled," Devich said, suppressing a smile at Gibson's tactics.

"How much cocaine did you take on July twenty-sixth, prior to your conversation with Ricky?" Gibson continued, looking at Jackie.

"The three of us divided the amount I told you."

"How much did *you* take?"

"I cannot recall exactly, sir."

"How many drags did you take?"

"I cannot recall that exactly, sir."

"Had you smoked any prior to the conversation?"

"Yes," said Phillips. "And during."

Jackie went on to say that after she and Henry Miller smoked "some" and Ricky less "because he was wounded," the conversation about the shootings took place.

"Did you continue to take hits during the conversation?"

"Yes."

"How about afterwards?"

"No, because we didn't have enough. But I can't recall with certainty."

"It was an emotional, upsetting time?"

"Yes."

"What did Ricky first say to you?"

" 'I killed my father.' "

"Those were his first words?" Gibson said doubtfully.

" 'I shot my father.' "

"What was his emotional condition then?"

"Well, he wasn't teary-eyed or anything," Phillips said flippantly.

"What was his next statement?"

"I remember breaking down when he told me that and I started to cry."

"Was Ricky emotional?"

"No," said Jackie. "He simply told me that with no emotion."

Eyeing her suspiciously, Gibson asked what her brother said to her next.

"He told me he went in and woke my father up, carrying a gun," Phillips said truculently. "He told my father there was a prowler. They walked around the house. Then they stood in the doorway. He shot my father, rounds were fired. Then he shot him again because he wasn't dead."

"And you say they were standing in the *doorway of the dining room*?" Gibson emphasized.

"Yes," Jackie said. "And as my father turned to go upstairs, he shot him."

"You gave some testimony at the preliminary hearing in this courtroom *under oath*," Gibson pointed out. "Remember?"

"Yes," Phillips said sullenly.

Announcing that he was reading from Volume II, page 34, Gibson opened one of the transcripts in front of him on the counsel table and said with deliberation: "Question by Watnick: 'What did Ricky say to you?' Phillips: 'He said there was gunfire. And that he was shot and my father was shot.' Watnick: 'Did he say how it occurred?' Phillips: 'They went through the house . . . and the gunfire went between the two of them.' Watnick: 'Did Ricky tell you who shot Henry Kyle?' Phillips: 'Ricky told me he did. That my *father shot at him,*' '' Gibson punctuated, '' 'and *he shot at him and they shot at each other.*' ''

"Were you trying to be accurate then?" the defense attorney queried, putting down the transcript and looking directly at Jackie.

"Yes, sir."

"There was no mention of a doorway or the dining room, was there?"

"That's correct," Jackie said apathetically. At the same time Lew Watnick sputtered an objection, arguing vociferously that Gibson was trying improperly to impeach his witness.

"Overruled," Devich said angrily, in one of his few displays of emotion during the course of the trial.

Gibson grilled even more forcefully: "And there was no mention of your father turning and being shot in the back, or about Ricky shooting twice, was there, Miss Phillips?"

"No," Jackie replied.

"As a mater of fact," he persisted, "the first time you've testified that Ricky shot twice is today, isn't it?"

"Yes, sir."

"Then Ricky told you what story he was going to tell the authorities," Gibson said sarcastically. "Is that the next thing you recollect?" Seeing her look of confusion, he added: "I just want the truth, Miss Phillips."

When Jackie did not answer, Gibson remarked, "Yesterday you said Ricky told you he and Scott were going to make up a story. . . . That's the first time you've ever said Ricky told you during the Rowland conversation that he and Scott conjured up a story about a prowler, isn't it?"

"I don't understand what you're trying to do," Phillips said, bewildered. "I've always said that Scott—"

Interrupting her, Gibson said sharply, "Did you mention Scott at the preliminary hearing?"

"I can't recall," said Phillips.

"So the first time was today," he said with finality.

Next Gibson asked Jackie about her testimony that Ricky told her about the gloves.

"Ricky told me that he wore gloves," Phillips repeated. "That he put on gloves when he shot him. He told me that."

"Told you *what*?" Gibson demanded.

"Goddang it, I told you," Jackie said irritably, "that he put on gloves."

"Your answer is vague," Gibson responded. "Exactly what did Ricky say to you about gloves?"

"I'm afraid your question is vague," Phillips retorted, adding insolently: "He told me he put on gloves so there wouldn't be powder burns when he shot him."

"Is there anything you wanna add to that?" Gibson coaxed. "Did he ever say *no* gloves?"

"No."

Again referring Jackie to her testimony at the preliminary hearing, Ricky's criminal lawyer asked, "Were you trying to be truthful then?"

"Kind of," said Phillips. "Please quit putting words in my mouth. I was trying to protect my brother."

"So you lied under oath?" Gibson queried.

"Objection," Watnick interjected.

"Sustained," muttered Devich.

"You said in January you didn't recall Ricky saying anything about gloves," the criminal lawyer pressed on. "Yesterday you said he told you he was wearing Playtex gloves. Today you didn't say Playtex in your recollection of Ricky's statement. What are you saying now?"

"He said he was wearing Playtex gloves," answered Phillips.

"This is the first time you've ever suggested it was Playtex gloves, isn't that correct, Miss Phillips?" Gibson said in exasperation.

"That's correct."

"Did he mention what color they were?" the defense attorney inquired.

"I can't recall."

Jackie told Gibson that Rick wanted her and Henry Miller to go to California to look for the gun, and then drew a map on Henry's stationery showing where he had thrown it.

Hearing Phillips say this, Gibson got out of his chair and

held up a giant calendar within view of the jury and Jackie. He pointed to Tuesday, July 26, 1983. According to Jackie, on that date Rick asked her and Miller to fly to Los Angeles to retrieve the gun.

"You saw Ricky on Saturday the twenty-third when you were in L.A.," he observed, counting back three days on the calendar. "How many times?"

"I think twice," said Phillips.

"Ricky never asked you to get the gun or the gloves then, did he?"

"No."

Gibson asked Jackie what Ricky said after that.

"I told him I wouldn't do that, and we took him back to his mother's."

"In January you said this conversation at Rowland had an emotional ending and all of you cried—"

"Everybody didn't cry," Jackie interrupted, in a flat voice.

"Let me guess," Gibson said dryly. "Ricky Kyle didn't cry?"

"You got it!" said Phillips. "*Shoot!*"

"Do you recall a conversation between you and your brother as to why he said he shot your father?"

"I don't recall a reason."

"In January you testified—"

"Just read what you've got," Phillips said tartly, glaring at Gibson.

"Do you want to break for the evening?" Judge Devich broke in, turning to look at Jackie.

"No, sir," she responded. "I want to get this over with." Then she chuckled, saying, "It's up to you. *Jesus!*"

Deciding a recess was in order, Devich dismissed Phillips and the jury with what appeared to be relief.

The next morning, Thursday, Jackie was dressed for the cameras in yet another black suit, made sexier by a shorter, straight skirt, sheer black stockings, and spike heels.

Pouring her long limbs into the witness box, Jackie heaved a sigh and ran her fingers through her shoulder-length blond hair. Observing her ennui, Judge Devich leaned over from the bench and handed her a glass of water. He said half apologetically, "I know this is difficult. . . ."

Gibson showed no such sympathy as he resumed his cross-examination. He provided Jackie with a copy of the transcript from her preliminary-hearing testimony and proceeded to grill her further on her account of Ricky's confession. He was able to point out several small inconsistencies in her testimony.

"This sucks," said Jackie, under her breath. "Shit. Son of a bitch."

"Miss Phillips," Judge Devich interjected, looking at her crossly. "I know this is unpleasant, but—"

Gibson asked Jackie where she and Henry Miller drove Ricky when they left Miller's house.

"To my father's condo," she replied. It was a "ten- to fifteen-minute drive."

"Did you go upstairs to Ricky's condominium?"

"No, we let him off at the front door."

"Did Henry Miller go up to see whoever was there?" Gibson persisted.

"I don't recall," said Phillips.

"He didn't?"

"It's possible, but I don't recall."

"How long were you in the car after your conversation with Ricky?"

"We discussed him killing our father. We got him out of our house, okay?" Jackie responded. "I can't answer something I don't recall exactly."

Gibson next quizzed Jackie about her relationship with Henry Miller.

"Before you went into the hospital," Gibson proceeded blithely, "the two of you used cocaine almost daily, didn't you?"

"We used cocaine a lot, yes, sir."

"Did Henry Miller ever work during your relationship with him?" Gibson asked skeptically.

"Some," answered Jackie.

"Was he under any personal financial difficulties at the time?" the defense attorney prodded.

"I object," interrupted Watnick. "That's irrelevant."

Judge Devich instructed Gibson to drop his line of questioning about Henry Miller's financial condition.

Obviously displeased, Gibson asked Jackie whether she saw Miller after she was released from the Orange County Care Unit in the spring of 1983.

"Yes," she replied, indicating she was "with him" through the day of her father's funeral, July 26.

"And did you both continue to use cocaine?"

"Yes."

"Did you do any work during that period of time?"

"No."

"Did Henry Miller?"

"Not on a regular basis."

"Weren't the two of you having financial difficulties?" Gibson persisted.

Looking at him with hatred, Phillips said insolently, "We weren't hungry, okay? We were *just fine*."

"You were just fine," Gibson shot back. "You had all the money you needed for cocaine and food, right?"

"Objection," Watnick said querulously.

"Sustained," ruled Devich, casting a wary eye at Gibson.

"Oh, thank you!" Jackie muttered, sighing loudly.

"You said you had a 'fairly substantial cocaine habit' before you went into the Care Unit," Gibson proceeded. "What exactly does that mean, in terms of cost?"

"I can't say exactly the cost. It differs. At times it was different."

"All right," said Gibson. "What was the low point?"

"A thousand dollars a month," said Phillips, causing several jurors' mouths to drop.

"That was the low point?" Gibson responded. "What was the high point?"

"Several thousand dollars a month."

"Some weeks didn't you spend as much as several thousand dollars a *week*?"

"Some weeks," Phillips said indifferently.

"How much did Henry Miller spend to support his habit?"

"The same as mine," said Jackie. "The same as I quoted."

"And neither of you were employed regularly?"

"That's right."

"How were you supporting your habit?"

"I had financial aid and money from my career."

"Who was furnishing this 'financial aid'?" asked Gibson, looking at her dubiously.

"Henry Miller and my family."

"Your family was giving you money to support your cocaine habit?"

"None," Phillips spit out. "How *dare* you? How *dare* you? At times my parents would give me money. When it was necessary for my bills."

"Did they give you an allowance?"

"No."

"Was it ever a set amount?"

"No."

"And you're saying you had funds from your modeling career to support your habit?"

"Yes."

"When did your modeling career end?"

"1980."

"And you had enough money from modeling up to 1980 to support a habit at this level?" Gibson queried, looking at her with disbelief.

"Sir, I worked since I was twelve years old," said Phillips.

"And you had enough money saved up to support a several thousand dollar a month cocaine habit?"

"Believe it or not. You got it."

"How extensive was your habit from May to July of 1983, when you got out of the Care Unit?"

"Sporadic use," said Jackie. "No more than several hundred a month."

"Were you getting any financial aid from your family then?"

"No."

"Who provided it?"

"Henry Miller."

"How much?"

"I don't have a big overhead so I can't give you an exact figure."

"Were you receiving financial aid from Henry Kyle?"

"I wanna think on that so I can answer it correctly," Phillips responded. "No," she said after a pause. "I turned it down."

"When you were with Ricky," Gibson changed the subject, "did you ever see him with physical bruises?"

"At one time I saw what's-his-name . . . Ricky with a bruise," Jackie said.

"Where did he get it?"

"I don't know. It was a little red dot on his cheek."

142

"Did you ever see him with black eyes?"

"I have never seen him with a black eye."

Pulling out the preliminary-hearing transcript, Gibson read Phillips her testimony saying that she saw Ricky with black eyes once.

"Does that refresh your recollection?" he asked.

"Yes," said Jackie, adding: "I didn't observe black eyes."

"Did you see any other physical injuries?" asked Gibson.

"Never."

"On Scott?"

"Never."

Viewing her with a combination of disbelief and disgust, Gibson asked: "Did you have any conversations with either of your brothers before July of 1983 regarding Henry Kyle's actions or activities toward you or Ricky?"

"Yes," said Jackie.

"Do you have an opinion regarding Henry Kyle's propensity for violence?" asked Gibson, no doubt hoping Phillips would repeat her testimony from the preliminary hearing that Kyle had physically and sexually abused her.

"Yes," responded Phillips.

"What is your opinion?"

"He expected a lot of his children."

Trying to get more, Gibson asked, "Did he have a potential for violence?"

"To protect his children he could be violent," Phillips said simply.

"Was he a violent man?" Gibson repeated, frustrated.

"He could be."

"As much as you or I . . . ?"

"I'm tired of that question."

"Did he have a level of violence equal to your own?" Gibson tried again.

"I'd be proud to say so," Phillips said arrogantly, throwing back her head.

"Was he a man of violent temper?"

"If the cause presented itself."

"Was he a *violent man*?" Gibson persisted, staring into Jackie's eyes.

"Yes," she finally conceded. "He was known to be. He had a reputation. To be a *man*."

"I think she's answered the question," Judge Devich interrupted, watching Jackie's histrionics.

"Thank you, your honor," she said gratefully.

"Did you discuss Henry Kyle's violence with Detective Grogan on July twenty-eighth?"

"I said that he could be crass."

"Meaning what?"

"Meaning he can be quick-tongued," Phillips responded, sticking out her tongue at Gibson.

"You don't recall having any other conversations with Bob Grogan about Henry Kyle's violence?"

"I don't recall them, sir. You can read it."

"Would the fact that one of his children was taking drugs provoke violence in him?"

"Yes."

"What would he do if he heard that Ricky were using cocaine?"

"He'd do something about it," said Jackie. "Like he did with me: He'd help me."

Reading from the transcript of Jackie's taped interview with Grogan, Gibson pointed out that she told the detective that Henry Kyle suspected Ricky was using coke, and then she said: "Don't worry about it . . . but sometimes my father goes wild over that."

"Is that a true statement that you made, Miss Phillips?"

Clearly bored, Jackie responded, "Naturally my father would be terribly upset about that."

Gibson then pointed out that, after she had testified against him at the preliminary hearings, Jackie visited Ricky at his condominium in Dallas in February 1984, when he was there with "one other person" (Doug Halley).

"You were mad at him; that's why you went over there, isn't it?"

"Yes," said Phillips.

"You yelled at him and then you left, didn't you?"

"You bet," Phillips said with hostility.

"It's true you said you'd come out here and do everything you could to do him in, isn't it?" Gibson said forcefully.

"You're lying through your teeth!" Jackie shrieked.

Sitting back down, Gibson said, "You said you were protecting your brother when you [first] talked to Detective Grogan, didn't you?"

"Isn't that sick?" said Phillips.

"Were you protecting your brother when you talked to Frank Wright?"

"No."

"Were you protecting him when you testified before the grand jury?"

"I wanted to," said Jackie.

"Were you protecting him when you testified at the preliminary hearing?"

"I object to the use of the word 'protect,'" interrupted Watnick, leaving Jackie to play with the buttons on her jacket.

When Devich ordered him to pursue a different line of questions, Gibson asked Jackie: "Were you aware of the extent of your father's wealth?"

"No, sir," said Phillips. "I knew he was wealthy."

"Did you know Henry Kyle was married to Vicki Yang in July of 1983?"

"My father never told me so."

"Did you *know* as of July of 1983?"

"I did not know it," said Jackie. "I was told it."

"Did you expect to inherit anything from your father in July of 1983?"

"No."

"Had you been told that?"

"Yes."

"What were you told?"

"That I was to get a small amount."

"How much?" Gibson demanded.

"From the only will found, ten thousand dollars," Jackie said churlishly.

"Let me explain it," Gibson said patronizingly. "I want to be fair with you."

"That would be wonderful," said Phillips.

"Isn't it true your father in effect disinherited you in his will?"

"My father left me a small amount for my own good," said Jackie, glaring at Ricky's lawyer. Then she blurted, "I knew my father was drafting a new will excluding his sons and including his widow, myself, and my half sister."

"Who told you that?" asked Gibson, looking at her with total disbelief.

"Ricky, and my father's best friend."

"When did they tell you this?" Gibson pursued, still incredulous.

"In the summer of 1982. Dale Swann was there, too."

"Where did this supposed conversation take place?" continued Gibson.

"At Preston Road. My father told me that, too."

Arching one eyebrow, Gibson said sarcastically, "Henry Kyle told *you* he was making a new will. . . . When did he tell you this, Miss Phillips?"

"Immediately prior to his death," Jackie said haughtily. "Within a few months prior to his death."

"When?" said Gibson.

"Starting in May."

"When you were having this every other week communication with him?" Gibson said sardonically.

"Yes," said Jackie.

"What did he tell you?"

"He said he was having trouble with his sons," responded Phillips, making a face. "They were not doing well. They weren't doing anything."

"What did he say to you about his will?" persisted Gibson.

"He told me specifically he would have to cut the boys out. That I would be taken care of. He said his widow would get something."

"Did he say his '*widow*'?" Gibson interrupted.

"How could he know he was going to die?" Jackie retorted, followed by snickers and laughter in the courtroom.

"*You* used the term 'widow,'" observed Gibson.

"That's what she is, unfortunately," snapped Phillips.

"Where did these conversations between you and Henry Kyle between the months of May and July concerning his will occur?" the criminal lawyer persisted.

"On the phone."

"Did he ever discuss it with you in person?"

"No."

"They were all on the phone. . . ." Gibson repeated.

"Yes."

"Did you tell Frank Wright about these alleged conversations with your father regarding his will when you were in his office after your interview with Detective Grogan?"

"No."

"Did you tell Detective Grogan?"

"No," said Jackie. "To the best I can recollect."

"Did you tell Grogan and the other prosecutors about it in October?" Gibson pressed.

"I do not recollect."

"Isn't today the first time you've ever said this?" Gibson said rebukingly.

"Bullshit!" fired Jackie.

"Who is the 'best friend' of your father's you say told you this, also?" Gibson continued.

"I didn't say he had a best friend with him," responded Phillips. "Did I?"

"You said Henry Kyle's best friend told you this in person," pointed out Gibson. "Are you saying something else now?"

"No one told me in person," said Jackie. "It was all on the phone."

"Who else knew about these conversations?"

"Henry Miller," offered Phillips.

"Did you tell him?"

"Henry Kyle spoke to him about it the Wednesday the last time I spoke with my father," said Jackie, breaking into tears.

"Did you ever tell Henry Miller about it?" Gibson said suggestively.

"No."

"Does anyone else know about these conversations?"

"No."

With a look of satisfaction, Gibson changed the subject, saying to Jackie: "Were you aware that your conversations with Bob Grogan and Frank Wright could cause trouble for Ricky?"

"Yes," she responded.

"And it's true, isn't it, that you hired your own attorneys afterwards to challenge Ricky's inheritance?"

"No," said Jackie.

"You *didn't* hire attorneys to challenge your brother's inheritance?" Gibson demanded.

"I hired civil attorneys as advised."

"To challenge Ricky's share in the will—"

"It was not a will, it was a settlement," Jackie interrupted.

"And you filed papers to challenge that inheritance, didn't you?" Gibson said.

"Yes."

"When did you file those papers?"

"I don't know the exact date."

Pointing to July 29, 1983, on a calendar he held up for the jury and Jackie, then to August 9, the date Phillips thought she met with Frank Wright, Gibson asked Jackie: "Isn't it a true statement that Ricky Kyle was in trouble after you made your statements to Bob Grogan and Frank Wright?"

"Objection," said Watnick.

"Isn't it true he was in some legal difficulties?" Gibson persisted.

"Yes, sir," responded Jackie.

"And it was after that that your civil attorneys filed papers seeking to disinherit Ricky Kyle, wasn't it?"

"No!" Phillips blurted. "You're sick!" Shaking her head back and forth, she made a face at Gibson.

"Isn't it true," he persisted, "that on August thirtieth you became an interested party intervening in the estate of Henry Kyle?"

"Yes," said Jackie, adding, "I don't remember dates. Between criminal and civil attorneys right now all y'all look alike to me."

On the following Monday, it was a far different Jackie Phillips who showed up in court. Her clothes were similar to those of the previous week—she wore a short blue jacket with a black collar to complement her white blouse and black skirt, this one pleated and hitting just below the knee.

But as she strolled into the courtroom past the cameras and reporters, she took deliberate steps, as if she were sleepwalking. Once on the stand, she could barely keep her eyes open or her head up.

Mike Gibson, however, showed no sympathy for her sluggish state and continued to hammer away with his copy of the preliminary hearing transcript. He referred Phillips to her testimony concerning the gloves.

"You testified at the preliminary hearing *under oath* during your testimony that morning, didn't you, Miss Phillips?" he inquired.

"Yes, sir."

"The answers you gave that afternoon—*also under oath*—

you told Mr. Watnick and the jurors here in this courtroom you made when you were tired and upset, didn't you?'' he continued.

"Yes, sir," said Jackie, pouting slightly.

"In the morning you said there was a glove; in the afternoon you said you didn't recall anything about it. And that was a lie, correct?"

"Yes," said Phillips.

"You lied to the judge under oath when you were tired and confused—"

"I was trying to protect my brother."

"Can you lie to those people," persisted Gibson, motioning toward the jury box, "anytime when you're tired?"

"Today I'm saying I was trying, *mistakenly*, to protect my brother," answered Phillips, with a look of disgust.

"You weren't subpoenaed to testify before the grand jury, were you?" the criminal lawyer pursued.

"No."

"Did you do *that* to protect your brother?"

"I don't understand," said Jackie, looking puzzled. "Do you mean to protect him from killing my father?"

"You're the one who keeps using the word 'protect,' " responded Gibson.

"I made a big mistake and I'm paying the dues right now," blurted Jackie. "Wasn't I a fool? I lost my father. *Can you understand that?*"

"How did you characterize your relationship with Henry Kyle to Detective Grogan?"

"That everything was fine," Jackie said flatly.

"Did you tell him about the fact that you had previous problems with your father?"

"Yes, sir."

Gibson read from her interview with Grogan: "Grogan: 'Did your father ever provide financial support for you?' Phillips: 'Henry never supported me. I got a garage apartment. I hid there and I was very sick.' "

"Is it not true your father never supported you?" demanded Gibson, putting down the transcript.

"No, sir, it's not."

Picking up the preliminary hearing transcript, Gibson then read Phillips's testimony in January that she and Henry Kyle did not have a "close and warm relationship." "And that in fact is the truth, isn't it?" he added.

"Over the past three and a half years it's a fact," said Jackie.

"In fact it was so bad you were prohibited from seeing the other members of your family, weren't you?" Gibson pummeled.

"Correct."

"It was so bad you were even prohibited from seeing your grandmother. . . ."

"Not based on our relationship," Phillips said heatedly. "That was not the reason."

"Is it true you couldn't see her?"

"Prior to my rehabilitation, yes, sir."

"And you say you were trying to rebuild your relationship with Henry Kyle after your rehabilitation?" Gibson said skeptically.

"Yes, sir."

"And you talked every other weekend?"

"Yes, sir."

"Did you ever talk to Vicki Kyle?"

"No."

"Did you have a feeling you were back in the family?"

"My name is Phillips," shot Jackie. "That is my family."

"You're not in the Kyle family?" inquired Gibson.

"He is my *biological* father," she emphasized.

"Isn't it true no one from Henry Kyle's family notified you of his funeral?"

"No one notified me of the funeral," admitted Jackie, still agitated.

"You had to read about it in the newspapers, didn't you?" Gibson said mockingly.

"I don't know how Mr. Miller and I found out," said Jackie. "Who was going to notify me: my father?"

"No," responded Gibson. "This family you were trying to get back together with." After a pause, he asked: "When did you hire attorneys to challenge Henry Kyle's will?"

"After my conversation with Frank Wright."

"And then you came out to California to testify to the grand jury . . ."

"Yes."

"No further questions."

"You came with Frank Wright to the grand-jury hearing,

didn't you?'' Watnick jumped in, as soon as Gibson finished his sentence.

"Yes," said Jackie.

"Did he *tell* you to come?" the DA queried.

"Yes."

"Before your rehabilitation," Watnick continued, "did your father tell you not to see certain family members?"

"Yes."

"Why?"

"Because he was having trouble with his boys," said Jackie, a look of satisfaction on her face.

"Did he say anything to you about your cocaine?"

"He never said that," responded Phillips. *"Not once."*

Having made those two points, Watnick passed his witness back to Gibson, who practically leaped out of his seat. Without even stopping to formulate a question to Jackie, Ricky's attorney opened the transcript of her July 29 interview with Detective Grogan and read from page 32. "Jackie to Grogan," he began. " 'I don't know. I wasn't allowed to see my brothers.' Grogan: 'By whom?' Jackie: 'Oh, Henry.' Grogan: 'Because you were screwing around with coke?' Jackie: 'Yeah.' "

After impeaching her for the umpteenth time, Gibson looked at Jackie with contempt and asked simply, "It's true, isn't it, that you've testified before that you were prohibited from seeing your brothers by Henry Kyle because of your drug use?"

"Yes," Phillips conceded.

"Do you recall your testimony last week regarding your opinion on Henry Kyle's propensity for violence, and you said, 'He could be a violent man'?" the defense attorney continued.

"Yes, sir," said Jackie, more subdued again.

"How old were you when you met Henry Kyle?"

"Eleven."

"And you testified that you saw him between the ages of eleven to fourteen, isn't that so?"

"Yes, sir."

"Isn't it true that you received certain physical attacks on you by Henry Kyle?"

"Yes."

"When did these start?"

"Soon after I met him."

"Were there various instances of physical harm?"

"Yes, sir."

"From the ages of eleven to fourteen, didn't he hit you with his fists?" Gibson asked, more intensely.

"With his hand, yes, sir," said Jackie.

"Did he kick you?"

"No."

"He *didn't* kick you?"

"No. The answer is no."

"Were you thrown out of a moving vehicle by him?"

"Yes."

"How long did this go on?"

"From about twelve to fourteen, sir."

"After the age of fourteen weren't you physically removed from Henry Kyle?" Gibson said forcefully.

"We were never together to begin with," Phillips responded. "And I was in boarding schools."

"Didn't you see him summers from the ages of fourteen to seventeen?"

"Yes."

"According to your testimony at the preliminary hearing, Miss Phillips, you said you were sent to boarding school to 'protect yourself,' do you recall that?"

"No."

Looking at Jackie's testimony from January, Gibson read to the jury: " 'I did not meet my father until I was eleven and the abuse began the year I met him. Then I was sent away to boarding school. I was no longer around him ever. . . . I protected myself.' "

Judge Devich had already instructed the defense that they were not allowed to question Jackie about her testimony that Kyle had also sexually molested her (because it was irrelevant to the murder case), so Gibson stopped reading at that point. He then asked Phillips: "Did you need any medical help after any of your injuries from Henry Kyle?"

"None," Jackie said with derision. *"Never. Never."*

"I'm through with this witness," announced Gibson, turning his head to give her one last disgusted look.

"You're excused now, Miss Phillips," Judge Devich said benevolently, after confirming that the DA had no more questions for her.

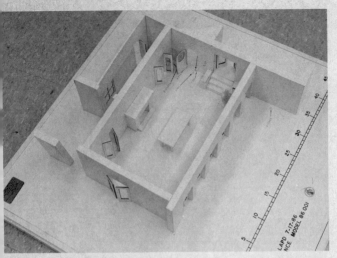

Defense exhibit model of dining-room area at Stone Canyon showing the location of Henry Kyle's body and the position of the doors at the time of the shooting *PHOTOGRAPH BY PAUL BISHOP*

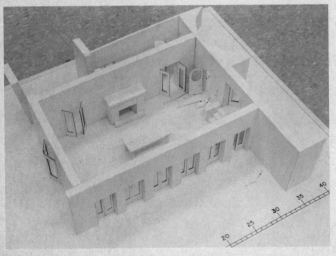

Different view of same model showing the open French door facing Sunset Boulevard *PHOTOGRAPH BY PAUL BISHOP*

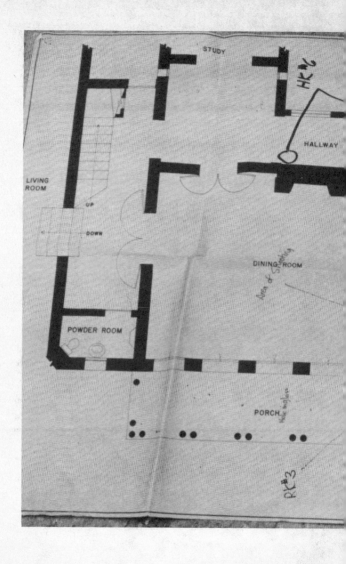

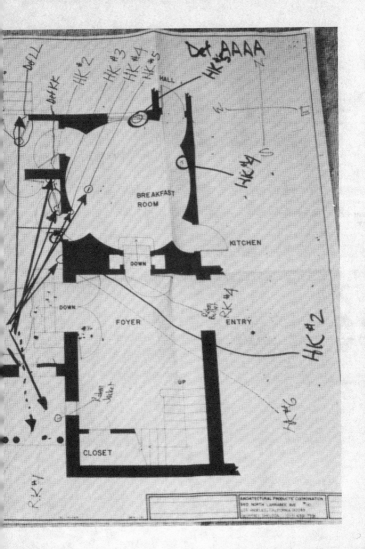

Architectural floor plan of the dining-room area showing Henry Kyle's shots (designated HK #1–6) and Ricky Kyle's shots (RK #1–3). Diagram by Architectural Products' Coordination for the defense. *PHOTOGRAPH BY PAUL BISHOP*

Side view of 110 Stone Canyon shortly after the shootings

PHOTOGRAPH BY R. L. OLIVER, COURTESY OF THE LOS ANGELES TIMES

Mike Gibson, Rick-
ey's lead counsel at
the first trial
COURTESY OF MIKE GIBSON

Steve Sumner and the
mannequin of Henry
Kyle prepared by Dr.
Cogan, with the arrow
representing the path
of the bullet that killed
Kyle
*PHOTOGRAPH BY
LESLIE ERGANIAN*

Above, John Vandevelde and Ricky Kyle at the second trial, with the courtyard and breakfast-room doors in the background

PHOTOGRAPH BY LESLIE ERGANIAN

Lew Watnick, the prosecutor at the first trial

COURTESY OF LEW WATNICK

Detective Bob Grogan (*in jogging suit*) with a friend
COURTESY OF BOB GROGAN

Hank Kyle and Madonna Wiese Kyle during their brief marriage, pictured by a lake in the Tennessee Valley Authority

COURTESY OF MADONNA WIESE ROSENFIELD

Kyle in the fighter plane he crashed, for which he received one of his Distinguished Flying Crosses

COURTESY OF MADONNA WIESE ROSENFIELD

Kyle as a marine in Korea at his tent base. In the background are helmets he used as washbasins and a cable spool where he kept toilet articles. *COURTESY OF MADONNA WIESE ROSENFIELD*

Carolyn Shamis
COURTESY OF CAROLYN SHAMIS

Below, the house at 9909 Preston Road in Dallas, rented by Larry Hagman at the time of the shootings
COURTESY OF CHARLOTTE KYLE WHATLEY

Henry Kyle and Charlotte Edwards Kyle at the Copa in 1962
COURTESY OF CHARLOTTE KYLE WHATLEY

Charlotte Kyle
Whatley in 1985.
*COURTESY OF
CHARLOTTE KYLE
WHATLEY*

Henry Kyle with
Mary Ann Viola on
holiday in Florida,
January 1975, just
before she broke off
their relationship
*PHOTOGRAPH
REPRODUCTION BY
PAUL BISHOP*

Jackie Phillips's portfolio picture in the Kim Dawson Modeling
Agency book in 1982   *BY PERMISSION OF KIM DAWSON*

Ricky, Kelly, and Justin Kyle at the time the mistrial was announced.

UNITED PRESS INTERNATIONAL

Ricky Kyle as a cadet at the Marine Military Academy in Harlingen, Texas

Below, Scott Kyle and Ricky Kyle in Atlanta, Christmas of 1984, the last time Scott and Ricky were together

Scott Kyle, Charlotte Kyle Whatley (holding Ricky's son, Justin), and Ricky Kyle at a friend's house in Atlanta, Christmas of 1984

14

THE NEXT WITNESS FOR THE
prosecution was Dallas criminal lawyer Frank Wright, to whom
Jackie and Henry Miller had first turned after being questioned
by the L.A. police about Quint Barnes's gun. True to his reputation for sartorial splendor, Wright was decked out in an expensive blue-serge suit and white dress shirt. As he strolled up
to the witness box, Wright nodded to the jurors and smiled at
the press.

Essentially, Watnick tried to establish, through his questioning of Wright, that Jackie initially tried to protect Rick and
had to be compelled to testify against him and turn over the
incriminating evidence of the map.

In his cross-examination Steve Sumner tried to show that
fear of being charged herself was Jackie's primary motive in
deciding to cooperate with the police. Sumner produced a copy
of a letter from Wright's business files. It demonstrated that
Jackie had had a meeting with a probate lawyer before mid-
August and was planning another. Sumner also tried to pin down
the exact dates of Jackie's and Henry Miller's meetings with
Wright, about which Wright acted confused.

Wright testified that he first heard from Miller in an "emergency" call on August 7, more than a week after Grogan questioned Jackie about the gun. They had two meetings afterward,
he said, on the eighth and the ninth. Wright claimed he had
made no notes at either meeting. Wright also testified that he
held on to the map for only "a day" before turning it over to

the police, and he showed Sumner a memo he had dictated to his files to prove this.

Henry Miller III took the stand, and like his former girlfriend, Jackie Phillips, he knew how to dress for an appearance in court. He had selected a dark-blue suit, white shirt and gold cuff links. The finishing touch was a silk handkerchief folded elegantly in his breast pocket. Miller's dark-blond hair was cut shorter than a GI's, albeit more fashionably.

Belying Miller's *Town and Country* appearance was his drug background, which had prompted a hearing outside the presence of the jury. Gibson had wanted Miller to waive his attorney-client privilege with Frank Wright, so Wright could testify about drug cases in which he'd represented Miller in the past. When Miller declined, Gibson told Judge Devich he planned to ask him on the witness stand about his "relationship and dealings with individuals still under investigation on drug-related offenses," and about his involvement in a 1981 federal criminal drug investigation, in which Frank Wright had represented him.

"We're not interested in a narcotics investigation," Watnick said angrily. "Just murder."

After listening to both sides argue the point, Judge Devich told Gibson that he would allow him to question the witness about his drug use and level of addiction ("basically what he had testified to at the preliminary hearing"), but not about his involvement as a witness in any prior drug-related cases—because Devich "didn't see the relevancy" to Rick Kyle's murder trial.

As Henry Miller III took the stand, the only visible clue to his previous cocaine problem was his weight. Like Jackie, Henry Miller was rail thin.

In his first few minutes on the stand, Miller confirmed what Henry Kyle's younger daughter had already said about their relationship: that the two met and started dating in January 1983, became engaged in July of that year (the month Kyle was shot), and broke off the engagement sometime later. He said he last saw Jackie five months earlier, in July or August 1984.

Miller said he "didn't know" Henry Kyle and had never met him or talked to him until the Tuesday before he was killed. On that day Miller testified, he telephoned Kyle to ask permission to rent Jackie's apartment to someone else because it was in an "unpleasant neighborhood," and she wanted to move in with him. Kyle returned the phone call, Miller stated, saying, "This is Henry Kyle." "He told me that he was very proud of Jackie, she had made an effort to get off drugs . . ." Miller said. "He was very happy about the relationship [with me] and felt like—that I was the only person that she had ever dated that could handle her." According to Miller, in the same conversation, Kyle told him he was "getting ready to change his will so that he could take care of Jackie."

By Miller's recollection, he and Jackie left Dallas for L.A. around 10:30 or 11:00 on Friday night, after Jackie's mother called to say Kyle had been killed. The "primary reason" they flew to California was because Jackie was "very, very concerned" that Rick had been hurt.

Back in Dallas on Tuesday, July 26, he and Jackie left for the funeral home "about an hour" before the services started, which he thought was at 10:00 or 11:00 A.M. They saw Ricky "very briefly" before they went into the chapel. "I think that we just came up and hugged each other," Miller volunteered. "And I was feeling very brotherly toward him and we expressed mutual concern."

The two of them were at the reception "between one and two hours," Miller testified. When they were about to leave, Rick asked if he could go with them. "He said he needed to get away, he needed to talk to us."

They drove to a restaurant called the Café Pacific about five minutes away, at "around three-thirty or four." Miller said he wasn't intoxicated, and Jackie and Rick didn't appear to be, either. At the restaurant, they had "a couple" of drinks (Miller couldn't remember what kind), and Jackie "kind of caught up on what Ricky had been doing. I think Jackie talked about, you know, how she couldn't believe that Henry Kyle wasn't going to be around anymore or something like that. It was hard to get that out of our minds."

About thirty to forty-five minutes later, Miller said, he drove the three of them to his apartment, where they arrived at "four, four-thirty, I would just guess." The three of them walked up "some back stairs" to his second-floor apartment and entered through the kitchen door. Then they went to the living room "and sat down. We may have stopped to mix a drink or something like that in the kitchen. And we sat down and started talking, because Ricky had said that he wanted to talk with us. And this is an area that I am not real comfortable with," Miller added, "but we went to get some cocaine."

According to Miller, he and Jackie and Rick had talked about using cocaine while they were at the Café Pacific, and "that was one of the reasons" they went to his apartment. He said they did not stop anywhere to get any because he "believed" he had some at home. "Shortly after" they arrived at his apartment, he testified, either he or Jackie made some free base out of one to two grams of cocaine. "I remember we were standing in the area right between my living room and dining room, the three of us, kind of in a little circle," he said. "And Ricky said, 'I have to really tell both of you something. I shot him.' "

"Did he say anything about when this shooting or killing was planned?" asked Watnick.

"Well," said Miller, "he said that he and Scotty had been planning it for quite some time, and I don't know exactly how long."

"Did he say anything about why he had killed his father?" the DA queried.

"Well, he made a statement that said 'I just couldn't take it anymore. I did it for all of us.' "

Miller said that the cocaine he and Jackie and Ricky free-based that afternoon "did not affect his perception or memory" of what occurred at his apartment. In contrast, however, he said he "couldn't recall" anything else that was said while they were at his house.

At 8:30 or 9:00, Miller testified, he and Jackie took Rick home to Preston Towers. Miller said he drove, and that he and Jackie went inside and visited "for a little while" with Ricky's mother and several other people who were at the high-rise.

Before he and Jackie made their statements to police, Miller testified, Jackie was "very upset and telling me and telling Frank Wright that she wasn't going to go through with it. She had just thrown up and she was really a wreck." According to Miller, he and Frank Wright had to "prompt" Jackie to turn over the map.

When they testified before the Los Angeles grand jury, he went on to say, Jackie was still upset and crying. "She cried a lot during this period," Miller observed.

* * *

The next day Mike Gibson spent the morning session and the better part of the afternoon in cross-examining Miller. Unlike Jackie, Miller remained calm and basically consistent throughout the defense attorney's questioning. Nevertheless, by the end of Thursday's testimony, Ricky's lead counsel had successfully raised several questions about the real-estate heir's credibility and motivation as a witness.

Gibson's first line of attack was Miller's relationship with Ricky. To rebut the impression the DA was trying to convey—that Henry was a "friend" and contemporary of Rick Kyle's, who felt "very brotherly" toward him—Gibson pointed out that Miller was thirty-seven years old to Ricky's twenty when they met, and that Miller was married and divorced with two children.

Next, Gibson revealed that Miller had arrived in Los Angeles the previous Saturday night to "prepare for his testimony." He had been "working with the prosecution and detectives" since then. Miller admitted he had spent Monday with Lew Watnick or his associate or "some of the detectives" rereading his testimony from the grand-jury proceeding and the preliminary hearing, and that he had "looked at some photographs."

Gibson then asked Miller about his relationship with Jackie Phillips. From the time they met in January 1983 Miller stated, until he admitted himself to the Orange County Care Unit on March 6, he and Jackie were together "almost constantly."

Throughout this two-month period, he testified, they were consuming "at least a couple of ounces a week, maybe more" of cocaine, which he estimated cost five thousand dollars a week, "minimum." On certain occasions during January and February, he said, their cocaine purchases could have been as high as seven or eight thousand a week. During this time, he testified, Jackie wasn't working and received no income from any sources. Miller said he was paying her bills and her living expenses, in addition to "providing the funds" for their cocaine and other drugs.

Miller admitted that he was "beginning to have financial problems" before he admitted himself to the hospital on March 6, and that he was selling "some art work and jewelry" to get money. He also testified that he and Jackie's half brother Jim Phillips arranged for Jackie to enter the hospital by a process called "intervention."

"Could you tell the ladies and gentlemen of the jury what

intervention is?" asked Gibson. "What it is, and what did you all do?"

"Well," said Miller, "I arranged for Jim Phillips, who lives here in Los Angeles, to meet me at the Care Unit in Orange County along with Dr. Persh, the director, and another member of his staff. And we, without telling Jackie that I had arranged this meeting, and while she was visiting me, we went into this meeting and expressed concern and care for her and told her that—I basically told her that I couldn't continue the relationship unless she got some help."

After the meeting, Miller said, Jackie checked herself into the hospital for "about five weeks."

From the time he met Jackie in January 1983 until Henry Kyle's death in July, Miller said, he was aware of only two telephone conversations between Jackie and her father. The first occurred at her apartment in January or February, he testified, and the second was "in June, around the time of her birthday." From May to July, he said, Jackie never saw her father as far as he knew.

"In January and February 1983," Gibson asked, "did you become aware of the amount of inheritance that Jackie Phillips would have under the will of her father, Henry Kyle?"

"I believe that she mentioned it," said Miller. "I'm not sure that it was during that time period, but it may have been."

"Isn't it a fact that it was mentioned and discussed that she was going to get a very nominal inheritance under the will of her father?" pressed Gibson.

"I believe that she said something to the effect, and I can't be sure whether it was January or February or subsequent to that time, that she had asked her father to cut her out of the will," Miller said.

"She had asked her father to *cut her out* of the will?" Gibson said incredulously.

"Yes."

"All right," said Gibson. "Do you know *when* she asked her father to cut her out of the will?"

"No."

Leaving that subject aside, Gibson switched to Henry's and Jackie's trip to Los Angeles after the shootings. He emphasized the fact that after having never visited the house before, Phillips and Miller went to Stone Canyon *twice* during the day and a half they were in California. He also pointed out that it was Jackie's idea to go to her father's mansion, and that once she got there, "the first place she wanted to go" was Henry Kyle's bedroom, where she asked to be left alone. Gibson insinuated that Jackie's real motive in going to Granada was to search for the briefcase, or even for cash, large amounts of which Kyle was known to keep around the house.

Gibson also noted that Rusty Dunn not only provided Henry and Jackie with a tour of Stone Canyon on Sunday, July 24, but also told them his version of what happened the night of the shootings.

For the next forty minutes or so of testimony, Gibson tried to determine from Miller the sequence and dates of his and Jackie's meetings with Frank Wright. By the end of the questioning, Miller had given so many contradictory answers that Gibson said he was "frankly confused." By that time, Miller was becoming visibly irritated, and finally said in exasperation that he "really didn't remember the exact time frames."

At this point Gibson suddenly turned to Miller and said abruptly, "Mr. Miller, can I ask you please, sir, where you have personally been residing in the last ninety days prior to coming to California for testimony?"

"At Timberlawn Hospital in Dallas," Miller responded.

"And how long were you in Timberlawn Hospital?"

"Since January of this year, '84."

"And when were you released?"

"I haven't been released," said Miller. "I'm still a patient there."

"You're on a furlough to come out here, is that correct?"

"Yes."

"And is that hospitalization for the treatment of the drug-addiction difficulties that you have had?"

"Yes."

When Gibson further questioned Miller about the events the day of the funeral, his previously solid testimony began to crumble.

Miller repeated his testimony that he and Jackie and Ricky discussed "obtaining cocaine or getting high" while they were at the Café Pacific after the funeral reception.

"Now do you recall, Mr. Miller, you leaving the table where Mr. Ricky Kyle and Jackie were at and going and making phone calls in an effort to secure some cocaine for that evening?'' Gibson asked next.

"I don't really recall."

"Do you recall Jackie Phillips leaving the table and going and making some phone calls in an effort to secure cocaine?"

"I don't really—really remember that, either," Miller said hesitantly.

"Do you recall Miss Phillips drinking martinis there at Café Pacific?"

"I'm not sure what we were drinking."

Continuing to press Miller, Gibson said, "Isn't it a fact, Mr. Miller, that after Miss Phillips was at the Café Pacific and made some phone calls, that she told you that she had in fact made a connection and you-all could get some cocaine for that evening, isn't that correct?"

"Objection," Watnick interrupted. "A fact not in evidence."

"Sustained," said Devich.

"Is it a fact," Gibson said instead, "that you, Miss Phillips, and Mr. Kyle left and went to Tom Blake's house in east Dallas to get some cocaine?"

"I'm not sure whether it was that particular afternoon or whether it was another time that we were together that we did that," said Miller.

"Isn't it a fact that you went to Tom Blake? Isn't he a source of cocaine?"

"I assume so," said Miller. "I never met him."

"Isn't he a source of cocaine for Jackie Phillips?" Gibson said with irritation.

"I've been told so, yes."

"Isn't it a fact, instead of going to Rowland, you went to his residence and Jackie Phillips went up to his house and talked with him while you and Rick Kyle stayed in the car?" Gibson glared.

"I don't know. It could be. I remember a time that that happened. I don't know whether it was after we left Café Pacific that afternoon or whether it was some other time when we were together," said Miller.

"Your memory today doesn't allow you to make the connection of it being on this date?"

"I don't make the connection that it was necessarily that afternoon."

"Isn't it a fact that on this very afternoon that you then left from there and went to a restaurant and bar called the San Francisco Rose on lower Greenville Avenue?"

"Here again, I don't make the connection with that afternoon," Miller replied.

"And do you recall," Gibson continued, "Jackie Phillips making some phone calls and telling you that you in fact had scored some cocaine for that evening?"

"Once again, I don't make the connection with that evening."

"Could you tell the ladies and gentlemen of the jury, then, where you obtained the cocaine that you say you and Jackie and Ricky ingested on the day of the funeral . . . if your memory will allow you to recall that?"

"I don't recall."

"Do you recall that on the day of the funeral, that you had to borrow or get three hundred dollars from Ricky to purchase the cocaine from someone in order for you and Jackie and Ricky to get high that evening?" Gibson persisted.

"No, I don't recall that, either."

"Those events in your mind today just do not sink in with what occurred on July twenty-sixth, 1983, is that correct?"

"That's correct."

At his apartment that day, Miller said, "either he or Jackie" cooked the cocaine. "I'm sure Ricky didn't," he observed. "I don't believe he knew how." The effects of the cocaine lasted until he and Jackie took Ricky home, Miller said, which "seemed like it was an hour or two, probably, maybe closer to two." He "couldn't recall" whether Ricky free-based less than he and Jackie due to his injury, nor could he recall whether the three of them "passed" the cocaine by inhaling the smoke from the pipe and blowing it into each other's mouths.

Miller reiterated that it was an "emotional" conversation with Ricky, and that he and Jackie were "shocked" that he was telling them what he did.

"Isn't it a fact," Gibson asked at that point, "that you really didn't believe what you had heard; isn't that a fair statement?"

"No, I don't think that's a fair statement."

"Ricky talks a lot, does he not?" asked Gibson.

"Yes."

"Ricky brags a lot?"

"Yes."

"Puff talk?"

"Yes, I believe so."

"And after you got the map, did you think there was any reason to save it, Mr. Miller?" concluded Gibson. "Isn't that the reason you threw it away, actually?"

"Well, I think the reason, to the best of my memory now, that I threw it away, I just really didn't want to have any part of it, whether it was true or not."

"Do you recall testifying in front of a judge here at the preliminary hearing in January of 1983?" Gibson said sharply.

"Yes," said Miller.

"Mr. Miller, let me show you what is Volume Five of the preliminary hearing and ask you to look at page eleven, please, sir," said Gibson, walking up to the witness stand with a transcript. "You were asked the question—I believe this was on cross-examination by me at the preliminary hearing. Question was: 'You would agree with me, Mr. Miller, if you looked at it closely, that it appears that the map has been crumpled up or folded up?' And your answer was: 'Yes, it was crumpled up.' And that's what you recall, isn't that correct?"

"That's correct," said Miller.

"And then if we skip down to the question at line fourteen: 'Do you recall basically when it was that you did that?' And your answer then was: 'Well, it sat on my desk for a couple of days, then I moved it to my bedroom on the TV, and I really didn't think there was much reason to save it. I didn't really put much, you know—' Question: 'You didn't put much stock in it?' Answer: 'I guess you could say that.' "

"Do you recall that being your answer under oath at the preliminary hearing, Mr. Miller?" asked Gibson, looking up at Miller.

"I recall that."

"Now isn't that true, Mr. Miller, that at the time, you didn't put much stock in what you say occurred there on July twenty-sixth, 1983?"

"Well," said Miller, "I think that—I would have to kind of go into a little bit more background. I felt like that, as the description of what happened continued, Ricky became a little bit more boastful and I didn't put much stock in his kind of boastful statements. But I did believe that he had actually done it, yes."

178

Miller said he "believed" Jackie recovered the map after their first meeting with Frank Wright. He also testified that after Grogan questioned her on July 29, Jackie telephoned him at his office and "asked him to pick her up." She was "angry and upset."

"Did she say to you, Mr. Miller, that she was suspected of being involved in the incidents that occurred out in California?"

"Well, she told me that the murder weapon had been stolen from a friend of hers, and if that involved her, yes."

"Okay," said Gibson. "The focus of her concern was the fact that a murder weapon had been found and it was connected with a friend of hers, is that correct?"

"Yes," said Miller. "She was more concerned about involving a friend of hers than anything."

"It's also true, however, though, she was somewhat concerned and scared for herself and the implications that that might have towards her, would that be a fair statement?"

"That would be a fair statement, too."

Afterward, Miller said, he called Frank Wright, who had been his attorney, and "made arrangements" for Jackie and him to meet with him. From that point, Miller conceded, Wright was representing both of them.

"And did he have an opportunity to talk with you during however many interviews you had with him concerning the law in California about accessory or accomplice to murder?"

"I recall a conversation where he was going to have to look into that," responded Miller, adding hastily, "His primary concern was suppression of evidence."

"I understand," said Gibson. "But he also looked up and had to check into the law of accessory or accomplice to murder in California; do you recall that?"

"I believe so."

"And again, that's part of him doing his job to ensure that you and Jackie were represented and protected to the best of his ability."

"Your honor," Watnick put in, "again, we're talking about what Mr. Wright did, and I think that—"

"Sustained," Devich interrupted.

"Thank you," muttered Watnick.

"Jackie Phillips and you," Gibson continued, in a firm voice, "to Mr. Wright, expressed some concern for any possible criminal liability that she and/or you might have as a result of the incident in California, isn't that a fair statement?"

"Well, we both knew that she hadn't done anything wrong," responded Miller, "so we just wanted to make sure everybody knew that."

"You wanted to find out if you had any trouble or difficulty, isn't that correct?"

"We wanted to make sure that we didn't, yes."

"And you would expect and you wanted Mr. Wright to protect you and do his job in representing you and Jackie Phillips, isn't that correct?"

"That's why we hired him."

During their meetings with Wright, Miller said, neither he nor Jackie brought up Henry Kyle's will or estate, and he "didn't believe" the three of them discussed it. He said Wright "made mention" of Jackie needing a probate lawyer for legal help concerning her father's will. He also said he "didn't know" whether Jackie sent Wright a copy of Kyle's will, or whether he and Jackie received a letter from Wright advising them to see a probate lawyer. When Gibson showed him a copy of the letter from Wright to him and Jackie, dated August 15, 1983, telling them that "at their earliest convenience, [they] should make another appointment with Mr. Passman" to "thoroughly discuss any and all details pertinent to the death of your father," Miller said, "Okay, I recall now what this is in reference to." After listening to the letter read aloud to the jury, Miller conceded that he "or his businesses" had used Sam Passman in the past, and that he made the arrangements for Jackie to meet with Passman.

"When did you make those arrangements, if you recall?"

"Well, it was obviously before August fifteenth," responded Miller. "I just would imagine that it was reasonably shortly, you know, before this."

Pressed further by Gibson, Miller testified that he telephoned Sam Passman first to make an appointment ("I wouldn't have just shown up in his office," he said dryly), and then he went with Jackie to see Passman, where they were joined by another attorney, George Nachtman. He "couldn't remember" the date of the meeting. After he and Jackie received the August fifteenth letter from Wright, he said, he "took Jackie down to meet with Mr. Nachtman" again. He "couldn't recall" that date.

"Now isn't it a fact, Mr. Miller, that at some point in time prior to August the thirtieth, 1983, Mr. Passman and Mr. Nachtman began to formally represent Miss Phillips?" Gibson demanded.

"Yes."

"And isn't it a fact that on August the thirtieth, 1983, the same day you're out in front of this grand jury, that they filed a document in probate court challenging the inheritance of Ricky Kyle?"

"I don't know."

"You don't know the date of the filing of that instrument?"

"I have no idea."

"Whatever the date of the filing of the documents by Mr. Passman and Mr. Nachtman, Jackie had changed her mind about wanting to be disinherited, wouldn't that be a fair statement?" Gibson said heatedly, with a penetrating gaze at Miller.

"Objection, your honor," Watnick said, rising halfway out of his chair.

"Sustained, sustained," muttered Devich.

In answer to Gibson's final question on the subject, Miller said he "didn't believe" Jackie received a copy of Henry Kyle's will or any documents concerning his estate at her condominium or his apartment before she met with Frank Wright or Detective Grogan.

At Gibson's request, Miller repeated his account that he had telephoned Kyle the Tuesday before he was killed to get his permission to lease Jackie's condo, and that Kyle had returned the call.

"Is that your recollection today?" Gibson asked, when he had finished.

"Yes," said Miller.

"Mr. Miller," Gibson said then, "back in January when you testified at the preliminary hearing you gave this testimony before the judge. . . ." Opening a transcript, Gibson said, "The question was: 'Now, the phone call, was that the first opportunity on the phone or in person for you to directly talk with Mr. Kyle?' And the answer you gave under oath was: 'The only time.' And the next question was: 'So this was a phone call just out of the blue, correct?' And your answer was: '*Out of the blue* at almost exactly five in the afternoon because I was—' "

Closing the transcript, Gibson said, "Is that how you answered it in January of 1983?"

"Yes, before I was interrupted," said Miller.

"Isn't it accurate, Mr. Miller, that the phone call was in fact out of the blue and it was a call unexpected to you at that time?"

"I don't believe it was," responded Miller. "My recollection now, after giving it considerable thought, is that he was returning my call, because I think the main reason I wanted to talk to him was about the condominium."

"But the condominium had been basically vacant since May, since Jackie was living with you, isn't that correct?"

"No, it wasn't vacant. She had her clothes and most of her stuff over there."

"She wasn't living over there, was she?"

"A few nights, she would stay there."

"Whether or not it was out of the blue, as you testified in January, or whether it was in response to a call by you," Gibson said forcefully, "your testimony to this jury is that Mr. Kyle, a person you have never met or talked with, called you two days before his death to discuss with you his personal details concerning his disposition of his estate, is that correct?"

"That was part of the conversation, yeah."

"After this conversation, where you indicated that this person you had never met talked with you about changes in his will, the end result of that, is it not, Mr. Miller, is in fact you then became a witness for Jackie Phillips—"

"Objection, your honor—" Watnick said angrily.

"—in her cause to challenge the inheritance of this young man as a result of that; correct?" Gibson continued.

"No," responded Miller.

"I have no further questions," said Gibson, turning away from Miller.

15

On Monday morning of the last week before the Christmas holidays, Lew Watnick called Rick Kyle's brother-in-law to the stand. Louis Douglas Halley IV (known as Doug), appeared to be in his late twenties. He had a slight build, medium-length sandy-brown hair, and a moustache. He was dressed neatly in a maroon windbreaker, khaki-type pants, and a knit shirt.

On the witness stand Halley said he had met Rick Kyle in Denton, Texas, in September of 1982, when Rick had started dating his sister, Kelly Moore. They "got along real well." He saw him again during his sister's Christmas break, when Rick stopped by with Scott Kyle to see Kelly in Midland, Texas (at Halley's stepfather's). The boys were on their way from Dallas to Los Angeles. Scott and Rick were driving Henry Kyle's Bentley at the time, Halley said. Scott brought about a gram of cocaine with him, Halley testified, and he and Scott and Rick snorted some of it that night.

Halley also saw Rick about ten months later, in October 1983, when Rick was in Midland, "shortly after the indictment." Halley said the two of them were at a restaurant, and that Rick said to him, "I'm not going to insult your intelligence. I'm sure you know what happened." They had "used a little marijuana."

In November 1983, Halley testified, Rick came to Midland on weekends "now and then," and the two of them used marijuana on occasion. They never talked about the shooting itself, Halley said, but he asked Rick about his defense, and Rick told him he "felt very optimistic." Halley said that around Thanksgiving, Rick told him his defense was going to be self-defense, and that they would be "bringing up his abused childhood." He also told him he'd "gone ahead and made a settlement on the will," and said he'd been cut from "forty-nine percent to eighteen percent," and that Scott was cut from "forty-nine percent to forty-five percent." "He thought he'd still get in excess of a couple million dollars," Halley said. Halley also testified that Rick mentioned that he and Scott were the beneficiaries of a "separate trust from the estate," but they wouldn't be getting any money for a few years because of an "age stipulation."

Next, Halley lived with Rick at the Preston Towers in Dallas, between March 13 and May 12, 1984.

Rick told him then that he killed his father, Halley testified. Asked by Watnick if Rick told him why, Halley said, "As far as a motivation, one reason, no. He said he did it when he did because Vicki was gone, and the fewer the people there the better."

Halley said Rick also told him that he and his brother planned it "that summer." Watnick asked if Rick felt his brother had "set him up to take the fall." Halley replied, "He was afraid to think such thoughts; he didn't like to think such thoughts." In addition, Halley testified that Rick told him Scott gave him the gun and said it was "unregistered and untraceable," that he had "checked it out." Rick said Scott stole it from a boyfriend of Jackie's—out of his car.

Rick was "leery" of Jackie and "what she could do," Halley testified. He tried to avoid her for "several different reasons"—first, because she was "unbalanced," and second, because she was a "prosecution witness" and he was "advised by his defense attorneys not to have conversations with her."

Halley said he "met" Jackie Phillips one morning at the high-rise when she started "screaming and beating at the door." Rick let her in "reluctantly." Halley was in the bedroom at the time. Jackie "jumped up in a huff and screamed at Rick, 'You're trying to frame me for murder!' Rick kind of laughed at it," Halley said. "She said, 'You're going to jail,' and Rick said he wasn't."

Halley also said that Rick described the murder: "He said Scott came into his room and asked if he was ready to do it, and Rick was surprised because Scott was supposed to be in his room—

:hat was part of the plan. Scott said, 'Are you sure you can do it?' " Halley continued. "Rick told him to go back upstairs."

Rick told him he "woke his father up and said he heard a prowler, and his father got his gun and they looked around." Rick said he had his gun "in his sweat suit. I asked him what happened before he shot him and Rick said 'nothing.' He said it was like his dad knew what was going to happen and turned around. I asked Rick why his father shot him, and he said that while he was getting his gun out from under his sweats, that Henry Kyle turned around with his gun raised." According to Halley, Rick told him he shot his father "just once," and that it was "under his left arm. He said he could prove his father shot first," Halley added.

"He said it ruined his plan that his father shot him, so he ran outside and threw the gun. He said the plan was to say it was a prowler."

Halley further testified that Rick told him that he was wearing "a surgical glove," and that he put it in the "trash container," Halley thought "in the kitchen. He thought investigators might have it and he was worried."

After the shooting, Halley went on to say, "Rick became worried" because he "couldn't remember whether he threw the gun with his right or left hand and he had only one glove and he thought his fingerprints might be on it, so he asked Jackie Phillips and Henry Miller to get the gun." He said he "didn't know the LAPD already had the gun" at the time. Rick told him he wore a glove, "because he knew a paraffin test could show how close the range was."

Asked if Rick talked about his inheritance, Halley replied, "What he said varied. At times he would be real upset that everybody was trying to cut in on it, at other times he told his lawyers that he didn't care—that they could just have it."

Halley said he last saw Rick on May 12, 1984. Watnick asked if he had any animosity toward him. He replied, "To a small degree. Not as much as I did after I was in Dallas."

Halley also testified that he "first talked to an officer about the case" in mid-October, when he met with Bob Grogan and John Rockwood. At that time, he said, he signed a statement.

For his cross-examination, which began after the lunch break, Gibson was even more antagonistic than he had been with Henry

Miller III and Jackie. He barely introduced himself to Halley (whom he kept referring to as "Mr. Holly" until Halley corrected him), and treated him with unvarnished scorn.

By the end of Gibson's hour or so of cross-examination, the jury learned that Halley was Kelly Moore's half brother, and that he considered his "permanent address" to be his father's residence in Norman, Oklahoma. He told Gibson he was twenty-seven years old, and that he was employed as a bartender at the Sheraton Norman in Norman, Oklahoma, where he was currently living in a trailer home with a female roommate. He said he was attending the University of Oklahoma.

Gibson asked if he had a job during the period he lived with Rick in Dallas, and Halley said no.

"So you spent considerable time at the condo, didn't you?" Gibson said accusingly.

"Yes," acknowledged Halley.

"And while you were there at the condo, you looked at a set of legal documents, didn't you, Mr. Halley," Gibson said stridently, ". . . some grand-jury proceedings?"

"No," said Halley.

"You looked at the preliminary-hearing transcript, too, didn't you?" Gibson said angrily. When Halley shook his head, the defense lawyer looked him in the eyes and said, "You also had an opportunity to read correspondence between Ricky Kyle and his attorneys, isn't that correct, Mr. Halley?"

"No," repeated Halley.

"And the settlement agreement?"

"No," Halley persisted, adding, "The only semilegal documents I read was a list of assets of the estate."

Next, Gibson noted that while Halley was staying at the high-rise, he contributed money to help pay the bills only once—$120 when he first got into town. He paid no rent, the defense attorney brought out, furnished groceries only once, never paid for the telephone or utility bills, and never provided drugs or alcohol.

"In fact," Gibson posited, "didn't Ricky Kyle ask you to leave in May or throw you out because you were taking advantage of him?"

"No," answered Halley, squirming slightly. "That's not correct."

According to Halley, Rick told him "more than once" that he had killed his father, and each time they were free-basing

186

cocaine. Rick also told him that "Jackie got him started" free-basing.

"Didn't a reporter come to your door at the Preston Towers once and ask to come in?" Gibson asked next.

"Yes," said Halley, looking around the courtroom. "She's sitting right over there," he added, pointing to a spectator.

"And didn't you tell her this case read like a Harold Robbins novel and you wanted her to write it?" Gibson demanded.

"No."

"You constantly talk about this case, don't you, Mr. Halley?"

"No."

"As a matter of fact, you find it fascinating, don't you?"

"I think it's interesting."

"Didn't you in fact tell a number of other people you were going to be subpoenaed as a witness in a big murder case?" Gibson said accusingly.

"I told a few people I work with at the Sheraton."

"In fact, you told them all about the details, didn't you?"

"I didn't tell them about my testimony."

"Didn't you also tell the patrons in the bar?" pushed Gibson. "Didn't you tell them you were excited about going out to L.A. to testify?"

"Excitedly, no," responded Halley.

"But you did talk about it, didn't you?"

"Yes," admitted Halley.

"Wasn't it in fact your plan to get a million dollars from Ricky Kyle to start a restaurant in October?" demanded Gibson, his voice rising in intensity.

"No," said Halley.

"Wasn't that your plan in March when you moved in with Ricky?"

"No," responded Halley. "I never had any such plan."

"You didn't have a plan to start a restaurant in Midland?" Gibson persisted.

"No."

"You didn't *take* a million dollars with you when you left Ricky's condominium in May, did you, Mr. Halley?" Gibson said after a pause. "He turned you down, didn't he?"

"I never asked him," said Halley.

"I have no further questions," Gibson said curtly.

16

TUESDAY'S SESSION STARTED OUT
rather less dramatically. As its first witness of the day, the prosecution called Detective Rick Jaques, one of the minor investigators in the Kyle shootings, to the stand, merely to get into evidence the fact that it was Jaques who found a holster in a garment bag in Rick Kyle's bedroom closet.

Sumner's cross was far more comprehensive. As part of his investigation of the main floor, Sumner brought out, Jaques searched the kitchen thoroughly, including the cabinets and the trash can. If he had found a glove with blood on it, Jaques conceded, he "would have recovered it."

On re-direct the prosecution asked Jaques whether he would have recovered a Playtex glove *without* blood on it, and the investigator said no, "based on his state of mind that a burglar did it."

On re-cross, Steve Sumner showed the investigator and the jury some police photographs of the crime scene, taken in the kitchen at Stone Canyon. After asking Jaques to point out that there were six blood droppings visible on the picture of the kitchen linoleum, "more or less in a line," about one to two and a half feet apart, the defense attorney then directed the detective to note for the jury that the distance between the nearest blood spot and the kitchen trash can was "about eight feet." This suggested, Sumner hoped, that Ricky had left a trail of blood on his flight out of the house—a flight, the defense maintained, that did not include the kitchen trash can.

Around 11:30, a little before the lunch break on Tuesday, the courtroom grew considerably more animated when Watnick announced Vicki Yang Kyle's name.

Even Ricky Kyle turned around to stare as the Taiwanese realtor walked up the aisle of Department 123, past the spectators' benches and jury box, to the witness stand, where she demurely took her seat.

In contrast to the image conveyed in the publicity surrounding the murder, Vicki Kyle came across as poised, self-contained, businesslike, and surprisingly down-to-earth. Her hair was cut about chin length in a pageboy style with bangs. She wore a short red jacket with a black bib cut in the shape of a V to match her black skirt.

An extremely solicitous Lew Watnick asked her to state her name for the jury, and Vicki responded, "Vee-kee Kyle," in a strange, childlike voice. Except when she spoke about financial matters—when her command of the language became nearly flawless—Vicki answered in slightly broken English.

While the jury looked on with obvious fascination, Vicki testified that she met Henry Kyle "around 1978," and that she was "going with him" from then until their marriage in November 1982. She told Watnick that she attempted to keep the marriage a secret "because my father would not approve that I married to Caucasian." She described her father as a "very conservative" businessman with "substantial property" in Taiwan. Vicki said further that her father invested in the United States through her. She also testified that she and Henry Kyle signed a prenuptial agreement "to keep their property separate."

When Watnick asked her about Henry Kyle's relationship with Rick, Vicki responded, "To me it was a normal father and son." She said she saw Kyle hit Rick once. "I didn't know the reason," she testified, "He hit Ricky's shoulder. . . . It was one punch." Watnick asked if Ricky and Kyle had "any discussion" afterward. "I remember Rick said, 'I'm sorry, Daddy.' My impression was Henry was mad that Ricky didn't tell the truth," she noted. "I asked him why and Henry said, 'He just lie.'" She never saw him hit Scott, and she testified, "I never [even] heard him yell at anybody."

On several occasions Kyle told her he was "very disappointed'' with Ricky. ''He said, 'Those boys could have gone to Harvard, Yale, or Princeton, but they were so lazy they didn't want to study to get into it.' '' Kyle ''didn't particularly expect'' Rick and Scott to do what he wanted, Vicki observed, as long as they were ''doing something straight, right.''

Before she left for Taiwan in June 1983, Vicki testified, Henry told her, ''We have to get our June will done.'' She said Kyle had told her on ''a number of occasions'' before then that he was going to cut Ricky out of his will (whenever he was disappointed with him), and it was ''her impression'' he already had. ''He said he worked too hard to let his children use his money for alcohol and dope.''

Vicki said that in the first part of 1983, Scott was living at Preston Road and going to school, and receiving an allowance of two hundred dollars a month from his father. Ricky was in Denton, at school she thought. He visited the house ''not very often but several times,'' and he came with his girlfriend, Kelly. At the time, Vicki testified, Rick was driving a new Mazda, which his father gave him when he got out of the Marine Corps. During that time, she said, she ''didn't see much of Ricky,'' and she never went with Henry to visit him in Denton.

After graduating, she testified, Ricky attended the University of Texas in Austin for one semester, then he came back to Dallas. Kyle told her ''Ricky got kicked out of school,'' and Henry was ''depressed'' about it. The next semester, Ricky attended Brookhaven Community College in Dallas and lived at home. Vicki didn't know if he received an allowance, and he ''told her that he worked.'' While he was at UT, Rick lived in a dormitory paid for by Kyle. ''Henry told me that he pay everything,'' she noted.

After one semester at Brookhaven, Ricky went into the Marine Corps, then he returned to the house on Preston Road ''a short while.'' From there, she said, he and Scott went to Atlanta to visit their mother the Christmas of 1981. Rick didn't come back with Scott after the holidays. He came back the following May (1982), when Henry went to Atlanta ''to pick him up.'' Afterward, she said, Rick went to North Texas State in Denton.

Watnick asked Vicki if ''the victim mentioned giving Rick certain options with respect to the rest of his life'' before and after he picked him up in Atlanta. ''Yes,'' Vicki responded. ''Henry said he'd give him a car and money and he'd be on his own, or he to go to college and he'd give him tuition and let him finish.''

Watnick's last questions concerned the living trust Kyle had set up for Rick and Scott. Vicki testified that she had ''seen a copy of the trust'' and that ''Henry told her'' it provided Rick and Scott each with sixty thousand dollars a year until Scott turned thirty-five, when they would receive the principal. The basis of the trust, she said, was Kyle's golf course in Kansas City. ''Every time he was disappointed and depressed'' with the boys, Kyle told her he ''wanted to dissolve or change the trust—mostly if they didn't make their grades,'' she observed, and ''every time they changed schools.'' Whenever he mentioned dissolving the trust, she said, she told him to ''leave that there.''

Wednesday morning Vicki showed up for court in another prim business suit (light-gray with white pinstripes).

Watnick's direct examination lasted most of the rest of the morning.

Vicki testified that when she returned from a trip to Taiwan on Wednesday afternoon, July 20, Rick picked her up at the airport and ''appeared normal. The conversation was, 'How are you doing with Daddy?' He said fine, they had come to some kind of an understanding, and everything was working out great.'' Vicki said she asked Ricky about Kelly, and he told her she was ''in Paris or San Francisco taking French cooking courses or something.'' Rick did not mention that Kelly had been in L.A. for a week or that she had stayed at the house. That night Ricky drove Vicki's daughter, Ellen, to Vicki's condominium in Salano Beach.

Vicki joined them the next day and that evening, she related, she and Ricky and some friends had dinner at a Chinese restaurant across the street from the condominium. Rick seemed ''rather happy with her company'' at dinner, she said, and answered questions about Stanford, which gave her the impression he was ''happy he got in and prepared to go.''

After dinner, Vicki ''offered Ricky to stay in condo'' because Henry and Scott were planning to come to Salano Beach the next day (Friday) to spend the weekend. Instead, Ricky returned to Stone Canyon. ''He said he had to go back,'' she said in her last piece of testimony on direct examination. ''He had something to do.''

When Judge Devich nodded to the defense team to begin its cross-examination, Mike Gibson dispensed with preliminary niceties.

"How old a young lady are you?" he said, his voice polite, but curt.

"Thirty-eight," responded Vicki.

Her bank account in San Diego was in the name of "Mrs. Vicki Yang," she acknowledged, when Gibson pointed it out. She "thought" Henry had opened an account in California after they were married, but she "didn't know for sure."

When Gibson asked about Kyle's move to California, she reiterated what she had told Lew Watnick that morning, saying it was "her impression he was retiring and slowing down," and that Henry "thought of" the move to Los Angeles as "a retirement." When Gibson mentioned that Kyle had formed a law partnership in Mesquite, Texas, in the spring of 1982, Vicki seemed surprised and said she "didn't know" about it. Then she added curtly, "I haven't seen the paper [proving it]."

Between April 1978 and March 1982, Vicki testified, Henry had visited her "once or twice a month" at her condo in Salano Beach, and she had visited him "once or twice a month" in Dallas.

"Did you ever meet Ann Meidel?" Gibson asked next, referring to the decorator Kyle had lived with at Preston Road from 1978 to 1980.

"No," said Vicki.

"Do you know who she is?" Gibson continued.

"The interior designer who remodeled Preston Road," Vicki said, with no change in expression.

"And didn't she live there at Mr. Kyle's house?" Gibson persisted, still hoping for some reaction.

"Yes," Vicki answered placidly.

"How about Patricia Blackman?" Gibson continued, naming another of Kyle's girlfriends during this period. "Did you meet her while she was staying at Preston Road?"

"No," said Vicki.

"Maryann Crutcher?"

"No."

"A lady by the name of Helen Boehrns, a manicurist?"

"Yes," responded Vicki. "I met her, but I didn't know she stayed at the house."

"Where did you meet her?" asked Gibson.

"At the barbershop in Preston Towers."

After answering Gibson's questions, Vicki testified that she "never really lived" with Kyle until February 1982, and before that, she only came to Dallas if he was in town.

Next, Vicki testified that she met Ricky for the first time during "the end of 1979 or early 1980," and conceded that she "didn't spend much time" with him. She said there was never a period of time when she and Ricky were living in the same residence at the same time, and agreed with Gibson that all the information she possessed about him came from Henry—"or Scott Kyle," she added.

Turning to her marriage to Henry Kyle in November 1982, Gibson said to Vicki, "Now that's what's called a 'secret marriage,' isn't that true?" Vicki acknowledged that she and Kyle didn't tell any of his children or his business associates that they were married "right away."

When Gibson emphasized the fact that she and Henry Kyle maintained completely separate finances, and that the only proof of their marriage was the marriage certificate, Vicki acknowledged that was true, then exclaimed, "But we planned to spend the rest of our life together."

Hearing that, Gibson responded cynically, "And the marriage certificate was the only paper to reflect that?"

"It was because we couldn't make our marriage open," she replied, looking frustrated.

"So it was a secret?" retorted Gibson.

"For the time being," Vicki said firmly. "That's why there was no bank account."

In that same context, Gibson noted that Vicki's airline tickets were made in the name of "Vicki Yang," as was her passport, and that she listed her condominium as her home address. "I never really lived in Stone Canyon," Vicki said in response. "More in my condo." When Ricky's defense lawyer pointed out that she paid for her plane tickets, not Henry Kyle, Vicki responded, "He gave me some money, but I don't remember whether I pay for this. . . ."

In her last testimony of the day Vicki told Gibson it was her impression that Ricky was "already out of the will" in July when Kyle was shot.

Thursday, December 20, the last day of court before a two-week Christmas break, was also Vicki Kyle's last day on the witness stand. She was attired in a feminine but professional burgundy-rose suit with a cream-colored blouse and matching rose pumps.

Gibson asked Vicki about the Stone Canyon property, which she had described as hers and Henry's "marital house," the house in which they had planned to live together. She said it was "their home" when the defense lawyer asked a second time. Gibson then handed her a copy of the deed to Granada, and asked her if she'd ever seen it before. Scrutinizing the document, Vicki said no. She expressed no emotion when Gibson pointed out that the property was deeded to "Henry Harrison Kyle, a single man" for $893,000. The date of the deed was April Fool's Day, 1983.

Gibson also noted that the title to the property was transferred to Country Club Management (Kyle's Kansas City holding and the corpus of his living trust for Rick and Scott) the same day Kyle purchased it. "So the title to your 'marital home' is actually in trust for the boys, is that right?" Gibson asked Vicki. "Right," she said brusquely, handing the deed back to Gibson.

When asked about Jackie, Vicki testified that the day of the funeral, she sat next to Jackie on a couch at the reception and talked. Gibson asked if Jackie seemed intoxicated or on drugs.

Vicki replied, "I can't say if she was intoxicated or on drugs, because I've never seen anyone drunk or on drugs."

Looking at her with disbelief, Gibson said, "You mean to say in your thirty-eight years you've never seen anyone drunk?"

"No," answered Vicki.

"You're a very fortunate lady," Gibson said, shaking his head.

Before passing the witness to Watnick, Gibson asked Vicki if it was true she had hired lawyers to represent her in connection with Kyle's estate. When she said yes, he pointed out that she had also challenged Ricky's inheritance, and that she wanted Kyle's will to be probated in California instead of Texas.

"You got a million-dollar insurance policy on Henry Kyle's life, too, isn't that right, Mrs. Kyle?" queried Gibson.

"Right," answered Vicki, who seemed angry for the first time.

"I have no further questions," noted Gibson.

When Vicki left the courtroom, Lew Watnick called Quint

Barnes to the stand to repeat his story about his missing gun. Under Sumner's questioning, however, Barnes testified that although he was with Scott several times during the period he dated Jackie, he never told Scott he had a gun in his trunk, and he never opened the trunk in Scott's presence.

George Joines, an antiques dealer, testified that a month after Kyle was killed, he found a box with sixteen rounds of ammunition "wedged" into a crawl space in the downstairs bedroom next to Rick's.

Watnick called Bob Grogan's junior detective, John Rockwood, to play the tape of Ricky's statement to Grogan. On cross-examination, Sumner got Rockwood to admit that the police found and took a photograph of "mud or muddy footprints" on the patio outside the open French doors—Bobby Green remembered sweeping that same patio earlier on the evening of the shooting. Rockwood also admitted that the courtyard door leading to Stone Canyon was open when the police arrived. Sumner insinuated these pieces of evidence pointed to the presence of a prowler.

The prosecution's next witness was Arland Ward, Henry Kyle's accountant and the executor of the estate. On the stand Ward revealed for the first time the terms of the November 1983 secret settlement among the heirs: Scott got 46.2645 percent, Ricky got 18 percent, Vicki got 13.7355 percent, Jackie got 11 percent, and Paula got 11 percent.

17

IN MID-JANUARY THE JURORS GOT
their first look at tennis pro Bobby Green. Green little resembled the stereotype of the blond, bronzed club tennis pro. He
was tall and gangly, with a Gomer Pyle earnestness about him—
right down to his accent, which was pure east Texas. As if to
underline this image, Green was wearing a red polyester leisure
suit with a maroon and white polka-dot tie. His black hair was
combed straight back from his forehead and slicked down to
within an inch of its life.

Green could hardly wait to answer the DA's questions about
Rick and Scott, and often blurted out his responses before Watnick could finish the questions.

The first thing Green told the DA was that he never saw
Henry Kyle strike Ricky, Rick never mentioned any injuries to
him, and he never saw any bruises on the boys. He heard a couple of "loud discussions" between Henry and Rick or Scott, but
"it was rare." He "saw" only one loud discussion, he testified.
"I admired his being a man very much under control," Green
said of Henry.

Did he ever hear Ricky threaten Henry? Green said, "Not
to Henry," but behind his back, "maybe" after an altercation.
Green recalled once when he and Rick were in the TV room on
Preston Road, and Rick said, "I'm gonna kill him. I'm gonna
kill him."

"Did you tell Henry Kyle?" questioned Watnick.

"It bothered me," Green volunteered. "I discussed it with

196

[Henry Kyle's friend] George Shore. And later I said, 'Henry, Ricky's been talkin' about you behind your back, and I don't like how Ricky's talkin' about you behind your back.' Henry said, 'Thank you, Bobby.' ''

"Did you tell Kyle about the death threat?" Watnick persisted.

"Not specifically," said Green.

When the DA asked if Rick said anything else derogatory about Kyle, Green responded, "Slight comments, but . . . he spoke derogatorily about his father—you know, I don't recall any exact comments. He just didn't talk respectful about his father."

"Could you give us an example?" Watnick pushed.

" 'Daddy does this or that and I'm not afraid of him.' ''

Green said he would describe the relationship between Henry and Scott as "normally a very warm father and son relationship . . . normal ups and downs between a father and son. A caring father," he went on to say, "and Scott also could be a joy to be around. Scott kept more to himself in his own comments and never said anything to me about his father.

"Rick and I got along," Green testified. "There were some tough spots when I got in between Rick and his father—the only touch and go between Rick and I . . . because I was very loyal and respectful of Henry. But I was concerned about Rick and Scott."

When asked how he got "between" Rick and Henry, Green said, "Different times when Rick would do things behind his father's back. . . . Henry seldom asked me because he didn't want to put me on the spot, but when he asked me I told him the truth."

"What are some examples?" asked Watnick.

"Henry would tell Rick not to turn loud music on," Green answered, looking straight at Ricky, "and as soon as Henry leaves—boom!—the loud music would go on."

Green said the reason Kyle asked him to move into Preston Road in 1980 was to "engage him as his resident tennis pro. He was a tennis enthusiast," Green remarked. "He enjoyed exercise. It was a help to me and a help to Henry. When I came in he kind of took me under his wing. . . ."

According to Green, Kyle "often" discussed his concern about his sons with him, and "more than once" said to him, "They're my sons. They always will be. I'll never give up on 'em.'' Green said that in early 1983 Henry told him, ''There's no way I can leave Rick a lot of money. He couldn't handle it.'' Green said Kyle told him, ''The jury's still out on Scott. But I know he can't handle it, either.'' According to Green, Kyle was ''in a very mellow tone'' at the time, ''very positive.''

Green said he arrived at Granada the day after the Fourth of July, 1983. ''Henry asked me to come. We had a business relationship and Henry had learned I had a degree in Radio-TV-Film, and he was going to make me his personal assistant at Four Star, but he thought it was better to get a well-rounded education at law school. He took me under his wing . . . he openly discussed the Four Star negotiations with me.''

Green said that ''rather than pay him,'' Henry was going to get him into law school, finance his legal studies, and print business cards that said ''Henry Kyle's personal assistant.''

''I was looking to Pepperdine University in Malibu. Henry wrote me a letter of recommendation.'' While he was staying at Stone Canyon that summer, he spent his time ''getting settled'' and contacting laws schools. ''I also helped Henry in preparing the grounds for a tennis court.''

Green recalled he overheard Rick's half of a phone conversation with Kelly Moore: ''Rick said, 'I just wanna bring you out here and show you all over again how much I love you. Daddy's doing so well, if we liquidate we'll have forty to fifty million. It's gonna be Kyle Brothers, Incorporated. I don't just wanna be rich. I wanna be famous.' ''

The following Wednesday, Kyle arrived home from a trip to Dallas and Green picked him up at LAX just before midnight. Henry was ''tired,'' Green testified, but didn't seem angry or upset. During the ride home from the airport, Henry allegedly said to him, ''Bobby, I'm preparing a new will and there's no way I can leave those rascals a lot of money. They can't handle it. You'll be in it and you'll be comfortable.'' Green said he told Kyle: ''You'd think they'd realize the opportunity they had in front of them,'' and Henry said, ''You'd think so, but things don't always turn out the way you think.''

Green said that when he and Henry got home from the airport, he was surprised to see Scott sleeping in the other bed in his upstairs bedroom because Scott had been sleeping in the second downstairs bedroom. The next morning, Thursday, Green testified, Henry came into his bedroom. "He looked surprised to see Scott there." At breakfast, Green testified, Henry said to Scott, "It's obvious Rick didn't do the things I asked. I'm pissed at both of you."

Green volunteered that sometime during that evening, he and Scott were at the dining-room table and Scott pulled a document from Four Star out of Kyle's open briefcase and told him, "These are some new movies Daddy's acquiring for distribution." Green continued: "Then he shuffled some more through the briefcase, and showed me George Shore's health-club brochure."

Later that night, "Rick came in grumblin', and appeared to be in a foul mood. He said to Scott, 'Where's Daddy?' and Scott motioned to Henry's room. Rick asked if he was asleep and Scott shrugged his shoulders. Rick looked at Scott and pinched him in the midsection while he was grinning at him. Then Scott said, 'I'm gonna hit it and go get a glass of milk.'" Green said a few minutes later (about midnight), he went to his bedroom and found Scott was in bed.

Green said he woke up later that night when Scott went to the bathroom, because he heard Scott flush the toilet. Scott was "gone a few mintues" in the hallway, and then came back to bed. Green testified that he kept his watch on the nightstand between the two beds, and when Scott got back into bed, Scott picked it up and "fiddled with it" to see the time.

A few minutes later, Green said, he was "wide awake" and noticed it was 3:46 A.M. A few minutes after that, "I heard shots going off." Green said that there was a "little bit of time between the first shots," and then a "succession of shots." "Scott yelled, 'Ricky,' three times right after the shots," Green claimed.

Concerning his claim against the estate for $72,000, Green told the DA that the money was for "three years in law school. In lieu of being paid, Henry was going to finance my legal studies, and twenty-four thousand a year was discussed. I felt that was a fair amount. That was my business relationship with Henry. That was our agreement."

Green's testimony had caused Steve Sumner to snicker, "Did Henry Kyle call *you* the night before the murder and tell you he was gonna write you in his will?! Jackie says Henry told *her* on Tuesday that he was gonna make a new will and put her in it. . . . Henry Miller says *he* talked to Kyle Tuesday afternoon—the only time in his life he ever talked to Kyle—and he told him he was changing his will to take care of Jackie. . . . Vicki testified that Henry told *her* in June he wanted to make a joint will for the two of them. . . . Now Bobby Green says Henry told him the night before he was killed that he was making a new will and Bobby would be in it. . . . Is there anybody he *didn't* say that to ?!''

On Tuesday morning, January 15, Sumner was in fine form. Of Ricky's three criminal defense lawyers, he had been selected to cross-examine Green, and his contempt for the tennis player was plain from the start.

After pointing out that Green was interviewed by Detectives Grogan and Rockwood twice, once on July 22, and later on July 25, Sumner said: ''Didn't you tell Grogan and Rockwood that the 'best part of your relationship with Henry Kyle was when Rick and Scott were away ?' ''

''I don't recall that,'' Green said with hostility.

'' 'Henry and I had a beautiful arrangement there in Dallas. . . .' '' Sumner said suggestively, reading from a transcript of Green's police interview. ''Did you say that ?''

''No,'' answered Green. ''I meant when the boys were there.''

''How about the time you said you and Henry had a beautiful arrangement and life-style when the boys were at private school ?'' Sumner continued, lifting one eyebrow.

''I don't recall my exact comments,'' Green said defensively. ''Henry was an exceptional person and we had become close friends. We got along as well as anybody could ever get along.''

''You pried into Rick's and Scott's lives, didn't you ?'' Sumner suddenly said with distaste.

''I would not,'' retorted Green, glaring at Rick's attorney. ''That's the last thing in the world I'd do. I was living my life. The last thing I was was a babysitter for two teen-aged boys—or a tattletale. But Henry knew I would tell him the truth.''

''In fact, you would actively seek out information, wouldn't you ?''

''I certainly would not.''

''Did you ever listen in on telephone conversations ?''

''Just what I overheard by being there.''

''Isn't it true you told Detective Grogan about a call or two you 'intercepted' ?'' Sumner asked.

"I remained on the line if I heard my name mentioned between Rick and Scott," Green said quickly.

"Is that 'any of your business'?" Sumner said in disgust.

"Yes, that's my business," Green snapped.

"Didn't you overhear Rick talking to Kelly at Stone Canyon?"

"I wasn't on that call."

"Do you deny that you told Detective Grogan, 'The reason I know it's Kelly is because I'm on the other end of the line. . . .'?" Sumner demanded.

"I didn't say that," Green blurted.

Shown a copy of the police transcript recording his statement, Green shifted in his seat and said, "Oh, back in '83? It was a long time ago."

"Oh, you were in shock?" Sumner said sarcastically.

"You don't have to raise your voice, Mr. Sumner," chided Green.

"Are you saying your memory is better now than it was in 1983?"

"I don't remember saying that," answered Green.

"You're saying now you *weren't* on the phone?"

"Right. I never listened on the phone, but it's a big house and you pick up the phone. And when I heard my name mentioned, then it's my business."

Steve Sumner cited Green's "supposed" conversation with Henry on the way home from the airport on Wednesday night, July 20.

". . . And he said he'd include you in his *will*?" Sumner asked, his voice dripping with sarcasm.

"Yes," responded Green, glowering.

"And that's the *first time* he'd said that to you. . . ."

"That's right."

"And there were no witnesses . . ." pursued Sumner, getting a "Yes."

"Was it common for Henry Kyle to refer to his sons as '*rascals*'?" he asked next, in reference to Green's testimony that Kyle told him there was "no way he could leave those rascals anything."

"No," answered Green. "He usually called them by name."

"Yesterday was the first time you've ever mentioned to anyone that Henry Kyle told you he was going to include you in his will, isn't it, Mr. Green?" Sumner said caustically.

"I told my family," responded Green.

"Did Henry Kyle say that same day that he planned to include Jackie Phillips?"

"No."

"Vicki?"

"No. He didn't go into anything else."

"I have no further questions," Sumner remarked.

The State's next witness was Peggy Fiderio, a fingerprint examiner for the Los Angeles Police Department. On direct examination by John Moulin, Fiderio testified that she didn't find any prints on the Rohm revolver—"consistent," Moulin suggested and she agreed, "with a person wearing a glove."

On cross-examination, Fiderio conceded to Gibson that examiners "don't always obtain prints," that there was "a lot of smudging" on the weapon, that fingerprints could be destroyed, and that "other things than wearing a glove" could affect print formation.

On Wednesday afternoon, Lew Watnick questioned Bob Grogan, who seemed as confident and self-assured as ever.

Grogan revealed, at last, what was written on the copy of Henry Kyle's 1978 will found on top of the stack of business papers in his open briefcase on the dining-room table at Stone Canyon: After telling reporters for a year and a half that Kyle had made "significant alterations" to the will, and that Rick's name was "deleted," Grogan finally revealed that Kyle made only two penciled changes. One was to eliminate his mother, Della Kyle, who had died in 1979. (Originally Kyle had left her $100,000 and her house.) The other was to cross out Rick's name merely from the disposition of his personal effects (jewelry, furniture, cars, etc.). The rest of the will, bequeathing the Henry Harrison Kyle Family Trust and all the other property in his estate—except Jackie's $10,000 and Paula's $100,000—to Rick and Scott, remained unchanged.

Grogan also said that he found "over six thousand dollars" in cash attached to a money clip on the bureau in Kyle's bedroom, and "another briefcase" in Rick's room. It contained notebooks, a business-reply card from Stanford, bills, letters to the Marine Corps from Henry Kyle, and two photographs, one of which showed Rick in Marine Corps fatigues.

On Thursday morning Grogan faced questions from the defense. Before court, he joked with reporters about his nubby brown and white sport coat, which had replaced his usual blue "witness suit." "Nah . . . I thought I'd wear brown today. I've got a lot of bullshit to go over. . . ."

When he took his seat on the witness stand a few minutes later, he answered smoothly, like an old pro.

"Do you recall," Gibson asked, "Bobby Green telling you, 'Rick knows I was an informant to his dad . . . I wouldn't cover up'?"

"Yes," Grogan said pleasantly. "I specifically recall it."

Gibson also asked the detective about his first interview with Jackie Phillips. Gibson asked the detective to read an excerpt from the transcript to show that Phillips was dealing drugs:

QUESTION (by Grogan): Do you know who he [Henry Kyle] was investigating?
JACKIE: Yes, sir.
GROGAN: Who?
JACKIE: He was investigating me and my business partner at that time. I was selling cocaine.

In his first interview with her, Grogan conceded, Jackie was "not quite candid." Had Grogan suggested she might "have some difficulties" if she was not cooperative? "I may have left that impression with her," Grogan admitted. His "line of questioning" suggested she "might have know about the gun," and indicated she would have problems if she wasn't truthful.

The next time he saw Phillips, on August 10, was the day he picked up the map and took hers and Henry Miller's statements at Frank Wright's office. Grogan said Wright first contacted him on August 8, when he telephoned to set up the meeting for the tenth.

Grogan told Gibson it was his decision whether or not to tape-record an interview, and that Jackie's statement on the tenth was not recorded at her request. He said he "could have" recorded it surreptitiously, but "didn't." Gibson asked if she was the only person in the investigation who was given that option. Grogan said, "Could be."

Before dismissing Grogan, Gibson asked him how the police learned about Doug Halley. Grogan testified that he got an "anonymous phone call from a male individual" just before the trial began in October. He was told he should "interview Doug Halley, a student at the University of Oklahoma," because he was "likely to discuss it because he was attending law enforcement classes at the University of Oklahoma." When Gibson suggested the "anonymous caller" was Halley himself, Grogan said he "didn't follow up" the source of the call, and that he flew to Norman on October 18 to interview Halley at his trailer park. He didn't record the interview, Grogan told Gibson, because he "didn't have his machine" with him.

18

AS ONE OF HIS FINAL WITNESSES,
Watnick questioned police ballistics expert Jimmy L. Trahin,
the man who Grogan contended could prove the State's case by
himself.

Trahin, a short, balding, lively gun enthusiast in his late forties, wore neckties with little rifles on them and addressed the
jurors as if they were his students. He often gestured excitedly
to explain a technical point.

During his testimony for the State, Trahin first explained
how he and his partner searched Stone Canyon for bullets and
fragments the day of the police investigation.

After analyzing the items and firing test shots, Trahin concluded that the bullets and fragments were fired from Henry
Kyle's Smith & Wesson, and from the Rohm revolver found in
the neighbor's yard. He said he "couldn't tell exactly which
shots were fired first," but in his opinion, Kyle (whom he referred to as "the victim") shot six times, all in a "northeasterly direction,"—that is, from the position where his body was
found, in front of the French doors, toward the Stone Canyon
entrance hall, the entry, and the breakfast room.

Trahin then identified Kyle's six shots, which he described
as follows:

- *Victim's shot #1:* Trahin said this shot hit the so-called
  "front" (or Stone Canyon) door, which led from the
  courtyard into an entrance hall off the dining room. The

bullet left a "small crease" in the door, "continuing on to an unknown location." The shot "could" have come from the Rohm since the projectile wasn't found, but since all of Kyle's other shots were fired in a northerly direction like this one, it was assumed to be Kyle's.

The rest of Kyle's shots (Victim's shots #2–6) were all fired in a downward direction, Trahin observed.

- *Victim's shot #2:* Trahin testified that this shot was fired in a northeasterly direction, slightly downward, and hit the door leading from the dining room to the breakfast room, imbedding itself there.
- *Victim's shot #3:* Fired in a northerly direction and downward, striking the northeastern wall of the dining room and ricocheting, then breaking into two pieces on the breakfast-room entryway floor.
- *Victim's shot #4:* Another northerly shot, which first hit the southeast wall of the dining room, then ricocheted downward and imbedded itself into the front door off Stone Canyon.
- *Victim's shot #5:* Passed through the breakfast-room doorway and hit the floor, then ricocheted off the floor and came up to hit the north breakfast-room window, where the jacket was found. Trahin said Kyle would have to have been positioned "very low down" when he fired this shot.
- *Victim's shot #6:* Another northerly, downward shot, which ricocheted into the doorjamb by the dining room, leaving a bullet casing on the floor.

Trahin said he believed four shots were fired from the Rohm; three he could "account for," and of those, two he had "definitely tied down." The two of which he was certain were the bullet through Kyle's body, and a spent bullet found in the floor between the dining room and the breakfast room. In addition, he said, there had to be "another shot" fired close to the victim's head to account for the tattooing on the left side of his face. Trahin said he had found a copper jacket from the Rohm ten feet from Kyle's body, on the patio floor outside the French doors, but no evidence of a fourth jacket.

In Trahin's opinion, Rick Kyle was struck in the elbow by Victim's shot #5 (or possibly, but less likely, #6), which he believed had intersected the shot by the Rohm into the floor between the dining and breakfast rooms. He said the "suspect's" downward shot into the floor was consistent with a "reflex shot" in reaction to being hit in the elbow by Kyle's bullet.

In reference to the holster police found in Rick Kyle's room at Stone Canyon, Trahin testified that there were "seven positive points of comparison" between the holster and the Rohm revolver found in the shrubbery. This proved that the Rohm was in the holster for "a limited period of time."

In his last ten minutes of testimony for the State, Trahin explained how he was able to tell how close a gun was held to the body of a victim by studying the amount of tattooing or stippling on the gunshot wound. In Trahin's opinion, Henry Kyle was fatally shot by a .38-caliber weapon "no further than six inches" away from his body, "one and a half to two inches minimum" (not a contact wound). Based on a gunshot-residue-pattern test using the Rohm, he observed, it was his opinion that the gun was "three to four inches" from Kyle. Trahin thus essentially nailed down two of the prosecution's key points: that Ricky Kyle was shot by Henry Kyle's .357 Magnum, and Henry Kyle was killed at close range by the Rohm revolver police found in the bushes almost exactly where Jackie Phillips and Henry Miller said Rick had told them it would be.

Ricky's lawyers, however, seemed as confident as ever about their case.

Shortly after Watnick had called Trahin to the stand, Rick's attorneys brought two of the actual doors from Stone Canyon to the courtroom, where they stood propped up against a wall behind the jury box.

Gibson's main point in his cross-examination of Trahin was the pattern of Kyle's shots. Using the enormous pair of white double doors, he had Trahin show the jury where the bullet from "Victim's shot #1" had barely creased the inside of the right-hand door at a height of six feet one inch. In order to make that indentation in the door, Gibson elicited from Trahin, Kyle had to have fired upward with the muzzle of his gun at a height of five feet, and the door (which opened to the inside) had to have been open at approximately a 60-degree angle. Trahin also conceded, when pushed by Gibson, that this shot was "more likely" fired while Kyle was erect.

All five of Kyle's other shots were fired in a downward, not upward direction, making impact at a height of three feet or less—as opposed to the six feet one inch indentation of the first shot.

The prosecution next called a handwriting expert with the Los Angeles Police Department named Bruce Greenwood.

Watnick's questions were short and to the point. On direct examination, Greenwood testified that after studying exemplars of Rick Kyle's handwriting, he was "confident and reasonably convinced" that the same person had "most probably" drawn the map showing where the gun was located.

Greenwood had also examined handwriting samples from Jackie Phillips and Henry Miller, and in his opinion there was "no evidence" to show that either one of them had drawn the diagram.

Mike Gibson's cross-examination, by contrast, took a full day and showed extensive preparation.

Gibson began by immediately pouncing on Greenwood's "most probably" opinion that Ricky drew the map.

"My opinion is only as good as the means to demonstrate it," Greenwood said defensively, not denying that he gave a "less than positive identification."

After intimating that Greenwood, as a "civilian employee of the police department," might have been influenced by information he received from detectives, Gibson went on to ask him in detail how he had formed his opinion. In response, Greenwood testified that he was first contacted about the case in September 1983, when Sergeant Rockwood brought him the map, along with an exemplar of Rick Kyle's handwriting. At the time, Greenwood said, Rockwood told him Rick was a suspect, and the police wanted to know if he had drawn the map. His report was "inconclusive," Greenwood testified, and he was "unable to determine if Rick did it." He said he didn't have enough of Rick's writing, and when he asked LAPD for additional samples, "they were reluctant to get more."

About a year later, he testified, Grogan and Rockwood brought him Rick's portfolio and told him there were writing samples in it. After studying those, Greenwood said, he formed the opinion that Ricky "most probably" drew the map.

Gibson noted that the police did not obtain samples of Jackie's or Miller's handwriting until October 1984. Greenwood testified that his opinion, based on those samples, was that a "different writer" from Jackie or Henry was "most probably" involved. Pressed further by Gibson, he conceded it was a "less than absolute" opinion.

It is interesting that Greenwood himself volunteered that he would "still like to see writing from anyone even remotely involved." After testifying, Greenwood was heard to say: "They [Watnick and Grogan] really made me look like a jerk up there. They didn't do their homework. They didn't do their job. Nobody likes to give an inconclusive opinion."

As the prosecution's case drew to a close, Watnick introduced a surprise witness from Paris. She was identified as Wendy Blum, the eighteen-year-old daughter of Henry Kyle's friend L.A. producer Harry Blum.

Wendy Blum was a cute girl with short dark hair—very wholesome and conservative-looking. She wore a plain gray skirt, black opaque stockings and shoes, and a royal-blue silk blouse with a red scarf around her neck. She seemed nervous as she explained that she was attending school in Paris on an exchange program. When Watnick asked if she knew the defendant, she looked over at Rick and smiled.

In her next few minutes on the stand, she testified that she met Henry Kyle first, because her dad "worked with him," and that she saw Kyle "often" at her house, because he "spent a lot of time" with her parents. Wendy said she met Rick at a New Year's Eve party at her house in 1982, and didn't see him again until June 1983, when she and a girlfriend attended the estate sale at Stone Canyon. Afterward, she said, she saw Rick on a "number of occasions: four or five times" at Crown Books in Westwood, where she worked, and "roughly eight or nine times" when they went out.

She said Rick told her he was planning to go to Stanford in the fall and "seemed pleased." Asked if he mentioned cocaine to her, she testified that it came up once "in passing" one of the first times they were together—"just that he used it."

Around July 4, Wendy testified, she and Rick went to Alice's Restaurant in Westwood together after she got off work. While they were there, they started talking about "family relationships—Henry, specifically. He stated that before the end of the summer he was gonna kill his father. He talked about being beaten, his poor relationship with Henry, not liking L.A. or being comfortable.

"I remember my reaction immediately afterward," Wendy said, looking upset. When Mike Gibson objected to her response, she said, "I asked him why he said that, and I was trying to discuss why he felt that way—if he could work out his feelings in another way. I was afraid of his aggression." Wendy said Rick told her, "He hates me," or words to that effect, that " 'he doesn't let people live the way they want to. Only if they live like him.' "

At the time, Wendy testified, "Rick was pensive and preoccupied. Every time we talked about Henry there was a lot going on in his head."

"Did he ever talk about Scott?" Watnick asked, breaking the stunned silence in the courtroom.

"He said that him and Scott were close, or had been, and both felt similarly about their father, but Scott needed his direct approval. When they agreed to do things, Scott sometimes backed out at the last minute, because he was afraid of Henry. He said Scott wanted it as much as he did, but would never do it." He called Scott a "coward."

Rick told her he moved to California "to get to know Henry better" before he went to school. The relationship "started deteriorating from the minute he arrived. His high hopes disintegrated."

"Did he ever say anything about his father's will?" Watnick said in a brittle tone.

"We had a conversation about Vicki," answered Wendy. "He said she was influencing him. His father was penciling him out," she added. "He had seen some pencil marks."

Blum said Rick "didn't like" Vicki because she "seemed conniving. She was a block in his relationship with Henry, since Rick and Vicki didn't get along, and Henry and Vicki were close." Wendy offered: "He said Vicki just wanted Henry for his money. In part, [Rick] didn't like her because she didn't like him. He didn't like David Bowie's song 'China Girl' because it reminded him of Vicki."

Wendy said she last talked to Rick the night after the murder, when she called him at the hospital to "ask if he was okay." She said he was "pretty groggy," and they didn't talk about Henry's death.

Asked to repeat what Rick told her about Scott, Blum testified: "Rick said, 'Scott agrees with me and wants to kill him, too, but he never would. Scott never would kill our father, so I have to do it, because he doesn't have the guts.'"

Mike Gibson handled Wendy's cross-examination for the defense, and he was the picture of politeness, though still determined.

After noting that Wendy had never met Scott or Vicki, and that she had no contact with Rick between New Year's and June 1983, he asked her about the time she spent with Rick in June and July.

Wendy acknowledged that she was "fuzzy" about her conversations with Rick, and that she "couldn't recall exact words." She remembered that they talked about his relationship with his father, and that Rick said he came back to California to "reestablish his relationship" with Henry. Rick had "high hopes" at first, but the "conflict and discord" started almost immediately.

According to Blum, Rick told her his father hit or beat him, verbally abused him, and belittled and demeaned him in front of other people. Several times, she said, she thought he had been beaten just before she saw him. Wendy said Rick talked more about "fear, frustration, anger, and a mix of emotions" than actual beatings. Had Rick told her about a threat Henry made to kill him? She said no, only that he "felt threatened by him." She said Rick felt his father was "strong enough to kill him," and that was "part of his fear of him."

Blum said Rick told her he was in a "dilemma" whether to stay or leave Los Angeles that summer because his relationship with his father had so deteriorated. He mentioned his desire to go to school, and said "the only way he could is if his father would help him financially." Rick told her Kyle disapproved of his ambitions to be a writer or an artist. Rick "made it clear he wanted his father's approval."

In response to several questions by Gibson, Wendy testified that Rick "never laid out the logistics" to kill his father, and he never said it was actually planned.

"Just that he wanted to?" Gibson asked.

"He said, 'By the end of the summer I'm going to kill my father.' He didn't show me plans. He didn't say he had a plan."

Wendy told Gibson Rick mentioned his father's will to her

"only once, maybe over lunch at Westwood." He "may have told her" he was "cut out," or that he was "written out," or that he was "penciled out. I remember the idea he was not gonna be in the will," she said, but conceded that she didn't know if she read the word "penciled" in the newspaper, or if Rick had told her that.

With that point established, Gibson passed the witness to Watnick, who asked Wendy if she was "concerned" about Rick's statement to her.

Wendy testified that she had later called a psychiatrist "to find out if I should have certain rights, certain responsibilities—if it was normal for Rick to have a death wish. I didn't know him very well," she added. Afterward, she suggested to Rick that he talk to a psychiatrist.

Marj Helper, the realtor who sold Kyle the house on Stone Canyon and a close friend of the Blums, later maintained that Wendy told her mother about Rick's statement, and that Sue Blum had told her husband, Harry.

"Harry called Henry the night he got in from Dallas, Wednesday," Helper told a reporter, "and said he had to talk to him, that it was very important. He wanted to warn him about Ricky. Henry said he was too tired, and he'd talk to him in the morning. That night he was killed. He was too late. And Harry just felt sick about it."

According to Sue Blum, when Wendy suggested to Rick that he see a psychiatrist, "he wasn't averse to it. He just said, 'Where would I get the money?'"

PART
THREE

19

THE STATE RESTED ITS CASE IN
the middle of the day on Thursday, January 31. Judge Devich
told the jurors to be back in court the following Tuesday morning, February 5, in order to give the defense a few days to contact its witnesses and prepare for its long-awaited opening
statement.

When Tuesday morning finally dawned, Department 123
seemed to come alive after a long sleep. Reporters who hadn't
been in court for weeks and virtually the entire contingent of
court-watchers showed up.

Rick Kyle's lawyers, and even Ricky himself, were dressed
in navy-blue business suits to mark the occasion. None of them
engaged in the usual early-morning banter, and their serious
mood seemed to rub off on everyone in the spectator section.
Judge Devich called the jury in and Mike Gibson walked over
to the lectern in front of the jury box to begin his opening statement. His wavy blond hair caught the reflection of the fluores-
cent lights, and the courtroom was as quiet as a church.

"Ladies and gentlemen," he said, in his characteristically
smooth tones, "I appreciate your patience. This has taken longer
than I think anyone anticipated, and we will make an effort to
present our case cogently and concisely. It's very important to
keep your attention up as you reach a very important decision.
Some of the evidence in the prosecution's case is to be used in
reaching that decision—through our cross-examinations.

"Henry Kyle's death," he went on to say, his voice suddenly

quiet, "was a justifiable homicide. A case of self-defense. A tragedy, not a crime, occurred on Stone Canyon Road on July twenty-second, 1983.

"It's very important that you keep a context and perspective on the evidence," he continued. "A glass of water can be half empty or half full."

Gibson told the jury he would take time at the beginning of his case to show the "historical relationship" between Ricky and others. "The evidence will show that Ricky Kyle was shuffled from parent to parent in his early years. His home environment was not like ours. He was in military school during his teen years, spending ten months away from his mother or father. All the while, Ricky was learning, watching, and experiencing Henry Kyle's way of living.

"Henry Kyle was volatile, violent, explosive," Gibson stated, emphasizing each adjective. "He had a Jekyll and Hyde personality. He could be concerned . . . and then at the flash of an eye express violence. He taught this to his sons. Henry Kyle was a trained marine killer, and proud of that aspect of his life, and he sought to instill that macho image in his children. . . .

"Ricky Kyle was physically abused by his father in a way I don't think any of us can comprehend," continued Gibson. "Verbally and physically demeaned. Henry Kyle instilled a fear—absolute and total—that's hard to comprehend in this sterile courtroom. From childhood to July of 1983," he said, gesturing toward Ricky, "this young man was in fear of his life—and it was genuine and reasonable under the circumstances."

Gibson told the jurors they would be hearing from neighbors who heard intruders on that "tragic day. Whoever they were woke Ricky up and caused him to get up," he said. "The neighbors heard basically the same thing Ricky did. Ricky then did as he was ordered to do: He got a gun, attributable to that room, for protection. He woke his father up. He didn't shoot him in bed silently. He allowed him to arm himself—with a .357 Magnum. They looked around the premises. Back in the house, Henry Kyle, at the French door, turned with his .357 Magnum, fully erect, and fired in the face and direction of Ricky Kyle.

"Thank God we have that bullet and door to show you," Gibson said, pointing to the white double doors still standing in the courtroom after Jim Trahin's testimony. "We have conclusive evidence to show that Henry Kyle shot first. It was medically impossible for him to shoot after he received his wound.

"Ricky Kyle, in that instant of terror, reacted," said Gibson, "and in the ensuing struggle with his father shot two or three times. We're not sure. Ricky's not sure.

"He fled to the back of the house," continued Gibson, who stopped, turned to his side, and motioned toward Ricky. "Only that young man can understand the terror and fright of what occurred in that room.

"He threw the weapon away. He panicked. He didn't hide it in a cool, calculated way. Then he crept back in the house, not knowing what to do. It's difficult for me to even articulate to you—you have to accept and understand what he did. He didn't tell anyone he shot his father. He told a story. He told the same story, essentially, over and over again, not knowing what to do, and that was clearly a reasonable reaction by a young man in the situation he was in. Once the terror subsided, he broke down and confided in a girlfriend the circumstances that occurred.

"We have witnesses who were at the funeral," Gibson related. "We know Jackie Phillips and Henry S. Miller ensnared this young man into their drug world over the last eighteen months. He felt he could turn to them for advice or help—rightly or wrongly. The *true* conversation after the funeral will be brought to you—that Ricky *reacted* to Henry Kyle.

"A map was drawn, by Rick, showing where, in panic and terror, he threw the gun. Jackie and Henry told him they'd help him find a way out of his dilemma. Then Detective Grogan scared Jackie Phillips to death," Gibson said flatly. "What was her reaction? Not mad at Ricky because he cold-bloodedly executed their father . . . not mad about what happened at the house . . . but mad because a *friend* of hers may be involved in a remote way—and *she* may be involved.

"She scurried around to get civil lawyers to help her challenge Ricky's inheritance," Gibson told the jury. "And she gained over a million dollars. The story she fabricated about what Rick told her will be shown to be not true—she sought to utilize it to her advantage. She and Henry Miller led Ricky down the road to being indicted.

"They took liberties with the truth *here*," Gibson pointed out, indicating Devich's courtroom. "Ricky had to deal with the pressures of the situation, at his tender age—and yes, he had difficulties. Others made the maximum effort to enhance their financial situation by scheming and devising ways to gain from the tragedy that occurred.

"This is a very difficult case," Gibson said in conclusion. "It requires understanding the complexity and the tender age of this young man. This was a tragedy, but a justifiable homicide. Henry Kyle set in motion the circumstances that brought about his own death."

During the lunch break, reaction to Gibson's opening statement was mixed. One of the court-watchers noted that Ricky's lawyers had been hinting to newspapers ever since the indictment that they would prove somebody *else* killed Henry Kyle. Now, he wondered whether Rick's attorneys were pleading self-defense to get around the ballistics evidence that Henry Kyle was killed with the stolen Rohm revolver, and that Rick was shot by his father.

Many had reservations about Henry Kyle's alleged brutality. The only evidence to support this so far was a few veiled comments from prosecution witnesses, and some anonymous quotes in the newspapers before the trial. Even Jackie, who had testified at the preliminary hearing that Kyle had molested her and abused Rick and Scott, virtually retracted her statements on the witness stand. Was Kyle's alleged violence a "defensive smoke-screen," as Lew Watnick called it, or "pure horseshit," as Bob Grogan described it?

The defense called as its first witness Walter Wainwright, a husky, fresh-faced twenty-two-year-old peach farmer from Reynolds, Georgia. He sported wavy blond hair and an air of country innocence. He was dressed, somewhat incongruously, in a black-and-white herringbone jacket with patch pockets and a yellow paisley tie.

In a thick Georgia accent peppered with "yes, sirs" and "no, sirs," Wainwright told the jury he was a "boyhood friend" of Rick's.

The summer he was fifteen, he testified, he flew to Dallas with Rick and Scott to spend three weeks at Henry Kyle's house. Rick and Scott went "to be with Henry and get to know him." While they were there, he said, they "played tennis or went to restaurants."

Wainwright told the jury about a time that summer when

218

he and Rick went to play tennis with Kyle, who was subsequently called away from the court on business. While they were waiting, Wainwright said, Rick bought Kyle a soft drink. When he got back, Kyle hit Ricky and said, "I told you never to drink a goddamned soft drink before you play tennis." Wainwright said Kyle then hit Rick again, on the back of the head. When he fell down, Kyle told him to "get up." Rick didn't say anything. Asked if *he* was scared, Wainwright said, "Very much. I felt like running."

Wainwright said he and Rick and Scott ate most of their meals in Dallas at restaurants Kyle owned. Whenever he introduced anyone there to his sons, Kyle would say, "These are my two bastards."

"He didn't take time to show Rick how to eat properly and he would get very upset at the way Ricky would eat. He hollered and cussed at him, 'Don't eat with a knife. Don't use your damn hands,' and so forth and so on." According to Wainwright, Kyle "hollered and cussed" at Rick "numerous" times.

Wainwright also told the jury about a time when he and Rick and Scott were watching television in the living room. Henry came in, "grabbed a bullwhip, and started poppin' it," telling them to "get up off their asses and do something constructive." Wainwright said Kyle hit him in the ear. "That's when I said it's time to go home," he testified, and added that he never saw Henry Kyle again.

Wainwright said Rick moved to Dallas when he was fifteen or sixteen, and afterward they saw each other "on occasion on holidays." Rick told him he was "afraid of his father."

After Kyle was shot, Wainwright said, he flew to Dallas to attend Kyle's funeral and reception. At the reception, Scott introduced him to Jackie Phillips and Henry Miller. Wainwright said he saw Jackie drink four drinks while they were in the kitchen together, and that she seemed "uptight and a little depressed." Later, outside by the pond, he saw her and Henry Miller "smoking a cigarette of marijuana." Wainwright said Jackie was "intoxicated and nervous" at the time, and was asking Miller to "call her coke connection there in Dallas. She told me how much money she was going through a week, that she was trying to quit, and it was a real problem." While he was talking to Jackie by the lake, Wainwright testified, Miller made two phone calls.

Wainwright said he also saw Rick at the reception, and that he seemed to be in shock. "He just told me he didn't know what was goin' on," Wainwright testified. "That he was confused."

On cross-examination, Watnick tried to downplay Wainwright's testimony by pointing out that Wainwright saw Kyle strike Rick only one time, that Rick played tennis "an hour and a half" later, and that Kyle never actually hit him with the bullwhip.

"It sure scared him," Wainwright volunteered.

"You didn't like Mr. Kyle, did you?" Watnick snapped.

"He was a fine man," Wainwright said without sarcasm, looking straight at Watnick and holding his head back proudly.

The defense's next witness, Mary Ann Viola, displayed none of Walter Wainwright's confidence as she took her seat in the witness box and nervously stated her name into the microphone.

Viola, a woman of forty-five or so, had pretty features and short, curly dark hair. She dressed simply in a plain blue-silk dress and wore little makeup. She testified, somewhat self-consciously, that she had dated Henry Kyle from February or March 1974 until January 1975. She said she met Rick and Scott that summer, when they were staying at their father's condominium in Dallas.

Viola told Steve Sumner that she and Kyle went to Florida together in January 1975. While they were there she ended the relationship "because of all the other women that I had just found out about." She "didn't want to date him anymore." After they got back to Dallas, she said, Kyle left for Kentucky, and he called her from there that spring. "I thought the relationship was over," she said quietly. "I don't think he did."

Viola said Kyle asked her to pick him up at the airport when he returned from Kentucky, and to have dinner with him that night. At dinner, she said, she repeated that she was not going to date him anymore. He became "angry" and started "clenching his teeth," but didn't say anything. The next day, he called her to say how close she was to his mother and to his boys, and how he had led them to believe it would be a long relationship. He didn't know what to tell them, and needed her help.

She agreed to drive him to the airport late that night (he was leaving for L.A.). When she got to Preston Towers, he didn't come down to the lobby, so she went up to his condo to get him.

Viola said she talked with Kyle in the living room, and he got up from the couch. "I thought he was going to the kitchen to get a drink. He turned away, and had his back to me, and all of a sudden he just wheeled around and hit me in the eye." When it happened, she was "surprised and very frightened"—she and Kyle were not having an argument at the time, and he didn't yell at her first. "He didn't say anything. He just turned around and hit me."

Viola "stumbled and knocked over a lamp," then she ran out of the apartment to the elevators. She was "upset and crying." Without saying a word, Kyle ran after her, grabbed her by the wrist, and dragged her back to the apartment.

Once they were back inside, he saw that her eye was already turning black. "My God, I've hurt you," he said. "I'm a boxer, and I know how to hit people without hurting them."

Viola stayed in the apartment, and "Henry started crying. We sat down on the sofa and he told me about things he'd never told me about his other wives and children."

The next day, Viola thought her nose was broken. When she told Kyle, he didn't believe her. She went to the doctor, anyway, and found out her nose was broken. Her wrist was sore, also, but not broken. The doctor wouldn't let her leave his office until she called the police or an attorney. She called an attorney, but she "didn't want to see him."

Afterward, Kyle attempted to see her, but she was "afraid." He came to her house the next day, anyway, and left some soup with one of her boys, who were in the front yard.

Sometime later, Viola testified, she got a "long letter" from Kyle. In it, Kyle told her that "if he had straightened out her thinking by hitting her, then he was glad he had. If not, then he was sorry he hurt her and wasted his time."

On cross, Watnick didn't attempt to dispute Viola's testimony. Instead he asked her if she'd ever seen Henry Kyle cry other than after he'd hit her. Viola thought for a moment, then said seriously, "When President Nixon resigned—or whatever he did. He was very upset about that." A few of the spectators in the courtroom tittered.

Viola also admitted that she "remained friends" with Kyle after he struck her, and that he was "fond of and affectionate" with her boys, who were younger than Rick and Scott.

On re-direct, Viola testified about a time when Henry, Scott, and Rick attended one of her son's baseball games in the summer of 1976. She said she couldn't hear what was being said, but she saw Henry try to hit Scott across the legs. Afterward, she testified, Scott dropped down to the ground, Henry kicked him in the leg, and dragged him to the car.

20

MIKE GIBSON'S FIRST WITNESS
Wednesday morning was June Burdette, an austere, heavyset
blonde in her early sixties. She was an employee of Jetco, Kyle's
oil-equipment company, from January 1963 to October 1981. She
first met Henry Kyle in the mid-seventies, when he took over
the company, and was "exposed to him" for about six years.

Ricky Kyle worked summers at Jetco, from the time he was
"thirteen or so" and continuing for about four years. According to Burdette, Kyle gave Rick "the most menial jobs available" (boxing and counting metal teeth, or driving a truck),
and checked up on him often. "He was most anxious that Rick
do his job in an exemplary way—almost possessed." Once, Rick
was "literally booted out of the shop" over a discrepancy in the
count of teeth in one of the boxes. Burdette testified she saw
Rick "on more than one occasion with evidence of having been
roughed up—swollen eye, cut lip, overall cuts and bruises on
his face."

On cross-examination, Watnick noted that Burdette was fired
from Jetco, and asked her whether Kyle wanted "all his employees" to work in an exemplary manner. "Yes," agreed Burdette. "But not to the same degree as he wanted Rick to."

As their next witness, Ricky's defense attorneys called a
mystery figure from Henry Kyle's past: Madonna Wiese. This
woman from California was married to Kyle for less than three
months in 1953 (between his marriages to Rheba Rice and Jackie
Glenn Garrison).

Wiese, a tall, stately blonde with chin-length hair flipped to one side, swept into the courtroom in an expensive, camel-colored coat. She took her seat on the witness stand with great dignity. Asked to state her name, she said, "Madonna Wiese Rosenfield," in a near-whisper.

"Mrs. Rosenfield," Steve Sumner said gently. "Could you speak up a little so the jury could hear you? You have a very soft voice."

Leaning into the microphone, Rosenfield said forcefully, "I can do better," and laughed along with the rest of the courtroom when her voice reverberated throughout the room.

While everybody followed her testimony with keen interest, Rosenfield told the jury she currently lived in Tempe, Arizona. She had been twenty-one years old when she met "Hank" Kyle, who was six years older than she, in "1950-something." She described Hank as a "lawyer and a fighter and reconnaissance pilot," and said he had been overseas fighting in the Korean War "most of" the two years before she married him.

"When were you and Henry Kyle married?" Sumner interrupted to ask her.

Rosenfield paused a second. "April twenty-something," she said, tilting her head to one side. "In—my goodness, 1940 . . . probably 1950s."

"How long were you married to him?"

"Approximately two months. Or that's how long I lived with him."

"Was the marriage difficult?"

"Absolutely. That's why it only lasted two months."

"Could you tell us what Henry Kyle was like before you married him?"

Rosenfield stopped to think. "Very charming and very interesting man. He was a bon vivant while we were dating. He charmed me to pieces to pursue me."

After they were married, Rosenfield testified, Kyle's personality changed. "He became very violent. I didn't have an opinion of my own that was valid. He said, 'Just shut up and smile.'

"If I didn't do what he asked, he would physically grab me and pinch me. The ultimate was to throw me into bed—I would say raped." Afterward, Rosenfield said, she was black-and-blue. "Even my ankles, torso, and legs."

Another time, Rosenfield testified, "we had one of our conflicts and he went to the bedroom and brought back a gun in a cloth and began wiping the gun and spinning it past my head. I was terrified, because I really felt he could kill me."

"Were there other incidents prior to this?" asked Sumner.

"Yes," responded Rosenfield. "He backed me to a door and held me."

"Do you recall what he said to you?" Sumner prodded.

"No," replied Rosenfield. "I just recall the terror and fear that I had. Then he hit the side of the door instead of my face, right past my ear."

"What did you do?" asked Sumner.

"Oh, I almost crumbled," Rosenfield said, shaking. "I had never been raised in that kind of violence. Then he asked me to kiss his hand," she said, breaking the tense silence in the courtroom. "Because look at what I made him do."

Rosenfield said "this kind of activity and conduct" went on "all during" the two months she lived with Hank. "I considered leaving him after the first such occasion because this was not my way of life," she testified, "but I was afraid to tell him. I was afraid for my life because of the physical abuse and his mental stability."

Rosenfield said when she finally did leave Kyle she planned it for several days. She left a note on Kyle's pillow, and flew home to her father's house in Los Angeles. "I felt I had escaped," she told the jury. "Hank called me there that night," she went on to say. "He told me that I had done a very terrible thing—that I'd left him . . . and I'd better have a lot of people around me from now on because he'd kill me. And I took that very seriously."

"Do you have an opinion about Henry Kyle's propensity for violence?" Sumner asked, when Rosenfield completed her testimony.

"Hank Kyle was a very violent man," she answered. "He wouldn't stop at anything—even my life. Just—a very cruel man and a very violent man."

No sooner had Madonna Wiese Rosenfield left the stand than the defense called another woman from Henry Kyle's past—Ann Meidel. She was the Palm Springs decorator he had pretended to marry in Mexico. Mike Gibson and Steve Sumner somehow managed to convince her to overcome her reluctance to talk, and she appeared confident and composed.

Like Rosenfield, Ann Meidel was a pretty, stylish blonde. Her hair was shoulder length and frosted, and she wore lots of large pieces of gold jewelry. She had a deep Palm Springs tan, shown off to good advantage with a striking lavender and black blouson-style silk dress with enormous padded shoulders and Romeo-and-Juliet puffed sleeves.

Madonna Rosenfield had happened to pass Meidel in the hall outside the courtroom between their two testimonies, and she said later it was like looking at herself. "It was a strange feeling. Hank probably went for the same types."

Once on the stand, Meidel described herself as an "architectural and interior designer." She said that she had lived in Palm Springs "off and on" for the past fifteen years, and "commuted" to Houston and Dallas for six of them.

Meidel told the jury she met Henry Kyle in "early summer" of 1978, and told the story of how Kyle had called her to redecorate his house in Dallas. Meidel said they didn't start dating until "late September," but Kyle began taking her to dinner and showing her his "business enterprises" in July and August.

Meidel said she was first introduced to Ricky at the Preston Road house in July 1978. He was "about fifteen" at the time. She said Rick was living permanently with Henry Kyle by then, and Scott was visiting for part of the summer from his mother's house in Georgia. That July and August, she testified, she and Rick "spent a lot of time together." The house was full of "dirt and dust," and there was only one couch, "so we sat together if we were in the house." Asked if they became friends, she replied, "Very much so."

Meidel told Steve Sumner that she saw Henry and Rick together that summer; and "I thought it was the greatest father-son relationship I'd ever seen."

"Now, during that period of time," Steve Sumner asked, "did your relationship with Henry Kyle become serious at any point?"

"Very serious," answered Meidel. "I was in love with him."

"And at that point did he ask you to marry him?" Sumner asked delicately.

"He asked my son to marry me—if he could marry me."

"And were you planning to do so?"

"Very much so."

"Now, during this period of time," Sumner went on, skipping past Kyle's fake marriage ceremony in Mexico, which Judge Devich had already ruled inadmissible, "did you learn anything about his personality that caused you to think he was a violent person?"

"Well," said Meidel, "I knew that he was a Tennessee hillbilly and I knew he had been in the Marine Corps and flown planes and killed Japs—you couldn't know the man and *not* know that, 'cause he always told his stories about his times in the hills in Tennessee, and they were always very entertaining— and people *loved* that about him. And I thought that he—I thought he was a Texas southern gentleman who was super athletic and great with the kids . . . and I thought he was the most brilliant man I'd ever met. I didn't know any other side then, but I did know he was raised a hillbilly."

"Did he ever show any of the other side to you?" asked Sumner. "With regard to acts of violence?"

"He showed a lot of things to me," Meidel said reflectively, "and *I* thought it was masculinity. He was a crack shot. He was a wonderful hunter. He was a boxer. He could play tennis. He could outrun all of our children. He was a super jock, an athlete . . . and what was he, a colonel in the Marine Corps? I mean, everything he showed me was great. I didn't think he *had* any weaknesses."

"Did something occur to change your opinion with respect to Henry Kyle's explosive capability?" Sumner prodded.

"Yes," said Meidel. "Well, I didn't think it was explosive, I thought it was his masculinity and his Marine Corps training."

"Tell us what happened."

Meidel paused. "As I remember it, we had a violent argument which came out of a—I don't know whether it was jealousy over another person I was involved with—the *only* other person I've been involved with in many, many years—or whether he was so disappointed that I had *had* that involvement. I don't know what provoked him, but either the jealousy of this man— which made him think that this man was maybe more powerful than he was—or the fact that I wasn't the Amazon that he thought I was, and that I had *had* a previous strong relationship . . . with a man who happened to be an Italian."

"Did that situation become quite physical and violent?"

"Well, I would always say something that would provoke

227

him. People that would not challenge him had no problem. But I wasn't that way, and I didn't know . . . how he was. So, I would provoke him. And when he said to me, 'How could you do that with an Italian?' I said to him, 'Well, you did it with a Jew,' and that did it. That provoked a *violent* argument—and I didn't know what it was.''

"Did you fight back?"

"Yes, I did."

"Ah . . ." Sumner stammered awkwardly. "Let me . . . could you describe it?"

"As I remember Henry's fights with me," Meidel said straightforwardly, "I never remember anything happening to my body. I never remember bruises, or beating me, or anything like that, but I remember that Henry fought like a person . . .'' Meidel searched for the right words. "A *man-to-man* fight. And I can't remember anything happening, except up above my shoulders. And I always was afraid he was gonna hurt my *face.* But I never remember a great big . . . at that particular time. It just really—we were having a female and male argument.''

"Now, did that—let me direct your attention to a period of time after that," said Sumner. "Did you go to Palm Springs after that?"

"Well, I got so mad at Henry that night that I hit him with a telephone," said Meidel. "And I think his face was scratched and bruised or something, and it embarrassed him very much. And he took me to the airport, and then he said he was leaving me at the airport to fly—well, I was leaving. I was going home. He went with me . . . because apparently—well, I found out later he didn't want anyone to see him looking like that, and he would have to explain it.''

"Did he shortly thereafter want you to go to San Francisco with him? And were you reluctant to do so?"

"Yes," said Meidel. "I told him—it was a bankers' meeting, and I told him I wouldn't go if he would do something that I didn't think was . . . proper.''

"Well," Sumner said, "did you tell him you were concerned about any more violence?" When Meidel didn't respond, Sumner said, "What did you tell him, ma'am, in regard to why you were reluctant to go to San Francisco?"

"Because I didn't want him to do anything that—I didn't want to have another argument—a physical argument," Meidel said hesitantly.

"Okay," said Sumner. "What'd he say?"

"He said he would not do anything if I would come," Meidel said, more forcefully. "And I wanted to go, so I went."

"And when you got there, what happened?"

"When I got there, he entertained me beautifully, with a lot of his banker friends. And we were dressed, and going out to dinner, to meet some people for dinner, and we entered into the elevator, and he laid a chop right into my stomach."

"What did you do?" asked Sumner.

"Well, I was very surprised," Meidel said. "And I remembered that I had discussed with some of my friends about a man that I suspected could be very strong and very, you know—if he could hurt me. And so I asked them what to do if a man does that to you, and they said, 'Well, hit him back.' Well," Meidel went on, "I asked him to take me back upstairs and to let me change my clothes, and I pushed him into the closet and pushed him clear down to the floor with a hanger. . . ."

Hearing the jury laugh, she added: "After that he was *wonderful!*"

Waiting for the laughter in the courtroom to die down, Sumner asked, "Now, after—with regard to the shot to the stomach, did he warn ya? Did you know that was coming?"

"Not at all," Meidel said quickly. "Everything was wonderful—we were dressed up, and goin' someplace great . . ."

"Were you arguing about anything?"

"No . . . I thought it was really a *joke*," Meidel said, still incredulous.

"Now, let me direct your attention to a—did you have occasion to go to Cuernavaca?" Sumner asked next. "Where is that?"

"Cuernavaca is the city of eternal spring in Mexico," Meidel explained, "and Henry had—he did *a lot*, set up a lot of wonderful business opportunities for me. And we were going down there—Henry was interested in some property, and a wealthy divorcée from Chicago was developing this property, and I was interested in doing the design work on the property—it was very beautiful. And so we were both down there as their guests, to play tennis, and to look over this Cuernavaca Racquet Club."

"And did any violence or fights occur in Cuernavaca?"

"Yes," said Meidel. "We had a wonderful time . . . and had finished dinner, or whatever, with these people, this woman—

she always had very interesting friends around. And Henry usually did not socialize afterward. He'd usually tell her we were going to retire. But he didn't that evening. He went back and sat with them and drank and talked . . . and I guess it made me jealous."

"How did you react?"

"Well, I don't remember, but I must have acted jealous," Meidel said. "Then he came back to the room and started another one of those arguments."

"Did it in fact get physical?"

"Yes, because he didn't want me to be noisy, and he didn't want me to embarrass him in front of those people. So it, again, was not a hitting, beating thing, but I can remember him holding me down, and trying to restrain me from screaming . . . and there was something that had to do with my face."

"Okay," said Sumner. "Now at this stage in your relationship, and this would be into '79, did your opinion change with regard to Henry Kyle's capability for violence?"

Meidel hesitated. "No," she said finally. "I always knew that he had been trained in the Marine Corps. I knew he had a very strong streak to him, but I began to suspect that he had a great disrespect for women, and started to sense things I didn't—couldn't figure out what it was. And I knew he really didn't want to do that to me or to anybody. But I saw it happening, and I started to sense things that I really had never been told about, or didn't know about."

"Did you in fact have a discussion with him with regard to his attitude, say, about killing?" Sumner posed.

"Did I talk to him?" Meidel responded. "Yes, he did talk to me about that."

"What did he say was his attitude about killing?"

"He said when he was in the Marine Corps, and he was flying those fighter planes, that—" Meidel interrupted herself. "We were talking about his background in Tennessee," she explained. "Where he'd hunted to eat, and how—what a disciplinarian his father was, and the strict life that he had led back there."

"What did he say with regard to his father's being a disciplinarian?"

"Well, he always said how he adored his father and was trying to live up to his father's expectations. And he would always say that if he didn't, that the father was so strong, and so capable of disciplining him, that it would be a—that his father would beat him. His father was considered a very strong mountain man.''

''Did he say his father would kill him?''

''He said his father would be . . .'' Meidel hesitated. ''He said that—as I remember it, he said that his father was either a sheriff or the constable in this community, and I can't tell you what the name of this community was, but I've been there. It's right next to Stomp Creek, where he went to grade school, and where he worked so hard, out on the farm. And he said that they would—the constable or the sheriff would come to get his father, and his father would go out and reprimand the criminals.''

''Did he say he killed them?''

''I'm not sure,'' said Meidel, ''but I think that the father, only through . . . to have justice be served . . . that the father was known for keeping peace in the hills, and the hill country. They were called 'hill people.' ''

''Did he go on and elaborate with regard to his—did he tell you about having a discussion with a chaplain in the Marine Corps with regard to killing people?'' Sumner asked gently. ''What did he say to you with regard to his attitude toward killing?''

''He said that when he went into the Marine Corps and was asked to leave the University of Tennessee, where he found out he could make so much money, and get away from his poor life in Tennessee, that right away he became one of their top—I don't know what they are, when they fly a fighter plane and shoot other planes down. And I guess he did shoot a couple planes down the Japanese were flying, and he said he went to the chaplain and asked the chaplain why it didn't bother him. Because it did not bother him to kill the enemy.''

''All right, now, let me ask you—you indicated that there were problems in your relationship with Henry Kyle's jealousy that you were describing?'' suggested Sumner.

''I thought at that time it was jealousy,'' Meidel said firmly, ''and then later on I realized that the thing that provoked his anger was his disappointment in the people he loved. And he was very disappointed in me.''

''Let me direct your attention to around the first part of

1979, and you were living at the house at that time on Preston Road. Now, up until February or March, into April, did you have an occasion where you left to go back to Palm Springs?"

"Yes," said Meidel. "Henry had a problem of putting people down verbally. After he found out where your weakness was, where his disappointment was about you, then he would use that point, and elaborate on it. And when were were playing tennis, he would start in on that—about this Italian man in my life, who I was in *love* with. I mean—"

"Let me stop and ask you some specific questions," Sumner interrupted. "When was the day this took place?"

"On Mother's Day—yes, it was May seventh. And he wouldn't stop this verbal . . . words, and I went up to take a shot, and I left. And flew back to California, and stayed out of his reach. Even with the crowd of people at the house, I went home for a week . . . to think. To think about what I was finding out about this man that I thought was the most wonderful person in the world," Meidel said softly.

"Did the boys live at the house during the summer of 1979?" Sumner asked next.

"Yes, both of them."

"Did you and Ricky develop a close relationship—"

"Yes," Meidel broke in, before Sumner could finish his question. "Very, very close."

"Did you ever observe any acts of violence by Henry Kyle toward Ricky Kyle in the summer of 1979?"

After a long pause, Meidel said, "I have heard about them— things that happened at Jetco and other places."

"Let me ask you specifically whether or not you ever saw Henry Kyle hit, strike, beat, whatever you describe it, Ricky Kyle during that time period," Sumner said resolutely.

"Yes," Meidel murmured, looking away.

"All right," Sumner said gently. "Tell us, generally, what you observed."

A hush fell over the courtroom.

"I think the reason I remember it so much is because Ricky was trying to protect *me*," Meidel said quietly. "Ricky and I were always very friendly to each other, and we did try to help each other out." Meidel paused. "I don't remember what the circumstances were, but Ricky had gone out to buy me [something], or to bring me home, or to do something to help me out of some kind of a difficult situation that I was in. And under the porte cochere on the house on Preston Road—and I don't know how I happened to be out there—I saw Henry . . .'' Meidel stopped, and began to cry. ''Hit Rick,'' she finished, covering her eyes with her hands.

Rick, who had been watching Meidel testify, turned away.

''Did he hit him with his fist, or open hand, or how'd he hit him?'' Steve Sumner asked, breaking the silence.

For a few moments, Meidel could not speak. ''Ricky would put his hands over his head,'' she said faintly, her voice still choked with emotion. ''And he would not fight. And then Henry would strike him,'' she whispered, crying again, ''but I don't remember how he did it.''

''Did he kick him then?''

''At that time he was on his way to the ground,'' Meidel answered, regaining her voice.

''Did he kick him when he was on the ground?''

''Yes, he did.''

''Did he hit him on his head, before he went down to the ground?''

''I remember Ricky's hands being over his head and I remember Henry going for the head, and I remember it was frightening . . . but I don't remember exactly how he struck people.''

''Did Ricky cry?''

''Ricky never cried,'' Meidel said, her voice breaking. ''He just said, 'Daddy, stop.' ''

Judge Devich handed Meidel a tissue.

''Did Henry Kyle say anything at all before he hit Ricky?'' Sumner asked, when Meidel composed herself. ''I mean, could you describe these instances—were they of an explosive nature, or sudden, or how would that come about?''

''They came about when somebody had done something wrong,'' Meidel said, more firmly. ''And it hurt and disappointed him inside. Then Henry would think about it for a couple of days and then out of the clear blue skies this volatile explosion would come.''

Meidel said she talked to both Henry and Ricky after the incident under the porte cochere. ''Henry felt terrible after he did that to either one of us,'' she testified. ''And Ricky cared very much about his father. I think he wanted to compete with his father. Both boys definitely loved their father," she added, her voice breaking again. "And he loved them so much—but he didn't know how to raise a family."

Meidel told the jury the reason Henry beat Rick under the porte cochere was because he caught him lying—to protect *her*. "Over some simple thing," she said, shaking her head. "It was my fault. He was protecting me." Meidel said she didn't remember whether Henry hit her when he found out, but she immediately packed and went to a health club, and tried to take the boys with her. "I couldn't for some reason," she recalled, "so I called them every half hour to see if they were all right, because I knew it was my fault they were in that kind of trouble." She said she called their mother "to tell her to come and take care of their children," but she couldn't reach her. "I determined that night that they shouldn't live there," she said.

Meidel told the jury she had "never been that frightened of Henry," and she was "in disbelief" that he could have an outburst like that when he was so quiet and soft-spoken at other times. Before then, she said, "I always jumped back at him whenever I could."

After she packed and moved to the health club, Meidel testified, Kyle began threatening her. "He told me if I ever tried to prove common-law marriage, that he would treat me like he didn't know me with our peers," she said. "And he said if I tried to prove that he was violent to the police, that he knew all of them. So I knew it was fruitless to pursue it."

During the summer of 1979, the summer she saw Henry beat Ricky, there was a "level of anxiety" in the house. "The boys would ask, 'Is Dad in a good mood or bad?' all the time, and we would think up ways to keep him in a good mood. I didn't think Ricky was that afraid of Henry," Meidel said wistfully. "He used to say, 'When I get big enough and strong enough and I can run faster, my father will never be able to hit me again.'"

According to Meidel, Henry gave Scott and Ricky "some money," but it was not enough to take care of their needs. "They did not shop and buy and do like a normal family," she explained. "The children did not have an allowance that children in their stature should have. They didn't have enough money." Meidel said she told Henry about it, "and he said he'd handle it."

During the summer of 1980, she said, both boys were at

Preston Road again, and the three of them were dressing up one day for a "happy occasion" with Henry. "Henry did do neat things with us."

Meidel said she and Henry had had two glasses of wine, and they were in Scott's room talking. "I said something to Henry in a fun way," she remembered, "something that hurt or insulted him about his mother, that made him very angry." She said he made a comment about her appearance, and she said, kiddingly, "I can't help it that your mother ran away with the choir director." Kyle became enraged, she said, "and I ended up in the bathroom with the telephone trying to call my son. There was no warning at all," she remembered. "We were having a wonderful time."

Afterward, she said, "there was blood all over everything. All over my hair and face, all over the towels the next day." Meidel was reluctant to talk about the specifics of what Kyle did to her, other than to say, "It was a terrible incident." Rick and Scott heard "the most of it," she testified, adding that "Henry sent the boys off" before he finished his attack. "I was disappointed they didn't go get help for me," she said.

The next morning, Meidel said with embarrassment, "I wouldn't come downstairs. Rick and Scott came up to comfort me. And that did it." Meidel said she never lived at Preston Road again. "I still finished the house," she said with determination. "Later. But after that, our relationship was platonic."

Meidel said she went to see a psychiatrist and a minister while she was still living with Henry to try to get help for him and herself. She told Sumner she also flew to Tennessee "to research Henry's background" in February or March 1980, a few months after the incident with Rick under the porte cochere. "I wanted to see how he was raised and try to find out what made him have this dual personality, and why he was like this. Because I cared." Meidel said Kyle wanted to find out, too. "He wanted to know what his problem was. While I was in Tennessee," she said, "I found out about his father."

Even after she left Henry in the summer of 1980, Meidel testified, she continued to communicate with him "always. Henry was my force," Meidel said poignantly. "He taught me business. Whenever I had a problem, I called him, and he always had an answer for me within twenty-four hours . . . and he was usually right. I depended on him."

Meidel said her design firm already had a contract with Henry to do the interior work at Stone Canyon, and she had visited the mansion several times to look it over. She recommended that Kyle live in a trailer on the property until the work was completed. "I couldn't believe he'd let the children stay in it. The house was really old and smelly and in terrible shape. I thought it was unhealthy to live in the house, and dangerous, and I told him so. The doors didn't even lock—you could have pushed the doors open with your foot."

Meidel told Steve Sumner Henry "always" kept guns around the house—beside his bed and in the gun case she had built for him, and that he kept a "sawed-off shotgun" under the driver's seat in his car. While she was living with him at Preston Road, she said, he got up "many times" at night with his gun to look around the house or outside when he heard noises. Once, unclothed, he got out of bed early in the morning to look for a prowler, and "almost shot" the maid, who was coming in a few minutes ahead of schedule.

Lew Watnick's cross-examination of Ann Meidel was relatively short, and brought out little that was new. He emphasized the fact that Meidel knew of only two instances when Kyle struck Rick from 1979 to 1980, and intimated that Meidel told Detective Rockwood during a police interview that they were "punishment." Meidel denied having said that, and repeated, "When we provoked Henry, Henry became angry and violent."

21

AFTER ANN MEIDEL'S AND MADONNA Rosenfield's dramatic testimony for the defense, Judge Devich's courtroom had a completely different atmosphere. Except for Lew Watnick, who was noticeably nervous and edgy, everyone from the court reporter to the bailiff to the hard-bitten journalists were more relaxed and good-humored. Even the skeptics among the veteran trial-watchers were viewing Ricky and his lawyers in a different light.

The morning session on Thursday, February 7, began with an appearance by Guy Bartoli, an architect friend of Henry Kyle's for twenty-three years. Bartoli was a short, distinguished-looking Italian with good manners and a soft-spoken way of answering questions.

Over the years, Bartoli testified, he observed Kyle's temper "many times. Henry was a very rude person and had a very violent temper. He could change from very pleasant to very violent almost instantaneously." Once, Bartoli recalled, Kyle "hit and felled to the floor a subcontractor who was working on a pool, and then just calmly walked off. I learned later that he was unhappy with him. But it just came out of the blue."

Bartoli said he met Rick and Scott for the first time the summer they were staying at Stone Canyon. His impression was that "Henry liked Scott, he didn't like Rick. He said demeaning things about him in front of me and other people. Many times . . . 'Here comes my bastard son,' and so forth. Rick was never disrespectful."

According to Bartoli, the summer he was working on the house with Kyle, Henry mentioned beating Ricky three times. The first was in early July 1983, at Bartoli's office. "He said he'd just beat up Ricky because he was lying and stealing," Bartoli testified. "I was very upset to hear it." A week later, the architect said, he was at Stone Canyon to review the progress on the house, and Henry said to him, "I had to beat up Ricky again because he stole from me." That night, Bartoli said, he and Kyle went out to dinner, and Bartoli suggested he "do something between him and his son." The third incident Kyle reported to Bartoli was in "late July. He said again that he had to beat Rick up—the same reason."

On cross-examination, Lew Watnick was almost hostilely aggressive. He made the point that Bartoli had never seen Rick with any "bruises, blood, contusions, or black eyes," and that Kyle beat him "because he had been lying, stealing, and disobeying him."

After the lunch break, Steve Sumner questioned Tresa Jereczek, a Polish domestic who worked in the house across the street from Granada. Jereczek told the jury that on the evening of July 21, she slept with her windows open in the servants' quarters, which faced Stone Canyon Drive. Sometime during the night, she was awakened by a "man and a woman's voices," and she got up and went to the window. "Shortly" after, she heard a "big shot" followed by a "little time," then "two small shots . . . quiet . . . and more shots." Then she heard "footsteps . . . it sounded like running," on asphalt. Then she heard sirens.

Following Jereczek to the stand was another neighbor of Kyle's, Derek Jones, who lived to the east on Sunset Boulevard. Jones's bedroom was on the west side of his house and faced the fence between his property and Granada.

Jones told Gibson he woke up on the twenty-second at about 2:30 A.M. in front of his television and then went to bed. He "couldn't get to sleep" and "kept looking at the time." Around 3:30 he "heard some heels in his driveway and a car door close." The windows in his bedroom were "at least cracked" at the time. The footsteps "sounded like a woman's."

Close to 4:00 A.M. he heard "crackling sounds" in the ivy. He also heard voices "between 3:30 and 4:00" that "might have been male." Jones said that in the morning there were tire marks in his driveway that had not been there before.

The testimony of these two neighbors, at the very least, corroborated Ricky's contention that he had heard suspicious noises in the area shortly before the shooting occurred.

The defense also brought in a former waiter friend of Doug Halley's who confirmed that Halley had proposed to "borrow a million dollars" from Rick to open up a restaurant. The waiter also said that Halley had told him a month before Grogan had received the "anonymous" tip that he "might have to testify" at a "big murder trial in California."

Tuesday morning Mike Gibson questioned a young married couple named Lon and Peggy Wallace, who had met Rick while attending North Texas State in Denton during the summer of 1982. Lon, a polite, serious twenty-four-year-old, was tall and thin, with dark hair worn sixties Beatle style. He worked as a software engineer in Plano, Texas.

Rick was living in a dorm that summer, Lon said, and he and Peggy saw him frequently after they were introduced. According to both Lon and Peggy, an outgoing woman with frosted brown hair, Rick seldom if ever mentioned his father, and neither of them had any idea he came from a wealthy background.

When the dorm closed for two weeks at the end of the summer session, Lon said, Rick had to move in with them before his apartment was ready. "He kinda lived out of his truck," Wallace testified, "an old red Ford pickup. So we didn't move him in, really." Once classes started in the fall, Peggy Wallace testified, she and Lon helped Rick move into a "run-down, small, ugly apartment" near the campus. "There was not a lot to move," Lon told the jury. Rick's bed was a mattress "from somewhere," and he used an old VW car seat propped up on bricks as a couch. Eventually, Lon said, Rick got a "worn but sturdy" table and four barstools from his father. According to Peggy, Rick dressed in "faded blue jeans and worn Oxford shirts" while he was at North Texas State, and kept his clothes in a loose dresser drawer in the back of his truck.

The fall of 1982, Lon Wallace said, he saw Rick "often." He and Peggy both said Rick seldom had money, and would sometimes ask Lon for cash. "He ran out of gas many times," Lon testified. "He claimed the gas gauge didn't work . . . whatever." For a time, Lon said, Rick worked for him carrying small refrigerators up to dorm rooms, or stacking them in trucks, for $3.50 an hour.

At some point in the fall, Lon testified, Rick's red pickup

was "not around"; he didn't know why. For a while afterward, Rick didn't have any transportation and had to get rides from people. "Eventually," Lon said, "he got an old black Trans Am—I don't know where."

Sometime that semester, Lon and Peggy remembered, Rick met Kelly Moore at Taco Night. "That was a big sort of thing for us," Peggy said, in her country accent, while jurors laughed in amusement. "It was three twenty-five a person." She and Lon bought Rick's ticket. "Many a time we paid for him just so we could have all our friends together. We didn't have any money to do anything," she added. Most of the time they "just visited" at each other's apartments.

In the spring of 1983, Lon said, Rick's financial condition "seemed to drop." An " '81 or so" Mazda RX7 he got from his father earlier in the spring was "gone," Lon said, and he was either evicted or "had to move" from his apartment because he had no rent money. Later, Lon testified, he learned that Rick had moved to California.

On Valentine's Day, the defense called Kelly Kyle. On the stand and off, Ricky's wife seemed a typical, sweet, small-town college girl.

She told the jurors it was her idea that Rick write his father and move out to California that summer, because she wanted him and Kyle to "rebuild" their relationship. She denied that she and Ricky ever had the "Kyle Brothers, Incorporated" conversation Bobby Green testified to overhearing. She told Steve Sumner that the first time she and Ricky were alone after the shootings, he cried and confessed that he shot his father, but said that Kyle shot first. She also said that her half brother Doug Halley was always asking questions about what happened, and once told her he "had a plan" where "she and the baby wouldn't suffer." After the shootings, Kelly testified, Jackie kept reassuring Rick that she and Henry Miller would "work it all out" for them.

On cross, John Moulin, who was obviously hostile to Kelly, emphasized that she had once broken off her engagement to Rick because she disapproved of his cocaine use. In general, Moulin tried to suggest that she was lying.

22

ON TUESDAY, FEBRUARY 19, THE
courtroom benches were filled to overflowing with journalists of
all description. Flashbulbs were popping, cords and wires from
TV cameras clogged the aisles.

The reason for the excitement was that the defense had decided to put Ricky Kyle on the stand. Mike Gibson and Steve
Sumner had been tossing the idea around in strategy sessions
for some weeks. In the end, they determined that Rick was the
only one who could address whatever questions remained in the
jurors' minds about the shooting—even though such testimony
was risky, since it exposed him to cross-examination. "We had
to put him on," Sumner said flatly. "Otherwise the jury would
have wondered."

Seeing Ricky take the stand, Watnick seemed to perk up,
and Grogan joshed with a reporter, "I don't know why the media wasn't here for *my* testimony."

When he was finally sworn in at approximately 10:45, Ricky
was solemn and extremely subdued. The tension in the room was
excruciating.

Mike Gibson began by asking Rick about his childhood. Rick
answered with an almost exaggerated politeness, saying "yes,
sir" and "no, sir" frequently. Rick told the jury his parents
were divorced when he was two, and that he lived in Reynolds,
Georgia, with his mother and brother, Scott, until he was fourteen.

He "first remembered meeting Henry Kyle" when he was
five or six. His father was in Georgia "on a trip." Afterward

Kyle "started taking" him and Scott for a couple of weeks in the summers. The first such trip was to Los Angeles when he was "five or six."

When he and Scott arrived, Rick said, they stayed at La Buena Vida (a singles complex Kyle owned with Don Tanner). During the trip, "Dad would just get angry at me and Scott for things like getting candy or soft drinks or playing around." Once his father hit him in the face and he fell off an iron staircase.

Rick said, "I became afraid of my father at that time." Before then "I had only been spanked."

After that summer, Rick said, he didn't see his father that much: "maybe one Thanksgiving," never at Christmas or on any other occasion. Kyle would call "once every month or two months," and he and Scott continued to visit him in the summers in Dallas.

Asked to recall any "outstanding acts of violence" by his father, Rick told about a time when he and Scott "ran downstairs with a basketball at Preston." Security called Kyle, he related, "and he took us outside beside the road and started hitting us." Rick said he started crying after his father hit him, "so he hit me for crying."

"Did he say anything to you?" Gibson said gently.

" 'You're a goddamn sissy. You're no fuckin' kid of mine. You'd better wipe that frown off your face or I'll give you a reason to frown.' "

"Did you eventually just stop crying because you knew it would just make it worse?"

"I stopped crying at fourteen," Rick said impassively.

When Gibson asked him how his father referred to him in front of other people, Rick said, "He would introduce me and Scott in derogatory ways—'little girls,' or 'little bastards.' "

"Were you afraid of him?" Gibson said emphatically.

Rick paused for a second. "I was always very nervous around my father," he said without emotion. "He was an explosive type of individual. I kept my distance as much as possible."

Rick told Gibson he "asked to go back" during the school year.

"Why?" asked his lawyer.

"After a year," said Rick, "the things that he did to us didn't seem as important."

"Did you love your father?" Gibson inquired, after a pause.

"Very much so," answered Rick.

Rick told the jury it was his decision to move to Dallas when he completed the ninth grade at Beechwood School in Reynolds, and that he called his father to ask his permission. "He was sort of apprehensive about it. But he said okay."

Rick arrived in Dallas on Father's Day when he was fourteen years old. Kyle let him make the decision about where to go to school. "He kept mentioning Marine Military Academy. He said he had friends who were trustees there." In late July, Rick said, he "decided on it," and his father was "very pleased." He chose the Marine Military Academy "because it would please my father, and I had to go to a school where I wasn't living at home—I felt it was a necessity."

"Why was that?"

"It was hard to study at home when my dad would hit me for reading a book," Rick said dully.

"Did he do that all the time?"

"On and off," said Rick. "He was different every day."

Rick said he met Ann Meidel during spring break in the tenth or eleventh grade, or "maybe the summer of 1979. She was a real fun lady," he said. "She'd been around. And she liked kids."

Gibson asked him to relate the episode under the porte cochere, and Rick said it began when Ann asked him to "pick up some nails." His father had "ordered him not to go anywhere in the car." When he got back, Kyle confronted him about leaving the house. "I told him I'd been to Seven-Eleven to get some orange juice," Rick said.

"Why didn't you tell the truth?"

"Because he'd hit Ann," Rick said flatly.

"So Henry Kyle hit you?"

"Yes."

"How?"

"He hit me in the face with his fist," Rick said in a monotone. "It seemed like forever."

"What did you do?"

"I screamed and put my arms over my head."

"Then what happened?"

"Then he'd knock me down. Then he'd kick me on the ground. I was afraid to get up," he continued, "so Dad grabbed me by

243

the leg and pulled me across the pavement. It skinned my arm."

"What happened next?"

"He pulled me in the house," Rick said. "Then Ann told him the truth and he choked Ann and twisted my arm."

"Did he say anything to Ann?"

"He told her not to make his kid have to lie for her."

"What was your reaction after this happened?"

"I was real upset about it, because I was afraid of what he was doing to Ann."

Afterward, Rick told the jury, Kyle told him to go upstairs and he heard Ann "screaming."

That same summer, Rick testified, he called his mother to tell her what had been happening, and she called Kyle. When he found out, "he grabbed me by the hair and said, 'Now tell me what you said behind my back.' Then he got back on the phone and said to my mother, 'Are you satisfied now, you slut?' " After that, Rick told the jury, he stopping telling his mother. "It didn't help," he explained. "Just made things worse."

Rick told Gibson he "did average" in school. "It was a lot easier to go to MMA than live with Dad." During spring break when he was in the eleventh grade at the Academy in March 1979, he said, he invited two of his classmates to stay at Preston Road in Dallas. While they were there, the three of them fell asleep in front of the TV, and Rick awoke "being hit in the face" by his father. "When I gathered my wits I asked him why. And he said, 'You're just a worthless punk. You're letting your friends sweat on my sofa.' " Then Kyle "just walked away and said he'd take care of me in the morning," Rick related.

"Was that the last time you invited friends to your father's house?"

"Yes. It humiliated me. It was very hard, because my friends would want to talk about it, and they'd tell people at school the kind of life I was leading and I didn't like that."

Concerning the beating that caused Ann Meidel to finally move out, Rick told Gibson it occurred while they were all dressing to go out to dinner. While he and Scott were in the kitchen, they heard Ann screaming, "Not my face! Not my face!"

"We were real excited and scared. We wanted to go up and help her, but we knew we couldn't." Rick said his father called down for him, "threw me a hundred-dollar bill and said, 'Go feed yourselves.' " When he and Scott came back to the house, he said, they heard Ann crying "the rest of the night. I didn't sleep real well that night," Rick testified.

The next morning Ann was "lying in bed" when he went upstairs to see her. "All of her hair was red with blood," he recounted. "There was blood on the walls, in the bed, on towels. I thought her arm was broken—it was in a very unusual position. I told her how sorry I was," Rick said softly, looking at the floor. "That I was so very sorry."

That incident, Rick testified, "had one of the strongest impacts in my life I'd ever seen . . . what he was capable of doing really scared me."

After lunch, Gibson asked his client about the period right after he graduated from MMA in May 1980, when he was making a decision about college.

"What was Henry Kyle's reaction," Gibson queried, "when you informed him of your decision to go to the University of Texas?"

"He was angry because I didn't get into Harvard or Yale or Annapolis," Rick replied.

"Did you apply to those schools?"

"No."

"Why not?"

"Because I didn't have the grades."

Before fall classes started, his father gave him enough rent money for one month, he told the jury, along with a $100 check for books and a $250 check for his tuition. "After a month," Rick said, "he told me it was too expensive so I broke my lease and moved into the Spanish district of Austin. It was very hard to get an apartment," he testified. "I walked three miles to the bus to get to school."

Rick said his father paid one month's rent for his new apartment—October. "Then he called me saying he was extremely fed up with Scott, and I was just like Scott so he was going to cut me off and quit wasting his money."

After the phone call, Kyle stopped sending him money and took his car away. He said he applied for jobs within walking distance, but it "just became impossible. I was very upset. It was the first time I was thrown out of the nest and I wasn't prepared for it at all."

"And do you know what your grades were at UT that semester?" Gibson queried.

"I assume I got all Fs," Rick said, "because I couldn't finish."

"Did you experiment with any drugs while you were at UT?" asked Gibson.

"I was given a line of cocaine by a girl once," said Rick. "That was it."

"Did you ever use marijuana?"

"No," answered Rick. "I had never even heard of cocaine until this girl gave it to me. We led a pretty sheltered life at MMA."

"Did you do any drinking while you were at the University of Texas?"

"Most of the drinking I did was at dorm parties," said Rick, "because I was seventeen."

Rick told the jury he made a "truce" with his father when he came back to Dallas at the end of 1980, and he enrolled at Brookhaven in January 1981—"a good community college" in Dallas.

Rick told the jury he had four impacted wisdom teeth removed that winter and was instructed "not to knock the sockets out and take it easy." The day they were removed, he said, he was in the kitchen on Preston Road and his father hit him. "I don't know what it was for. He hit me in the jaw and said, 'I'm gonna knock all your goddamn teeth out so you won't have to worry about it.'" Afterward, Rick testified, "My ribs were bruised and my face was swollen. Then Dad left for work."

"Why didn't you go to the hospital?"

"Dad said he didn't believe in doctors or hospitals. It never came to my mind to go, because of what the doctors might ask."

"Were you afraid to go to the police?" Gibson persisted.

"Yes."

"Why?"

"Dad told me a few times if I ever went to the police, he'd kill me."

The morning after his father hit him in the jaw, Rick said, Kyle took him to school "and said he'd beat the hell out of me that night. I was embarrassed to go to class because of the bruises."

"What did you do?" asked Gibson.

"I went to a field and cried a little bit, and read a book. I do that quite often," he added. "I go off by myself."

"How did you do in school that semester?"

"Very badly. Dad would make me do things for him at work sometimes. It was the worst period in my life as far as beatings—it was the longest time I was under the same roof with Dad."

"Why did you join the Marines?" Gibson asked.

"It was a way for me to please my father," Rick replied. "My father bragged heavily of his days in the Marines. I wanted my father to love me and accept me for who I was. I wanted to get in his good graces."

"What was his reaction when you told him you had joined the Marine Corps?" Gibson inquired.

"He didn't say a thing," Rick testified. "He got up from the table and went upstairs."

The next morning, Rick said, the recruiter picked him up and took him to the airport. Before the plane left, "Dad appeared."

"What did Henry Kyle say or do when he showed up at the airport?" queried Gibson.

"He was nice," responded Ricky, in a subdued voice. "He said, 'Make me proud of you. Do your best.'"

Rick told jurors he returned to Preston Road on Halloween after completing his Marine reserve training in New Jersey, and that his plans were "to wait in Dallas until the school semester was over, then start in the spring session." At Christmas, he and Scott drove to Atlanta to spend the holidays with their mother.

"I decided on the drive to Atlanta to go to Georgia State University," Rick told Gibson. "I had an idea to ask Dad for money for books and tuition."

After he arrived in Atlanta, Rick testified, there were "many phone calls" with Kyle about his attending Georgia State. "He was mad at first," Rick recalled. "Then he said he would send a check to the school." Rick said he applied for admission, but Kyle never sent the money. "I called him the day of the deadline and he cussed me out and told me to get home and he'd beat the hell out of me. I hung up, and he called me back and said, 'Anybody who hangs up on me I'll kill.' I hung up again," Rick said evenly. "Dad called back and we had the same conversation. I hung up. Then he called back and my mother took the call.

"I reached a point where I had to do something," Rick told the jurors. "Go to school or get out. Not live with my mother— I was too old to do that." Rick said he and Charlotte "had problems" when he was staying there, and that his money "dwindled away" by May.

"What did you do then?" Gibson said sternly.

"I took a ring of my mother's and I took it to a place where they took it on consignment and sold it," Rick answered, looking at his attorney, then over at the jurors.

"Then what happened?" asked Gibson.

"My mother found out and told Scott, and Scott called Dad."

"Why did you take your mother's ring?"

"I needed the money to go out and get an apartment," Rick replied. "And it was a stupid way to do it, but I did it."

Rick said he was at a friend's house one day when he got a call from Scott saying that their mother needed help with her car. When he got to the house, Rick testified, Kyle was there. "He said, 'You're goin' back to Dallas. You got two choices: get money for a job or go to school broke,'" Rick related. "I said I'd rather go to school broke."

He and his father "drove all night" back to Dallas, Rick told the jurors, and he called North Texas State and started school "very quickly," in the summer of 1982. Kyle took his car away and gave him a truck. He was given no spending money, and his father wrote out checks for his meal ticket and dorm.

Before continuing with his chronology of the 1982–1983 school year, Gibson backtracked to ask Rick when he first met his half sister Jackie Phillips.

"I met Jackie during spring break when I was in the eleventh grade," Rick answered. "When I met Ann [Meidel]."

"Do you remember how she was introduced to you?" asked Gibson.

"Dad brought me into the study and said, 'I never told you about this girl, but here's your sister,'" Rick said flatly.

Plainly fascinated, a few jurors looked up from the notes they were taking.

"What did *you* say?"

"I said hello," Rick responded. "It was an awkward situation because we were kin, yet we didn't know each other."

Rick said he next saw Jackie in August 1982, about three years later, when he noticed a girl by the pool at Preston Road, and Bobby Green told him, "It's your sister."

"What was your reaction?"

"I was very interested," Rick said simply.

"What did you do?"

"We talked," Rick replied. "Getting-to-know-each-other talk. She said she had done some modeling in San Francisco, and she was curious why my hair was so short."

Jackie invited him to her garage apartment that evening, and when he got there, he said, "she handed me a glass pipe and said, 'Smoke this'" [free-base cocaine].

"What was your impression of Jackie Phillips at the time you met her?"

Rick grew thoughtful. "She was really unique," he said slowly, "and to me, she was an exciting person, because she'd done and seen a lot of things. And I was intrigued by her . . . and the drugs, and the whole atmosphere."

During the fall of 1982, Rick told the jurors, Jackie Phillips "would call me up and ask if I wanted to come over and get high with her. Sometimes I did." While he was at her apartment, he said, "she'd have coke from a boyfriend." Once when she called him, "Scott was there." Rick said Jackie provided the cocaine. "I liked it," he stated, "and I liked being around Jackie. It was an exciting sort of atmosphere to be around her. She was a little bit crazy, but it was fun."

Around Christmas, 1982, Rick testified, he got a call from Kyle. "He said, 'Bring me my money, bring me my truck, and my furniture.' Then he hung up." Rick said he loaded his bed frame, "a big table, and two chairs," parked the truck in his father's driveway, left him his money in an envelope, and was driven to Denton by a friend. Afterward, he said, he "continued on" with the spring semester.

"What was your attitude at school that spring after that happened?"

"I wanted to do good, to make him proud of me, but I messed up. I made some mistakes."

Eventually, he "just withdrew because I was very worried about bills, and about Kelly continuing her classes, because we were so close. I became disinterested in school, basically," he testified. "I looked for some jobs, but didn't put a lot of effort into it."

Rick said he "saw Jackie Phillips" that semester, and she

invited him to come down to Dallas after Christmas to meet her new boyfriend, Henry Miller. When he got to her condominium, Rick testified, she and Henry were "at the table with scales, weighing out bags of cocaine." Rick told the jury the three of them free-based cocaine together during the spring semester, "always at Jackie's," with "Henry's coke."

"How did that affect your schooling?"

"It hurt it, because I would stay there and not make it to Monday-morning class, because I would be too drained from the weekend."

Rick said he began to get calls from Jackie asking him to come in midweek, and that his "sleeping and eating were irregular."

In April or May, Rick had a "change in attitude. I wanted to do something to try and get my relationship back with my dad," he said quietly, "so I sat down and wrote a very long letter. I told him how much I cared about him and wanted to be part of the family." Rick said he put the letter in Kyle's mailbox at Preston Road, and after four or five hours, "I thought it over and decided he wouldn't understand . . . so I got the letter back."

Rick told the jury he decided to "tell Dad I was accepted at Stanford."

"Why did you decide to tell him that?"

"It was a way for him to accept me," responded Rick. "But it was a bad way."

"That was a lie, right?" prodded Gibson.

"Yes, sir," Rick said softly.

Kelly, he testified, was "totally against" the idea. "I made up totally new grades and classes," Rick stated. "It was just an attempt to be able to get money to go to school in San Francisco—not Stanford."

"Was it your hope in going out to California that you and your father would get your relationship back?" asked Gibson.

"Those were my hopes," Rick said with a trace of irony.

Wednesday, February 20—the day Rick was expected to tell the jury his account of how he killed his father—was wet, cold, and gray. The weather seemed to echo the mood in the courtroom. For his second day on the stand, Rick was dressed in a navy jacket, white shirt, gray trousers, and striped tie. His face was puffy and pallid, with dark circles under his eyes, as if he had been crying.

Bob Grogan made a point of arriving early Wednesday so he wouldn't miss a word of Rick's testimony. When court began, he was sitting in his usual chair behind Lew Watnick and John Moulin.

Mike Gibson began by asking Rick Kyle if it was Henry Kyle's practice to wake him up when he heard a disturbance in the house.

Ricky said his dad had awakened him "a few times" at 9909 Preston Road because he thought he heard something, and that Kyle "always" had a gun. "It was usually a noise Dad heard. It was an old house, and it made noises." During their burglar checks, his father was "usually nude. Once he had a bathrobe," Rick noted. The two of them would "walk the house, and once Dad was satisfied, go to sleep." Rick said it was a "rule" for every room to have a weapon.

Once he came home from a friend's house around midnight and saw through the kitchen window his father "loading his .357, and he had another weapon. I became concerned. I wanted to let him know it was me." A little while later, "Dad had me drive him to Highland Park [an affluent suburb of Dallas] and circle a block and slow down in front of one house. Then we stopped and Dad walked to the door with the gun in his hand, opened the screen and tried the knob. He couldn't open it. Then he looked inside the window." Before they left, "Dad said, 'I want you to watch me kill some drug dealers. They're not in now, but I'm gonna kill that motherfucker someday.' "

"What did you think about that experience?" queried Gibson, while the jurors looked on intently.

"I didn't really know what to think about it, to tell you the truth," Rick responded. "I thought it was very strange . . . it was sort of a relief that nothing happened."

After he moved to Stone Canyon, Rick testified, his relationship with Kyle "deteriorated" and his father became "more abusive."

Before his trip to Dallas, Kyle came home from work to pack and caught Rick reading a book. "I jumped up, and Dad hit me on the side of the head. He sort of broadsided me, and knocked me dizzy. He started rolling up his sleeves and took off his jacket and he said, 'I'm gonna kick the shit out of you like a man.' I said, 'Daddy, I'm not gonna fight you. I'd rather leave.' And he said, 'You'll do what I tell you to.' I began to wash dishes. While I was washing the dishes, Dad said, 'I'm not gonna even come close to you, because I'm afraid if I do, I'll kill you.'"

When Vicki returned from Taiwan on Wednesday of the following week, Rick said, she "tried to decide all afternoon what to do with Ellen." She eventually asked Rick to drive Ellen to San Diego that night, and when his father got in from Dallas that night, he and Vicki called him. "I was to return to L.A. [the next day], and Ellen's father was to pick up Ellen the next morning. Dad said I was to maybe take a train, and to stick around the condo and wait for instructions."

That Thursday morning, Rick said, his father called him again to say that Vicki was driving Scott's car to San Diego that day "and I was to drive Scott's car back [to Stone Canyon] that night and leave the Cadillac for Vicki."

When Vicki arrived in San Diego that afternoon, Rick said, she told him to wait for the traffic to die down before going back, and they had a "pleasant" dinner.

That night, the night of the shooting, Rick said, he arrived home at Granada between eleven and eleven-thirty. Before he got to the house, he stopped at a grocery store for some orange juice for breakfast. "I didn't know if there was any orange juice there," he said. When he got home, Rick told the jurors, he put the juice in the icebox and went to his bedroom, where Scott and Bobby were watching TV.

"I asked Bobby if Dad was awake and he said he'd gone to bed at nine. Then I asked Scott about Daddy's mood that day—it was sort of a typical question we always asked. His moods changed so quickly, we kept track for each other." Rick said he had "a lot of concern" about his father when he got back, because he was afraid Bobby had told him that Kelly had been at the house, and because of the large phone bill. "If he ever saw a long-distance phone call we made, he hit us.

"Scott said he wasn't in a good mood, and I said, 'I guess we'll find out why tomorrow.'" Scott left the room first, followed by Bobby "two to three minutes later." Rick said he went to sleep around midnight, and the next thing he remembered was hearing "noises outside."

"What did you hear?" asked his lawyer.

"I remember I heard a sound like crunching leaves, like someone in the bushes."

"Where at?"

Rick paused and the courtroom was completely silent for a moment. "It was outside my window, or outside, rather," he said finally.

"What did you do?"

"I sat up in bed for a little bit, and I listened, and the noises continued," Rick said, the words coming out slowly.

"Then what did you do?"

Rick paused again. "I went to the window . . . of my bedroom, and looked out. And I couldn't see anything. And then I heard it again, so I put on a warm-up suit that I had . . ."

As Rick's voice trailed off, Gibson said, "Where was that warm-up? Why did you not put on the clothes you had on the night before?"

"I had just thrown them in the dirty clothes," Rick responded, "and the warm-up suit was at the foot of my bed."

"What were you going to do?"

"I was going to investigate, and then I was going to wake up my dad, to get him to go with me."

"Well, what did you do next?"

"I went and got a gun that was underneath my bed," Rick said with deliberation.

"Well, let's talk about that for a minute, Ricky," Gibson interjected. "Where had you received or gotten that gun?"

"From my brother," answered Rick. "From Scott."

"Tell the ladies and gentlemen of the jury when it was and under what circumstances you recall receiving that gun."

The jurors leaned forward in their seats.

"It was maybe a week after Scott arrived," Rick said evenly. "We were down in my bedroom, and it was—we were having a conversation about the problems with security, at the house."

"Had you had problems there?"

"Yes, sir."

"Did you have your car stolen?"

"Yes, sir."

"When did you have your car stolen?"

"The first night I was there."

"Did you ever get it back?"

Rick paused. "I *saw* it again. And it was totaled. Someone wrapped it around a pole."

"Were there other instances where there were people around the yard?"

"Yes, sir."

Gibson hesitated a second, then asked, "What *was* the conversation you and Scott had about the gun?"

"I told him that I needed some kind of protection. 'I wish I had something downstairs.'"

"And had you before, at 9909, always had something for protection?"

"Usually I did. And at 9909, we had fairly good security. I mean, we had a locking gate, and the whole bit—and locking doors."

"Okay. Now were you the only one sleeping downstairs?"

"Yes, sir, I was."

"So what happened after the conversation with Scott?"

"Scott left the room, and he came back, and he had a gun and a holster, and handed it to me and said, 'You can use this if you want.'"

"Did you take it?"

"Yes, sir, I did."

"What did you do with it?"

"I took it out of its holster," Rick said slowly, "and I looked at it, and I saw that it had bullets inside it, and I took the holster and just threw it in the garment bag, and I put the gun underneath my bed."

The silence in the courtroom deepened as Rick finally got to what everyone was waiting to hear.

"I went up to my dad's bedroom . . ."

"Upstairs?" asked Gibson.

"Yes, sir."

"Was the door open?"

"Yes, sir, it was halfway open."

"Was your dad asleep?"

"Yes, sir."

"Why don't you tell the jury what you did."

"I went over to him and shook the bed, and he woke up real quickly."

"What'd you say?"

"I said, 'Dad, I think I hear someone outside.'"

"What'd your father do?"

"He grabbed his .357 Magnum . . ."

"Where was his .357 Magnum?"

"Ah . . . I understood it to be on the night table by his

254

bed," Rick responded, "but he just reached over and grabbed it, and I wasn't paying any attention, to tell you the truth."

"What did y'all do next?"

"He got up out of bed and said, 'Come on,' and we went downstairs to the Stone Canyon doors."

"Did he have his clothes on at that time?"

"No, sir, he didn't."

"Where did you go?"

"I was instructed by him at that time to turn on the lights and open the door."

"And then did you go out into the courtyard?"

"Yes, sir."

"What happened?"

"He threw the door open and ran out. I went out after him. We ran to the beginning of the driveway, to the end of the courtyard."

"And then what?"

Rick paused. "Then we looked around, and I didn't see anything unusual. I don't think he did, either."

"Did he say anything to you? Or talk or communicate to you at all?"

"No, sir."

"What was the next thing that happened?"

"He turned to go back inside the house."

"Did you follow him?"

"Yes, sir."

"What happened after that?"

"Mmmm . . ." Rick pondered. "We went through the doors, to the dining room."

"Did you shut the doors when you came back in?" Gibson asked, pointing to the double doors still propped against one of the walls in the courtroom.

"I don't remember shutting them."

"And where did you go—what happened next?"

"We walked into the dining room, and I noticed that one of the French doors was open partway."

"It was . . ." commented Gibson. "How light was it in that room?"

"It was pretty dark . . . it was dark."

"What did you see—what could you see, as best you recall?"

"I could see objects silhouetted," Rick said softly. "I could

255

see my dad's silhouette, and the table in the room against the French glass doors, because there was a soft light from the street, on Sunset.''

"Could you describe for the jury what happened next?"

"He walked to the doors, and I came behind him," Rick said slowly, then stopped.

"And what happened?"

"And then he turned, and he came up with his arm and shot," Rick testified, his voice breaking.

"Where did the shot go? Do you know?"

"No, sir," Rick responded, choking back tears.

"In your direction?" Gibson said gently.

"Yes, sir," Rick said, with a sob.

"What do you recall doing next?"

"I just jumped . . . and I shot."

"And then what?"

"And then I . . . I tried to get away from him," Rick said, in a flat voice.

"What do you mean, you tried to get away from him?"

"I started swingin' my arms," Rick said, crying. "I was pushin', I was just tryin' to get away . . . I—the gun went off again . . ."

"What gun?"

"The gun I had."

"Then what?"

"I ran. I ran around to the side of the garage."

"What did you do then?"

There was a long pause, then Rick said, "I looked around."

"What were you looking at? What were you looking for?"

"I was lookin' for Dad to come out the doors . . ."

"Why were you looking for your dad to come out of the doors?"

"I didn't know what I had done," Rick responded, his voice breaking again. "I didn't know what happened. And . . . I stood there for a second."

"How did you feel? What were you thinking?"

"I don't remember. I just remember I was scared. And I remember I saw blood coming out of my arm . . . my sweat suit."

"Then what did you do?"

"I walked to the side of the house, and I looked down and I saw the gun, and I threw it."

"Why?"

"I don't know," Rick said softly, gazing off into space.

"What did you do then?"

"I went back into the house," Rick whispered, crying again.

"How did you get back into the house?"

"Through the kitchen door."

"What did you do when you got inside the house?"

"I ducked down below the cabinets in the kitchen."

"Do you recall what you were thinking at the time?"

"I don't remember. I was just scared."

"What happened next?"

"I saw Rusty walk by the door."

"What did you do when you saw Rusty?"

"I went to him."

"What did you say to him?"

"I said the first thing that came to mind: I said that I'd been shot, and I think there's somebody in the house."

"Why didn't you tell him what had happened?"

"I didn't know what else to do," Rick said quietly. "I was scared."

"Where did you go next?"

"Rusty said, 'Get upstairs,' and we did. We went up to his room."

"And who was upstairs? Did you see your brother, Scott?"

"Yes, sir, I did."

"Did you see anybody else?"

"Yes, sir. Bob Green."

"Do you remember what you did up there in that room?"

"I remember that I was asked questions—people were askin' me questions, but I don't remember much of what I said."

"What people were asking you questions?"

"Bob . . . Rusty . . . Scott. I remember that I told them that it was an intruder, and I don't remember much else."

"Why would you tell them that it was an intruder? Do you know?"

"Yes, sir," Rick said softly.

"Why?"

"Because I was scared."

"Did you think you may have just shot your father?"

"Yes, sir."

"Did you think your father was trying to shoot you?"

"Yes, sir."

257

"Did you understand what had gone on?"

"Not really, to tell you the truth," Rick said bemusedly.

With reference to his conversation with Jackie and Henry Miller at Miller's condo after the funeral, Rick testified that he made gin and tonics for the three of them when they arrived, and that the cocaine "affected him pretty hard. I was nauseated and in a cold sweat," he told Gibson. Rick said he asked Jackie to take the pipe when they started free-basing, "and she told me to sit back and relax. I told them I needed to tell them what really happened that night," he testified.

"What did you say to them?"

"I told them that Daddy shot at me and I shot back."

"What was their reaction?"

After a long silence, Rick answered, "They sat there for a second. I was crying, Jackie started crying. She came over and hugged me, Henry came over, and we sort of all held onto each other for a second, and I remember them saying it was gonna be all right. It wasn't my fault. It was all right. They understood."

"What was the next part of the conversation?"

"After we calmed down a little bit, I told them that I had a problem. That I'd panicked and I'd thrown the gun away, and I didn't know where I'd thrown it, but I knew close to where I had, and I told them that if I could get the gun back I thought I might not be in such bad trouble."

"What did they say?"

"I think Henry was the one who said, 'What can we do? How can we help?' And I told him that I had been over by the side of the house, and that's all that I remember, basically. Where I had been, over by the barbecue pit, by the side of the house— and then that's about all I remember about where I was. And I threw the gun into the neighbor's yard . . . and Henry was confused about that, and asked me to make a drawing."

"Did you?"

"Yes, sir. He handed me a piece of his stationery and I made a drawing."

Rick told the jury the names were not on the diagram when he first drew it. "Henry asked me to label the house and Sunset," he testified, adding that he put in the star to show where he "thought the gun might have been. They said they'd go get the gun for me and everything was going to be okay."

Then, Rick testified, "Jackie talked about abuse she'd received when she was younger. It was an emotional situation. We were all pretty drained." They were at Henry's apartment for "a couple of hours," and they discussed the shootings once. According to Rick, Henry and Jackie took him back to Preston Towers around nine. Jackie made a phone call from the condo and told him she'd "scored more coke and would come back later. I said I was tired."

Over the course of the next few days, Rick "called Jackie to see if they were gonna do what they said, and I kept getting an answering machine." That Friday (July 29, the day Grogan and Rockwood questioned Phillips about the Rohm) Jackie telephoned him saying, "Get your ass over here." When he got to the condo, Jackie and Henry were smoking free base; then Henry left. Jackie was "real mad. She said, 'How in the world did you get Quint Barnes's gun?' And I said, 'Who's Quint Barnes?' "

In early August [1983], Rick testified, he and Kelly went to see Jackie at her Holly Hills condominium. While they were there he and Jackie had a conversation in the kitchen while Kelly was in the den. According to Rick, "[Jackie] said that she would take care of everything, that she would tell the police the truth, and for me not to worry. And I just said okay." As he and Kelly were leaving, he testified, "she kissed both of us and said, 'Don't you kids worry. I'll take care of everything for you.' "

After he was indicted in August, Rick said, he enrolled at North Texas for the fall semester of 1983. "I made one day of class," he testified.

"Why was that?" asked Mike Gibson.

"When I got to school, my picture was on the front page of the newspaper, which is read by everyone, and it made it very hard to go to class."

Gibson asked what he knew about Henry Kyle's will and trust fund. Rick testified: "I was told when he cut me off at UT that I was out of the will. And then he would make statements that 'I've already cut you out of the will' many, many times—and I really didn't care or pay attention to it."

"What did you think your status was?" Gibson asked.

"I didn't think that I was in the will," answered Rick.

Regarding Doug Halley, Rick testified, he got a phone call from Kelly in March of 1984 "asking me if I would mind if Doug came to stay with me for about a month until he got a job. Because he was her brother, I agreed." Rick said he "really didn't know" Halley that well, and once he arrived, Doug "went only one day to look for a job." While Halley was staying with him, Rick said, "I had almost everything involved in the case in the condo, including the grand-jury and preliminary-hearing transcripts, and financial statements from the estate." The majority of the papers were kept in an unlocked cabinet in the den, and others were on the coffee table "laying out sometimes. I saw Doug reading them a few times." Halley "asked him questions about what happened in California quite often. I would tell him I couldn't talk about it and had to deal with it."

Rick said Doug used cocaine with him—but never made a financial contribution toward its purchase. Halley also borrowed money from him. "A few days after he arrived," Rick said, "he mentioned starting a restaurant, and plans that he had, and said he needed a million dollars to get it goin'. And I said, 'Doug, I don't have a million dollars,' and he said, 'Oh, okay, right.'" Afterward, Rick testified, "he continued to mention the case, but finally gave up because I wouldn't talk about it." Halley "asked questions about country clubs and restaurants and stuff, and he would give his suggestions and I would blow them off." He "appeared familiar" with Kyle's country clubs, Rick testified, "and it had to be from reading the documents.

"I asked Doug to leave in May," Rick told the jury, "because I had had enough of Doug. He was a very, very dirty person. He didn't take showers. He threw trash behind the sofa, and ruined it." At the time, Rick recalled, Halley was "mad." At no time, Rick testified, did he ever tell Halley he killed his father, or that Scott planned it, or that he used surgical gloves. Rick said he hadn't seen Doug since he moved out, until he testified in December.

Before passing Rick to Lew Watnick for cross-examination, Gibson asked his client one last time if, when his father turned toward him in the dining room, he thought he was going to kill him.

"Yes, sir," answered Rick, saying he was "afraid for his life."

"Did you love your father?" Gibson asked.

Rick looked down, then faced his attorney and said, in a small, quavering voice: "I loved my father very much . . . and

. . . what happened is something that I'm gonna have to live with for the rest of my life.

"And I wish he were alive today . . ." he added, his voice trembling, "because he was a fine man in some ways, but I couldn't understand him."

"All right, ladies and gentlemen," Judge Devich interjected, breaking the tension in the room. "Let's take a short break, and Mr. Watnick can take up his cross-examination at three o'clock."

23

WHEN RICKY RESUMED THE STAND,
Lew Watnick turned to him and said, "Mr. Kyle, telling lies is
a way of life with you, isn't it?"

Rick didn't flinch. "No, sir," he said evenly.

Watnick glared at Rick. "You told Rusty Dunn and the others a prowler shot your father, and that was a lie, wasn't it?"
he continued, in a piercing, nasal tone.

The jury looked back at Rick. "Yes, sir," he responded.

"You told them Henry Kyle awakened *you,* and that was a
lie, too, wasn't it, Mr. Kyle?"

"Yes, sir."

"In fact," he went on, "everything you told Rusty Dunn
and Bobby Green about the shooting was a lie." The DA stared
at Rick. "You never once asked about the condition of your
father, did you?"

"I did," Rick retorted.

"When was that, Mr. Kyle?" quizzed Watnick.

"I asked Rusty to go find Dad . . . so did Scott," responded
Rick. "And I asked one of the policemen, 'Where's my father?,'
ten or fifteen minutes later."

Watnick became more aggressive. "You were afraid to see
your father, weren't you, Mr. Kyle?" he barked. "You didn't
try." Looking back down at his notes, he said, "You told police
officers a prowler shot your father, and that was a lie. You told
Detective Jaques the same thing. That, too, was a lie,
wasn't it?"

"Yes, sir," Rick replied.

"Did you tell the doctors or nurses at UCLA Medical Center a prowler shot Henry Kyle?"

"I don't recall telling the doctors or nurses," Rick said calmly.

"You told the police you never had a gun, and that was a lie, wasn't it?" Watnick said insistently.

"Yes, sir."

"You told Rusty you'd never had a gun, and that was a lie, too," the DA continued. "Didn't you say, 'I am trying to help you guys as much as I can,' to police?" he pushed.

"I guess so," said Rick.

"Were you lying then?"

"I suppose you could say I was," Rick answered. "I don't know why I told the police that."

"Were you trying to deceive them?" the DA snarled.

"Yes, sir," said Rick. "I told them a story."

"Why did you tell the police Henry Kyle woke *you*?" the DA persisted.

"I made up a story, and I wanted to say what I said before, and I couldn't recall what I said, so I just made it up," Rick answered.

"You planned the prowler story, didn't you?" Watnick grilled.

"No, sir," Rick said lackadaisically. "I made it up as I went along."

"Did you tell your mother what happened?"

"No, sir," said Rick. "I lied to her, too."

Moving on to Rick's birthday letter to his father, Watnick said, "Most of that was a lie, too, wasn't it?"

"Yes, sir," acknowledged Rick.

"To mislead and deceive your father?"

"Yes, sir."

"In fact, you've never made the dean's list anywhere, have you, Mr. Kyle?" the DA said with hostility.

"I once made the dean's list at MMA," Rick volunteered.

Watnick looked up at him suspiciously. "You did?" he said immediately. "When was that?"

"I got something known as a 'superior reef,'" Rick said lethargically, while Mike Gibson went straight to his briefcase to dig frantically through papers. "For a high B average."

Watnick eyed Rick with a look of triumph. "You never made

a high B average, did you?'' he said with disgust.

Rick returned his gaze. ''I don't know, sir,'' he said politely, ''but I got a superior reef.''

Hearing that, Watnick asked Judge Devich if he could approach the bench. Gibson and Sumner went up to join him, and after a few minutes of private consultation, Watnick returned to the lectern with Rick's transcript from MMA.

''All right, Mr. Kyle,'' he said, when Gibson and Sumner had taken their seats. ''Now when do you say you received this reef?''

''My eleventh-grade year,'' responded Rick, adding, ''It doesn't reflect whether I *deserved* the reef, but I did get one.''

Pulling out Rick's eleventh-grade transcript, Watnick read aloud for the jury: ''C in Military Science, D in English, B in American History, D in German, C in Spanish, and B in Biology. B in Military Science, second semester, C in English, B in History, C in German, D in Spanish, and B in Biology. And you're saying you got a reef for having a high B average for this year?'' he asked, setting down the grade report.

''I received the reef . . .'' Rick said steadfastly. ''And I didn't question it.''

On Thursday morning, Rick was more sullen and, on occasion, showed flashes of temper toward the DA.

Watnick asked Rick about the Mazda RX7 he got from Kyle when he completed his Marine training in November of '81.

''How much does an RX-Seven cost?'' the DA inquired.

''Eleven thousand dollars.''

''And your father bought the car for you?''

''It was a gift, as well as a means of transportation for me,'' Rick answered.

''It was a pretty expensive gift, wasn't it?'' queried Watnick.

''Yes, sir,'' Rick said stolidly.

When he arrived at Stone Canyon, Rick told Watnick, he and Rusty Dunn ''became friends. Not only that, I liked him. He was an interesting person.'' Did he ask Rusty to buy cocaine for him? ''It was a mutual agreement where we both were to purchase some.''

''Where did you get the money to pay for it?'' asked the DA.

''It might have come from my father,'' Rick said, ''I'm not really sure.''

On further questioning, Rick said he "assumed" he got the money from Kyle, since his father was his "only source of income," other than the "lamp incident. I wasn't allowed to get a job," he told the DA.

Rick told Watnick he and his father had had "some, but not many" conflicts over drinking and smoking before he moved to California. "He would hit me years later over a drinking incident in the eleventh grade," he explained.

"Did you and your father have conflicts over your drug use?" the DA asked, with an accusatory look.

"My father never told me anything about knowing anything about my using drugs," Rick said slowly and deliberately.

"How about lying?" Watnick asked. "Did you and he have any confrontations about your lying when you were in California?"

"I don't remember any lying problems at Stone Canyon," Rick answered. "We fought about my not making my bed or doing the dishes."

"What did Rusty Dunn mean when he said Henry Kyle yelled at you about 'drinking, smoking, and lying'?" Watnick demanded.

"He would bring it up anytime he had a conflict. Many times, it was not spawned by anything I had done."

"What did your father mean when he said you had to live by 'his rules'?"

"I'm not sure what he referred to," Rick said, bemused. "That was the problem. His rules were always changing."

"Did Henry Kyle ever tell you not to bring drugs into the house?" the DA fired back.

"He never said that," Rick replied, "but he told Rusty not to bring his 'clammy drug friends' into the house."

"Did he tell you not to use cigarettes and alcohol?"

"Yes, sir, he did."

Asked to explain the "lamp incident," Rick said, "That was a big misunderstanding all the way around. It was not stolen." Rick said he did take the lamp, and that he denied knowing anything about it in front of Rusty.

"Why did you lie to Rusty about it?" the DA interrogated.

"Because he was in the house and would have told Dad, and I wanted to tell Dad in my way without Rusty's help and influence."

Rick said he told Rusty three weeks later that he had sold

the lamp, and that he had the money "for a day or two. Dad understood. We took a walk and I explained it to him and I think he understood. He thought it was crystal, not glass . . . he didn't think I got a good price."

"What about your statement to Rusty that you had a pot farm in Denton?" Watnick brought up next.

"That was a joke," Rick said, with a half snicker. "I didn't know what else to say at the time about the money [from the lamp]."

"Did you tell Rusty Dunn Vicki was a 'threat to your inheritance'?"

"No, sir, I did not."

"Are you saying Rusty was lying?"

"No, sir," said Rick. "He assumed things after the fact. I never had any discussions about my inheritance with anyone, because I didn't think I was going to *get* an inheritance.

"I did tell Wendy Blum I didn't like Vicki," he said a few minutes later, "but I don't remember saying anything about Dad's money."

"Why didn't you like her?"

"Because she was trying to put a wedge between me and my father," Rick said sullenly.

"Did you dislike her 'very much'?"

"No, sir," Rick said distractedly. "I didn't have anything to *do* with her, really."

"Did you ever say anything to Jackie Phillips about Vicki 'taking money out of your pocket'?" Watnick said with a sneer.

"No, sir," answered Ricky. "I remember Jackie telling *us* something about Vicki taking money out of *her* pocket," he added disdainfully. "She got into a frenzy about Vicki dating Dad."

"Did your father ever say you were lazy?" Watnick continued.

"Yes, sir," said Rick. "But he used more harsh language."

"Did you tell Rusty that the reason you and Henry Kyle clashed was because you were 'just like your father'?"

"Yes," Rick replied. "Dad said that, too."

Rick denied that he ever told Rusty Dunn he "had to come up with the perfect murder. I have no idea how Rusty came up with that. I probably said, 'I could kill Dad,' in my anger and frustration, but I never meant to carry it out." Rick also denied saying to Rusty he "had to invent a car accident," or something similar. "I think he was mistaken," he testified.

"Did you ever tell him if you killed Henry Kyle 'people would come out of the woodwork cheering'?" Watnick quizzed.

"I don't remember saying that."

"How many times did you mention killing your father to Rusty?"

"I can't remember."

"Do you remember telling him at the hospital, 'Be careful what you say'?" the DA persisted.

"Yes, sir, I remember that," answered Rick.

"Why did you tell him to be careful what he said?"

"I was very scared," Rick said. "Anything he would say . . . I'm not sure I used the term 'Be careful,' but I said something to that effect."

"Did you tell Kelly Moore your father was worth forty or fifty million dollars?" the DA said accusingly.

"No, sir," said Rick.

"Did you tell Kelly Moore it would 'soon be Kyle Brothers, Incorporated'?"

"No, sir, I didn't. On that particular statement, I think that Bobby Green was lying."

"Did you ever tell Bobby Green, 'I don't just wanna be rich. I wanna be famous'?"

"That's just silly," Rick responded. "That's Bobby."

"You don't like Bobby Green very much, do you?" Watnick snapped.

Rick looked back at the DA. "I really don't care about Bobby Green to like or dislike," he said flatly.

"Dad told him to teach us tennis, but he wasn't a very good instructor to me, so I quit," Rick went on to say, adding, "I had been told he was an informant by my brother, Scott. He also made up things to tell my father."

"You didn't do what your father asked you to do, and that's what Bobby Green would tell him, isn't that right, Mr. Kyle?"

Rick paused for an instant. "My biggest mistake," he said, slowly and carefully, "is I've tried to live my own life under other people's rules. On some things that are basic human rights, I should be able to make my own decisions."

After the lunch break Watnick read from an introspective memo Rick wrote to himself in March of 1983. " 'I have a warrant out for my arrest because I cannot pay the ticket. I would be able to pay my ticket, however, my thirst for cocaine caused me to spend all my money and go $100 into debt. . . .

"Is that true, Mr. Kyle?" Watnick stopped to ask. "That you were spending so much money on cocaine in March of 1983 that you couldn't pay a ticket and there was a warrant out for your arrest?"

"No, sir, that's not true," Rick said gloomily. "I was not spending money on cocaine in March."

"Then why did you write that?"

"It was the beginning of a story about things that happened or didn't happen in prior times."

Watnick picked up the memo again. " 'I just called my girl-friend and she answered the phone with an exuberant "Brian!" ' " he read. "Are you saying that didn't happen?"

"It was a made-up statement," Rick responded.

"Who is Brian?" asked the DA.

"He was her boyfriend in high school, years before me," Rick said wearily. "Kelly was living with me at the time," he added, "so I don't know why I would have been calling her."

Watnick read some more. " 'I broke away from my father with a false sense of pride and security. . . . I stole from him and blew all of it on bad cocaine deals and partying.'

"That's what you really did with the money you took from Henry Kyle, isn't it, Mr. Kyle?" the DA asked, glowering.

"I stole it, and spent a good deal of it at Jackie's on co-caine."

"And 'bad cocaine deals' referred to the fact that you were dealing, didn't it?"

"No, sir, it did not," said Rick. "That was just a figure of speech. I meant the amount of money I blew at Jackie's on base."

"Then Jackie Phillips didn't pay for all the cocaine?" Wat-nick trumpeted.

"No, sir, in January—but I never denied that fact."

"Mr. Kyle," the DA interrupted, "you testified that Jackie Phillips supplied all the cocaine you used in the spring of 1983."

"Jackie indeed supplied all the cocaine—or Henry Miller," Rick said staunchly. "But I helped purchase it, and there's a difference in the two words to me."

According to Rick, "Henry had seven ounces lying around" the first time he met him, "and we would smoke and he would deal. They had a continuous smoking going,'' he said of Miller and Jackie. "I would come for a day or two and they would still be up from the previous weekend.'' Rick said he "would volunteer to pay Henry Miller sometimes—he was real loose with his cocaine and his money.''

Looking at the memo again, Watnick said, "You then wrote, 'At this moment I'm going to rip off my sister, who is barely surviving.' Do you remember that, Mr. Kyle?''

"A lot of that is just rough-draft things I never turned in and haven't seen until now,'' Rick replied. "Some was just figments of my imagination.''

"'The Marines are likely to give me a dishonorable discharge,''' Watnick read. "Is that true, Mr. Kyle?''

"No, sir, it was not,'' responded Rick.

"'Some might consider me neurotic, sick, barbaric, or without consideration or feelings,''' the DA continued, reading from the memo. "'If I don't stop I'll surely become an addict and that I cannot afford.'''

Putting the memo on the lectern, Watnick stared at Rick and said, "And this contains truth and story, is that correct, Mr. Kyle?''

"Yes, sir, that's correct,'' Rick replied.

Moving on, Watnick reminded the jury that the defendant had been through basic training for the Marine reserves, and "knew about weapons'' and "marine skills.''

"You also learned how to kill the enemy, isn't that correct, Mr. Kyle?'' he postulated.

"Yes, sir, that's correct,'' Rick responded, adding, "how to fight in a battle.''

Next, the DA asked Rick to repeat how he stole his mother's diamond ring, commenting, when he had finished: "You don't care how you get your money . . . if you want it, you take it, don't you, Mr. Kyle?''

"No, sir,'' Rick said impassively.

Rick told Watnick he apologized to Charlotte Whatley "in the room'' with his father when Kyle drove to Atlanta to pick him up, and that they were "all crying. It was a bad situation,'' he said contritely. "Something I'm embarrassed and ashamed of.''

"The same as when you stole a seventy-five-hundred-dollar check from your father?'' Watnick said cynically.

"Yes, sir,'' maintained Rick.

"Did you steal any other items from 9909 Preston Road?" the DA queried.

"I've taken some change my father left lying around the house."

"What was that?"

"Some grocery money he would leave in the kitchen," Rick elaborated. "Five or ten dollars."

"That was 'change' to you?" Watnick challenged.

"It was change to my father," Rick retorted. "To me, it was a movie."

Asked about his relationship with Wendy Blum, Rick told Watnick they became friends in June 1983.

"Did you tell her that before the end of the summer you would kill your father?"

"No, sir, I did not."

"Are you saying Wendy Blum was lying?"

Rick looked at the DA. "I'm afraid she was mistaken," he said quietly.

"You didn't say anything to Wendy Blum about killing your father before the end of the summer?"

The jury looked at Rick with interest.

"I might have said, 'I'm so mad I could kill my father.' Said out of anger or frustration. I didn't say before the end of the summer."

"So Wendy Blum was simply 'mistaken' about what she says she heard you say?" the DA pressed.

"I can't remember the specifics about conversations like Wendy can—or thinks she can," Rick said slowly, "but I'm afraid she's mistaken."

"Did you tell her you were gonna have to kill your father because Scott wouldn't have the guts?"

"I don't remember telling Wendy that Scott wouldn't have the guts, or any of that conversation," Rick responded. "I have made statements that Scott would do whatever Dad asked him to do and then get mad. And that I wouldn't play tennis with him, whereas Scott would go on and play."

Recalling the events right before the shooting, Rick told Watnick his gun was "in full view" when he was looking over the house and driveway with his father, and that he was "not trying to hide it."

"And you say your father said, 'Oh, God, no'?"

Rick looked puzzled. "I've been struggling with trying to remember who said it," he remarked. "If I said it or if Dad said it."

Rick told the DA he didn't know how close he was to his father when he shot him. Afterward, he testified, "I started struggling with Dad somehow . . . it felt like he was sort of on top of me or something. I remember just swinging my arms and trying to push him off of me. It felt like he was right on top of me. I didn't know I was shot until I reached the garage. I recalled being shot later—it didn't feel like what I thought a shot felt like."

Then, Rick said, he ran toward the kitchen and out of the house. He still held the gun in his right hand until he got to the garage, he told the DA. "I remember my arm hurting, and I may have changed the gun to the other hand. I really don't remember that well."

"Did you throw the gun with your left hand?" asked Watnick.

"I think I remember chunking it up with my left arm," Rick replied, screwing up his face in thought.

"And it's true that you were wearing a glove at the time, isn't it, Mr. Kyle?"

"No, sir, that's not true."

"And you told Doug Halley you might have left fingerprints on the gun because you switched hands?"

"No, sir, that's not true."

"It's also true, isn't it, Mr. Kyle, that the positions you used in your statements to police were the positions you were in . . . ?" Watnick said forcefully.

"No, sir, that is not true."

". . . and the 'third person' was you?"

"No, sir," Rick said dully. "I just thought it up as I went along. I only had two facts in my head," he continued. "Where Dad was, and where I ran out of."

In his final line of questioning, Watnick turned to the settlement among Kyle's heirs.

"Your share of the estate from the will went from fortynine percent to eighteen percent," Watnick said forcefully.

"Yes, sir . . ."

"You signed this to make sure that you would inherit something from your father's estate, didn't you, Mr. Kyle?" Watnick demanded.

"My major concern was to pay my attorneys," Rick said hotly. "I didn't care if I got a dime out of this."

"Did you believe, at the time you signed this agreement and agreed to the eighteen percent, that the other heirs to the estate could prevent you from inheriting from your father's will and your father's estate if you were partly responsible for his death?" the DA asked, glaring at Rick.

"Your honor, again, this calls for speculation as to what other parties might or might not do," Gibson interrupted, rising to face the judge.

"Overruled . . . he can answer it," responded Devich. "You can answer it, Mr. Kyle."

The jurors turned to look at Rick. There was silence for a moment, and then he said, "I'm not particularly sure about that. I remember that my discussions were concerned about having the money available to pay my attorneys. And whether or not they could take the money if I was convicted or not didn't matter beyond paying my attorneys."

"Isn't it a fair statement that you believed that unless you signed this agreement, the other heirs might prevent you from taking any part of the estate?" Watnick persisted.

"It wasn't any concern of mine because I'm not guilty, and I didn't feel like I had to worry about that," Rick said firmly.

"You weren't worried about whether or not you were gonna be in the estate?"

"Only enough to pay my attorneys."

"And that's the reason you cut your share from forty-nine percent to eighteen?"

"Yes, sir."

"Mr. Kyle, did you believe when you signed the agreement cutting your share from forty-nine percent to eighteen percent that the other heirs of the estate would be prevented from contesting this disposition of your father's estate?"

"As well as myself, yes, sir," Rick responded.

"One last area, Mr. Kyle," Watnick noted. "Did anyone force or compel you to come to California to 110 Stone Canyon in June of 1983?"

"No, sir, that was my decision," Rick answered quietly.

"Did anyone *ask* you to come to California to 110 Stone Canyon in June of 1983?"

"No, sir, they didn't."

"Did anyone force you to *stay* in California after June of 1983?"

"No, sir, they didn't," Rick responded, in a near whisper.

"I have no further questions," said Watnick.

Mike Gibson began his re-direct by asking Rick about the writings in his portfolio.

"Were these from a time when you were doing a lot of introspective writing?" he asked.

"Yes, they were," Rick said gloomily.

Handing him a copy of one of his journals, Gibson asked Ricky to tell the jury the circumstances in which he wrote it.

"This was written during a time I hadn't seen Dad and wanted to be part of the family," he responded, looking over the memo. "What I thought of Dad . . ."

"This is concerning your relationship with your father?"

"Yes, sir, it is."

"That entire document is in your writing, is it not?"

"It is."

"Would you please read for the jury that writing?" Gibson entreated, walking back to his chair at the counsel table.

"Yes, sir," said Rick, adjusting his position in the witness stand. "On the top it has a date, '4/4,' and then it says . . ." Rick paused, then began reading in a somber, melancholy voice: " 'Easter weekend. Another Memorial happening that will inevitably change my life. The days have suddenly taken upon an amber color that reflects back to the family. The family—why is it so important now? Was it ever before? How wonderful to think that we might be a family. But what does Dad want? What has he ever wanted? He wants me and Scott, but he's not willing to accept us on our own terms. He feels he has to keep us with money—his only power. Without money he is the weakest person I know. The saddest fact is that he doesn't know that he can only be admired or resented for his success, but he can never be loved for it—' "

"Slow down . . ." Gibson said gently.

"Yes, sir," said Rick, and then continued with his reading. " 'He can only be loved for his humanity,' " he recited, more slowly. "'He has a complete lack of self-esteem, however he continues to be so very egotistical about himself. Might that be a sign of his insecurity? It breaks my heart to think of him being so unhappy. He is so busy, and always has been, to just stop resenting the struggles that he has been forced to overcome and begin to enjoy the life he is living now.'"

24

On Wednesday, February 27, things were back to normal in Department 123. The press entourage on hand for Ricky's testimony had left. Only the regular court-watchers remained to hear the defense's next witness: I'ni (pronounced "Eenie") Chen, a pretty, personable woman, who had worked as a draftswoman for Kyle's architect and friend, Guy Bartoli. Chen testified that Bartoli had assigned her in June 1983 to do the measurements and drawings for the renovation at 110 Stone Canyon. She set up a temporary office and drawing board in the west end of the house, and spent "at least eight or nine hours a day" there, Monday through Friday, until July.

Chen, who was being questioned by Steve Sumner, testified that she first met Ricky at the house in "early June," and that they became friends. She saw him "just about every day" and they also socialized together from time to time, at the beach, at several restaurants, a club, and a friend's house.

Chen said Ricky told her "a lot of things about his past, including that he had been physically abused by his father." In July, she and Guy Bartoli had a conversation about it, and afterward, "I called Ricky to ask him if he was all right and if things were okay. He didn't really want to talk about it. I asked him if his father had beat him." When Rick didn't respond, she said, "I pursued it, asking him if he was okay. He said, 'It happened. Those things happen.'"

A few nights before Kyle senior left on his trip to Dallas, I'ni testified, she and he had dinner with the Bartolis at Chasen's. Chen said she had never been alone with Kyle before that night. She met him at Granada and they drove together to the restaurant in his car. Rusty and Rick were cleaning the garage when she arrived, and Kyle was "cursing" at Rick for stopping work. "He said, 'That damn kid never does what I tell him to. He's not like Scott.' He said he had just beat him. I told him violence doesn't help. And he said, 'That's the only way to handle Rick. It's the only way Rick will behave.' "

At Chasen's, I'ni told Sumner, "Mr. Kyle pulled out his wad when the check came" and placed it on the table. "Mr. Bartoli told him not to flaunt his money, and he said, 'I'm not afraid of anybody, because I know nobody would touch a big Texan like me,' " she repeated in a mock Texas accent, causing the jurors to laugh along with her.

Chen said Kyle decided to stop at the Bel Air Hotel on the way home for a nightcap, and "insisted" they take a walk through the grounds first. During the walk, she testified, "several times he grabbed me to him and forced me to kiss him." Afterward, she testified, Kyle had two drinks with her in the lounge and they "spent quite a while talking." When they got to Stone Canyon and her car, Chen told the jurors, Kyle "kept me in his car, and twice he dragged me over and forced me to his side of the car and forced me to kiss him. Each time I grabbed the car door, he grabbed my hand and forced me to stick it inside his pants." Chen said she "thanked him for dinner and left."

The next day, she told Rick about it.

"What did he say?" Sumner asked.

"He was not surprised," Chen testified. "He expected it. He said he knew his father had raped Jackie, his half sister when she was—"

"Objection!" Lew Watnick fairly screamed, while the jurors sat with their mouths half open. For the next several minutes, Judge Devich conferred at the bench with the DA and Ricky's defense lawyers. He repeated his prohibition about bringing up Jackie's alleged sexual abuse. Although no one in the courtroom could hear what he was saying, his displeasure with Sumner was obvious.

When he sent the attorneys back to their seats, Devich turned to the jury and said sternly, "You are instructed to disregard what you just heard. It is not to be deemed as evidence in this court, and you are admonished not to discuss it or consider it in any respect. Mr. Sumner, please continue.''

Chen told the jury she saw Henry Kyle the day after their dinner at Chasen's, and that he asked her to go to Dallas with him on his upcoming trip. ''I declined. He called me at least once a day before he left for Dallas,'' she related, ''trying to persuade me to go with him. He told me he'd be gone a week to ten days.''

The day before Kyle left for Dallas, Chen testified, she was at Granada and talked to Ricky. ''He said Mr. Kyle had tried to hit him again, and how he was very much afraid of him at that point and didn't know what would happen. Rick said that he had blocked his strike and Mr. Kyle was very upset and said he wanted to kill him. Rick said if he ever hit him back Mr. Kyle would kill him rather than lose. He said he didn't want to hit him back because Mr. Kyle was his father and he loved him.'' According to I'ni, Rick mentioned several times that he was afraid of his father. ''He said his father had threatened to kill him and he believed him.''

I'ni told Sumner that Kyle called her on Thursday the twenty-first, after he got back from Dallas. He told her he came back early ''because the boys weren't behaving.''

The rest of Wednesday and all of Thursday, the jury was kept outside the courtroom while Gibson and Watnick argued over whether the defense could call a clinical and forensic psychologist, Dr. Rex Beaber, to testify about Rick's perception of Kyle's actions at the time of the shootings.

Gibson wanted Dr. Beaber to explain to the jury that because of his history of abuse, Rick had a ''heightened level of anxiety'' or a ''lower threshold to interpret'' his father's behavior or anticipate violence under the circumstances, and that his inability to recall all the facts was consistent with stress.

Watnick, on the other hand, argued vociferously that Rick's state of mind, on which Dr. Beaber would offer his opinion, was ''directly in the province of the jury,'' and if Beaber was allowed to testify, it would be ''telling the jury what the verdict should be.''

''This testimony could really hurt us,'' Watnick's associate, John Moulin, said nervously during a break in the hearing on Thursday morning. ''Essentially, it's gonna boil down to: Do you believe the defendant? If you do, it's not guilty; if you don't, it's guilty.''

To reinforce their position, Watnick and Moulin called in the State's expert in examining medical witnesses, Dino Fulgoni, to cross-examine Dr. Beaber. After several hours of Fulgoni's pummeling, Judge Devich ruled in favor of the State. ''I get the feeling in courts today that the field of psychiatry is attempting to take over what courts are, and juries,'' he commented, in making his decision. ''There comes a time we have to put a stop to that type of practice. This is a critical area, and I have reservations. . . . Whether Rick acted in a reasonable manner is essentially the jury's determination. The jury's seen Rick on the stand. They can evaluate.''

On Monday morning, March 4, John Vandevelde called to the stand Larry Fletcher, a ballistics specialist for the defense.

Unlike Jim Trahin, the prosecution's expert, who, with his gun-motif necktie and corduroy jacket, looked like a walking advertisement for the National Rifle Association, Larry Fletcher was mild-mannered, reserved, and almost accountantlike. He had testified as an expert witness in more than a thousand cases, mostly for the prosecution and police agencies.

After rattling off his credentials in a Texas twang, Fletcher explained that he had based his report on his examination of Trahin's testimony, Kyle's autopsy reports, diagrams, casings, firearms, the doors at Granada, residue tests, and the bullets in the box, in addition to his own testing with a Rohm. His conclusion, he testified, was that the bullets originated from the ''same general area'' as Trahin testified, and that the shots from Henry Kyle's gun were in ''two separate groupings'': the single, high, separate shot grazing the door leading into the courtyard, and the five low shots in a group.

Discussing further the high shot into the door, Fletcher testified that he was able to ''actually see the path of the bullet'' for that shot, as opposed to the lower shots, and based on his findings, the muzzle of Kyle's gun would have to have been at a height of five feet six inches to account for the graze in the door. (Trahin's calculation was five feet one-half inch, plus or minus two inches.)

''In your opinion, was the high shot consistent with Henry Kyle being crouched?'' Vandevelde asked, when he had finished.

"No," said Fletcher. "The angle would be different if Henry Kyle had been lower."

"How about the low shots?" asked Vandevelde. "Do you think someone standing erect could have fired the five low shots?"

"I don't think so."

"Do you have an opinion as to the usual reaction of a person shot in a darkened room while standing?"

"He would immediately have some type of immediate reaction," Fletcher said, unbothered by the gesticulations of Trahin, who was sitting next to Watnick, observing. "Either make himself as small as possible, or try to protect himself."

"They wouldn't stand up," Vandevelde repeated for emphasis. "Or draw erect . . . but make themselves as small as possible by crouching or trying to hide?"

"That's correct," Flectcher repeated, implying that the shot Kyle fired while standing had to be the first shot.

Late in the day on Wednesday, the defense called one of its last witnesses, Dr. Robert Bucklin, a distinguished forensic pathologist, to corroborate Larry Fletcher's testimony about the order of the shots.

Bucklin, a tall, wiry physician with snow-white hair, wire-rimmed glasses, and a neatly trimmed Van Dyke beard, possessed a string of credentials impressive enough to cause particular apprehension to Lew Watnick: In particular, he was the supervising pathologist for Lawrence Cogan, who performed Kyle's autopsy and testified for the state.

Gibson handed the pathologist the mannequin with the arrow through its torso to indicate the path of the fatal bullet, according to Cogan's calculations. When asked about the entrance wound, Bucklin pointed to the black circle on the mannequin, "in what Dr. Cogan called the back," he said pointedly. According to Bucklin, Kyle's gunshot wound was actually "two inches further to the front" than Cogan had testified and had shown on the mannequin. "This is too close to the back," he said, fingering Cogan's mark. "It should be closer to the posterior of the arm." From his examination, he testified, he thought the shot that killed Kyle was "more to the side than the back."

Bucklin said the coroner's placement of the exit wound was "pretty accurate," but his autopsy report that both wounds were fourteen inches from Kyle's head was "impossible." If they were at the same height, he testified, the arrow showing the path of the bullet as going upward was inaccurate, and should have been "in a more horizontal plane."

Bucklin described the wounds to Kyle's head as "strong but not severe," and not enough to render him unconscious, in his opinion. By his analysis, the head wounds were "quite random," and "indicative of a glancing-type blow." They could have been caused by someone either in front of or behind Kyle, but the sites of the blows would have been "difficult to reach" if Kyle had been standing erect and someone was behind him; they were "consistent with" a person in front of Kyle swinging randomly toward his head—just as Ricky testified.

When court reconvened on Monday morning, March 11, Gibson called to the stand James A. Johnson, the operations officer for the Marine Military Academy. He confirmed that Rick Kyle had indeed been on the dean's list for the quarter ending December 20, 1977, as Rick had told Lew Watnick on cross-examination the week before.

After Johnson's brief testimony, Dr. Bucklin returned to the witness box. When Gibson asked him if he was sure about the location of the entrance wound, Bucklin stated an emphatic yes, saying that "by Dr. Cogan's own measurements and from the photographs," it was "definitely" more of a side wound.

Dr. Bucklin then went on to trace the path of the bullet, testifying that it hit the sixth rib and went through the left lung, and caused hemorrhaging along the track. Bucklin said it also damaged the pulmonary vessel and veins, the pericardial sac, and the right lung. The most serious injuries, he testified, were to the pulmonary blood vessels, which would have caused Kyle's death. According to Bucklin, it would have taken "four to five heartbeats" to fill Kyle's pericardial sac to the limit with blood, thereby preventing his heart from beating. After he was shot, the pathologist testified, Kyle's general circulation would have slowed and finally stopped, and he would have gradually lost consciousness to the point of coma. This would have had a direct effect on his muscle control and strength. The decline, in Bucklin's words, was "fairly rapid."

"Let me give you a couple of hypotheticals, Dr. Bucklin," Gibson interjected at that point. "Were there any medical injuries preventing Henry Kyle *before he was hit* from turning around and firing at a height of five feet six inches?"

"No," replied the pathologist.

"Assume the shot occurred," Gibson went on. "And from then on, Henry Kyle was engaged in physical activity, and after four to five heartbeats slumped down. Would he have been medically able to stand back up and discharge a .357 Magnum at five foot six inches?"

"It would have been medically unlikely or medically unreasonable," Bucklin said with certainty.

"Why?" asked Gibson.

"Because he began bleeding after the fatal shot, and after four or five heartbeats his heart would have been full. Then he would have been deprived of the necessary oxygen to the brain, and he wouldn't have been physically able to elevate his body from a slump."

"What if he had engaged in this physical activity and then dropped to his knee?" Gibson persisted. "Would he have been able to stand up and fire the gun at a height of five foot six inches?"

"That's even more exaggerated than the previous scenario," replied Bucklin. "A person becomes disoriented after a fatal hit, and the volitional use of the muscles diminishes and leads to a possibility of slumping."

Ricky's attorneys next read an affidavit signed by George Nachtman, Jackie Phillips's Dallas estate lawyer.

In the affidavit, Nachtman said Henry Miller III first called him about representing Jackie with respect to her fathe 's will on *August 1,* 1983—the Monday after the Friday Grogan questioned her about the gun, and a week *before* she and Miller said they contacted their criminal lawyer, Frank Wright.

As its final witness the defense recalled for a third time Dr. Bucklin, to bring to light some new information.

When Bucklin took the stand, he informed the jurors that he had just found out from the prosecutors that Dr. Cogan had saved certain tissue from Henry Kyle's atrium, lungs, and coronary arteries. These included the part of Kyle's heart pierced by the fatal bullet. Since his previous testimony, he had examined the tissue in Dr. Cogan's presence, and had some new findings to report: The bullet actually entered Kyle's heart—not just the pericardial sac, as the coroner had reported—and it had passed "completely through the left atrium."

According to Bucklin, there was no reference in the coroner's notes or autopsy report to an injury to Kyle's heart.

"Can you think of any explanation how it was missed?" Gibson inquired.

"I don't know how it was overlooked," Bucklin said without hesitation. "It just seems to me so obvious . . . a hole that large."

After examining the tissue, Bucklin testified, he felt Kyle's injuries were "much more significant than I thought a week ago. Then I was contemplating a hole to the pulmonary artery and blood in the pericardial sac. Now there's that and a major, more debilitating defect involving the left atrium."

"Does that have any effect on your opinion?" prompted Gibson.

"It supports and solidifies it," Bucklin said firmly. "It adds great substance."

"Would you say Henry Kyle's injuries were greater than you originally thought?"

"Very much greater."

"Dr. Bucklin," Gibson said confidently, "let me ask you a couple of hypothetical questions."

"All right," said Bucklin.

"Was there anything, from a medical standpoint, to prevent Henry Kyle, before he was shot, from turning and raising his arm to between five feet and five feet nine inches and firing a shot that hit the courtyard door at a height of six foot one inch?"

"No."

"If he'd received the fatal wound, went down—either crouching or on his knees—would it have been medically probable for him to *stand back up* and fire a .357 Magnum with his arm at a height of between five feet and five feet nine inches?" Gibson pressed.

"Bolstered by the fact that the bullet went through the heart," Bucklin responded, "it was highly unlikely medically that Henry Kyle could have stood up and reacted this way."

Gibson's two final points were to emphasize the pathologist's statements that his recent discoveries added a "tremendous amount of knowledge" about what had occurred and that Kyle did not die instantaneously, and could have fired five shots while crouching, in the direction of the breakfast room door.

On cross, Watnick ignored Bucklin's new medical testimony and asked the pathologist, "If Henry Kyle were turning with his arm upward between five feet and five feet nine inches, and he was struck with the fatal bullet, could he have pulled the trigger *as he was turning*?''

Bucklin paused to think.

''Or immediately thereafter?'' the DA suggested.

''In that sense, yes,'' Bucklin said doubtfully.

Watnick's other hypothetical scenario considered the possibility that Kyle and Rick ''shot almost simultaneously.'' In that case, Bucklin conceded, it was ''possible from a purely medical point of view'' for Kyle to stand and fire at a height of five feet to five feet nine inches, ''if it was during the one or two second interval after he was shot and before the blood filled his pericardial sac.''

''You can't tell the jury or anyone else exactly what Henry Kyle did after his fatal wound, can you?'' the DA said defensively.

''No,'' Bucklin answered simply.

''No further questions,'' Watnick muttered.

With Bucklin off the stand, Devich informed the jury that the only thing remaining was the closing arguments.

25

IN OBSERVANCE OF THE OCCASION, Lew Watnick used the lectern and a microphone.

"This is the beginning of the end," he began, as jurors crossed their arms and looked at him skeptically. Calling Ricky Kyle a "chronic, habitual and probably pathological liar," he then accused the defense attorneys of manipulating their case to fit the State's evidence. That is why, he said, they waited until their opening statement to admit their client shot his father—"because they realized the prowler theory just wouldn't fly."

"The People believe the defendant, Rick Kyle, intentionally planned, and with premeditation, murdered his father," the DA said coldly. "With evil intent."

For the first hour or so of his argument, Watnick outlined how he believed the shootings occurred, suggesting that if Henry Kyle had not shot Rick in the elbow, Rick would have hidden the Rohm gun in his room and pretended to have been asleep. The incident would have been blamed on a prowler, just as he and Scott planned. "To me, this is almost like the hand of God," the DA said dramatically.

The night of the murder, the DA said, Ricky hid the Rohm revolver in the pocket of his warm-up ("Why would he put on a jacket and warm-up on a hot July evening?"), awakened his father, and the two of them looked around the house for the nonexistent prowler. If the Rohm had been in plain sight, Watnick told the jurors, Henry Kyle would never have turned and fired at his son.

Kyle then lowered his guard, Rick took out his gun, and his father "either sensed or heard something" and turned and got his weapon ready. "Probably Henry Kyle was facing the terrace to Sunset, turning to his left, and he was struck in the left back as he was turning," the DA contended. "All one motion." If his arm had been up already, Watnick maintained, the fatal bullet would have hit his arm. The DA twisted and contorted his body awkwardly to demonstrate: It was "impossible" for Kyle to have fired first. As a reflex, as he was turning, Kyle fired his gun. "The first shot was in an upward direction," Watnick noted. "He would have shot parallel or down if it had been under normal circumstances."

After shooting Kyle in the back, Ricky clubbed him over the head and took at least one more shot, then ran away as his father was going down. Kyle fired five more times. He probably never really knew his son had shot him, the DA theorized, but fired back by instinct. "By sheer luck or the grace of God, he struck his murderer in the arm.

"It's illogical that the victim fired at the defendant first," Watnick insisted, because Kyle was an excellent shot, and he and Rick were close to each other. Besides, what was his motive? "There's only one word to describe it. An execution."

The DA discredited the defense's expert witnesses, Dr. Bucklin and Larry Fletcher, by insinuating that they were paid off. "I suggest very strongly, that you can buy almost any expert opinion if you have enough money to spend." He proposed that the matters they testified about could only be determined by "common sense"—in contradiction to what Bob Grogan had been telling reporters before the trial: that the State could prove who shot whom and who shot first.

Watnick admitted that Dr. Cogan "made a mistake" by missing the wound to Kyle's heart, and called it "regrettable and a shame. But what does it really mean?" he asked the jury. Cogan and Bucklin agreed death was not instantaneous; therefore Kyle could have fired the high shot either before or after the fatal wound. Watnick pointed out that Kyle was able to fire three or four additional rounds, regardless.

"Then there's the murder weapon," Watnick observed, stressing that the defense didn't admit Ricky had the Rohm or used it to kill his father until the State had rested its case. "That's because there was such overwhelming evidence they had no other choice," he said flatly. Ricky admitted on the witness stand that he got the gun from Scott, and this corroborated the testimonies of Jackie, Henry Miller, Wendy Blum, and Doug Halley.

In the second stage of his summation, Watnick focused on the events preceding July 22. He asked the jury why the defendant had come to California. The answer, he said, could be found in the Happy Birthday letter, which he called a "complete deception and intentional fraud." Once Rick moved into Stone Canyon, the DA argued, he did not behave like someone trying to get back into his father's good graces, or like a frightened, abused person. "There's only one explanation for that letter. The defendant needed money . . . he and Scott planned to kill their father, and now their father was in California."

For the next hour or so, the DA discussed the testimony of Rusty Dunn and Bobby Green. Neither said he had seen any evidence of beatings, only verbal altercations. Rusty testified Rick had mentioned killing his father to him six times over the summer, and had once discussed planning the "perfect murder."

Vicki Kyle said she never saw Henry hit Rick or Scott either. She was aware, though, of her husband's disappointment in Ricky and his "drinking, lying, et cetera." In the DA's view, the timing with respect to Vicki's absences from Granada and the shooting was critical. Vicki arrived back in LA from Taiwan the night before the murder, and left for San Diego the next day. The shooting occurred the night after she left, Watnick told jurors, because it was "the only time Kyle was there without her."

Wendy Blum was an important witness, the prosecutor went on to assert, because the defendant told her his timetable for killing his father by the end of the summer. By that date, Watnick told the jury, Ricky would have to admit that his admission to Stanford was a "gigantic and premeditated lie." His father would have "really kicked him out and cut him off."

Moreover, Watnick said, Wendy Blum corroborated Scott's complicity, and that Rick knew he would be penciled out of the will. His statements made such an impact on her that she called her psychiatrist.

Watnick brought up the ammunition box next, and noted that it was placed in the crawl space sometime after June. The defendant was the "only one with reasonable access to the crawlspace and a motive to hide the box.

"Let's look at the defendant's actions *after* the killing," the DA said, moving on to Rick's conversation with Jackie Phillips and Henry Miller after the funeral. "You decide if Jackie and Henry are truthful," he directed. To their credit, he observed, they did not try to lie about the fact that they were free-basing that evening, or that they had been treated for cocaine addiction. Furthermore, their testimony had been corroborated by the defendant himself: He admitted that he had drawn the map. "The crucial issue," the prosecutor said, "is not whether he told them, but whether he told them it was self-defense."

While conceding that Jackie was "very high-strung and emotional," Watnick pointed out that she was initially reluctant to talk to the police. She didn't tell Grogan about Rick's confession or the diagram when the police first questioned her on the twenty-ninth, the DA emphasized. She "broke down frequently," and "only with great reluctance" testified at the grand-jury proceeding and the preliminary hearing.

Jackie and Henry had no reason to "throw in" that Ricky told them the gun was untraceable, or that he was wearing a glove; they had actually been told these things. The police didn't find a glove, Watnick said, "because they weren't looking for one . . . they were looking for a prowler."

While admitting there were "inconsistencies" in Jackie's and Henry's testimony, the prosecution argued there was "nothing inconsistent" in what they had said about the murder.

During his discussion of Jackie, Watnick mentioned the settlement agreement, and claimed the important facts about it were that Rick was willing to cut his share from one half to eighteen percent "so rapidly," and that it was kept a secret.

For the next thirty minutes, the prosecutor discussed in detail Ricky's statements to Doug Halley, whom he described as a "reluctant witness." He suggested it was Rick's habit to talk about his feelings when he was using cocaine. Halley knew things only the defendant could know, Watnick said, which proved that Rick told Halley "exactly what happened on the night of the murder.

"You decide if Doug Halley, Wendy Blum, Rusty Dunn, and Bobby Green all lied to you," he told jurors.

For the rest of his summation, Watnick focused on Ricky. He began with an attack on the defense's contention that Rick was a victim of child abuse. "First you need to have a child," he scoffed. "The defendant is not and was not a child. He was a twenty-year-old ex-marine. . . . If he was worried about abuse, why did he come to California and why did he stay? The defendant was at 110 Stone Canyon, strictly speaking, for money and for murder."

Ricky's lawyers "changed the focus" from the defendant to the victim, to show that Kyle was a "violent, horrible person.

"The defense created a gigantic lie to show it was self-defense. . . . Rick Kyle came back because he didn't like his life away from his father. He wanted to be famous as well as rich, and now he's both: famous for having killed his father, and rich."

In the last minutes of his closing argument, the DA recounted Rick's thefts from both parents, his forged transcript, and the Happy Birthday letter. After his arrival in California, "he continued to smoke, lie, cheat, take cocaine, and steal from his father." Finally, the DA said, he shot Henry Kyle in the back, then lied to police, medical personnel, an attorney, and his mother.

"This is the character of the defendant," Watnick concluded, putting down his notes and scowling at the jurors. "Now he's asking you to believe his testimony . . . also that his half sister, brother-in-law, and Henry Miller are not only liars, but perjurers.

"The physical facts and motives behind the killing of Henry Kyle senior pointed to one logical conclusion: The defendant willfully planned and executed his father. It was murder in the first degree."

Appearing relieved, Watnick picked up his notes and walked back to his seat at the counsel table a few feet away.

"Mr. Gibson?" directed Judge Devich. "Your closing?"

Gibson, who had been making notes throughout most of Watnick's final argument, looked up immediately. "Yes, your honor," he said, getting up and walking briskly past the lectern to the front of the courtroom, where he stood beside the jury box.

"Ladies and gentlemen," he said solemnly and with self-assurance, "I am here to aid you in the serious decision you make next week. You have to decide a case that affects this young man's life."

For nearly forty-five minutes, Gibson carefully went over

the legal principles that the jury was supposed to consider. Under the law, he advised, the prosecution had to prove its case to a moral certainty. If there was even the slightest reasonable doubt, the verdict had to be not guilty.

Gibson reminded jurors how Lew Watnick said no one could tell them what happened in that room. "He's *got* to tell you," the defense attorney emphasized. Watnick also had to prove the shooting was not self-defense, and that the events in the dining room did not happen as the defense suggested.

"I feel compelled to respond to a few of Mr. Watnick's comments," he said seriously. "He suggested that Ricky and we perjured ourselves and fabricated a defense to fit the facts. I've never been accused of this in my life, and I'm offended by it." The reason they waited to reveal their defense was to test and challenge the State's evidence. Watnick's accusations were an attempt to "divert" the jury from the prosecution's weak case.

Gibson asked the jurors to consider Ricky's background when they determined whether he acted reasonably in firing at his father. That was why the defense put on witnesses showing Henry Kyle's volatility and brutality. Gibson offered several possible explanations for why Kyle had shot at his son: The most logical was that Kyle thought he'd heard a prowler by the courtyard door. Gibson reminded the jurors there was uncontested evidence of a third party around the house that night—two neighbors had heard suspicious sounds, mudprints had been found on the patio, the French door was open, and something had caused Rusty Dunn's dog to bark. Another possibility—"not logical," Gibson conceded—was that Kyle turned and fired to scare Ricky, perhaps because Bobby Green had told him about Kelly's visit on their way home from the airport. Or, the lawyer suggested, Kyle might have turned and fired to kill Rick. That was the most remote possibility, he admitted, since Henry Kyle would not have missed.

The physical evidence, Gibson contended, supported Henry Kyle's firing first, in the direction of the courtyard door.

It was expert witnesses Bucklin's and Fletcher's testimony that caused the State to change from labeling the incident as an "execution" to a "simultaneous shooting," because they had to "salvage their case." The evidence, however, proved it couldn't be a simultaneous shooting, he maintained. The only two people awake that night—Tresa Jereczek and Bobby Green—heard a distinct pause between the first two shots. Jereczek maintained that the first shot was louder than the others—which would suggest the sound had been caused by Kyle's gun, because it was larger and fired in the direction of the house where Jereczek was staying. Gibson castigated Watnick for suggesting that either expert was "paid off"; they were paid for their time and expenses only, just as Cogan and Grogan were.

Leaving the physical evidence aside, Ricky's lawyer ripped into the State's case, which he pointed out was based primarily on memories. Memories are frail, he suggested, and conversations can be misunderstood. The State's primary witnesses had heard Ricky's confessions while they were free-basing cocaine. Jackie and Henry Miller, he observed, couldn't even recall where they ate or which car they drove that day.

Gibson ridiculed Watnick's statement that Rick "had to do it" on July 22 "because no one was around"—Vicki Kyle had been in Taiwan for forty days before that.

Also, Gibson noted, the "murder weapon" was in the family TV room, the holster had not been hidden, and there was no evidence of a glove, all of which "belies a plan."

If there had been a plan, Gibson said, Ricky would have asked Jackie and Henry to get the glove, bullets, gun, and holster—not just the gun. Moreover, Rick would more likely have asked Scott, who was in California with him, and who visited him at the hospital—particularly if they were co-conspirators.

Gibson went on to attack the motives of the State's main witnesses. He noted that five other parties signed the settlement agreement. If Jackie really believed Rick confessed to murdering their father, Gibson argued, she would never have signed an agreement giving him any of Kyle's money. She was motivated, he said, by greed.

Rick's lawyer advised the jury to consider Jackie and Henry Miller as essentially the same witness. He outlined their motives to lie in court. Jackie, he said, was unemployed and dealing drugs, while Henry was hocking his art to pay bills. "They clearly had a motive to lie and fabricate," Gibson said. "Jackie Phillips is a millionairess today by her own actions."

The defense attorney turned to Doug Halley next, and said Halley was "up for the highest bidder." If Rick had confessed murder to him, Gibson said, Halley would have gone to the police, and protected his sister from marrying him. Instead, he tried to get a million dollars from Rick, and placed an "anon-ymous" call to Grogan to testify.

Ricky Kyle, Gibson said, grew up in the "tyranny and boot camp" of Henry Kyle. He reminded jurors how Ricky had learned at age eleven not to cry because he'd get hit again. "Ricky's been crying from the day he went to MMA to July twenty-second, 1983, to somehow gain his father's respect," Gibson pleaded, "and the letter he wrote and I read to you shows it."

Gibson admitted the Stanford letter was "wrong, not under-standable," but Rick couldn't talk to his father "the way you or I could."

Gibson told the jury Ricky lied about what happened be-cause he was "scared to death," and afterward he "stuck with one lie like a little kid." He couldn't confide in friends of the man he killed, Gibson argued, but he did eventually "misplace his trust" and tell Jackie, with whom he had a "mutual bond of their father's violence. He was a scared young man asking for help," the defense attorney said.

Gibson closed his argument with an emotional appeal to the jurors. "I'm giving this young man's life to you," he said qui-etly. "I beg and plead for you to do the right thing. Godspeed." Then he bowed his head and walked back to the counsel table.

26

ON MONDAY MORNING, APRIL 1, THE
defense attorneys and prosecutors got their first glimpse at what
was to become one of the more unusual jury deliberations in
their recent memories. One of the jurors, a middle-aged housewife named Marian Walecki, sent Judge Devich a note explaining that she had fired a gun over the weekend to test the ballistics
evidence in the case. She asked if she could share the results
with the other jurors. After reading the note, Devich immediately considered declaring a mistrial, since jurors are not allowed to consider evidence outside the case. However, he
decided—since Walecki hadn't discussed the experiment with
the rest of the jury—simply to disqualify her for juror miscon-
duct. She was replaced with the only remaining alternate, Grace
Williams, a fifty-five-year-old retired store clerk.

By mid-April, there was still no verdict. All sorts of rumors
circulated about the jury, and the condition of the defendant.
Steve Sumner admitted Ricky was "just having a tough time."
Sumner claimed also that there was an off-duty LAPD officer
"hanging around outside the Bel-Air Sands," where Rick was
staying. He was "watching who was going in and what he was
doing." As a result, Sumner said, he and Gibson moved Ricky,
under an assumed name, to another hotel. "I'm sure Grogan
was behind it," he said.

On Friday, April 19, the sixteenth day of deliberations,
Marshall Lai, an IRS employee elected foreman by the other
jurors, sent Judge Devich a note saying they were "hopelessly

blocked" on a "primary issue." As it happened, Mike Gibson was in Dallas that day, and Steve Sumner asked the judge if he would postpone a public announcement of a mistrial until Monday, so Gibson could be present.

Devich agreed to the request, and on Monday morning, April 22, his courtroom was a madhouse. Photographers and reporters tripped over each other to get seats on the benches. Ricky Kyle appeared, his face puffy and bloated. He had put on five to ten pounds in the month since closing arguments.

At the judge's signal, jury foreman Lai stood up self-consciously and said, "I don't feel we'll ever have a unanimous verdict as to guilty or not guilty." When Devich asked him to reveal the sticking point, Lai said quickly, "Who shot first."

Just as Devich was about to formally declare a mistrial, Marshall Lai stood back up and said, with a nervous, embarrassed laugh, "Some of the jurors are saying they would like additional time all of a sudden."

Judge Devich told Lai and the other jurors to go back to the jury room and continue their deliberations.

Late in the day, the jury submitted a list of thirteen or fourteen questions they wanted answered from the trial record—mostly they concerned the time between gunshots, the pathologists' testimony, and any testimony from witnesses who heard Rick or Scott talk about killing their father.

On Monday morning, the twenty-ninth, Lai announced that the jurors were absolutely and hopelessly deadlocked.

The final vote, to the obvious shock of the three regular court-watchers, who had predicted a not-guilty verdict, was ten to two: ten for first-degree murder, two for acquittal.

Sitting at the counsel table, Ricky slumped over and sobbed briefly at the judge's announcement.

Lew Watnick looked tired and haggard as he emerged from the courtroom. He stopped short of confirming the State would retry Rick Kyle, but said he "expected" that would happen. "We did have what I would consider overwhelming evidence," he said wearily.

Only two of the jurors would discuss the deliberations with newspaper reporters afterward. They were, in fact, the two holdouts who had voted to acquit Rick: Marilyn Williams, an attractive, intelligent thirty-seven-year-old nurse and housewife, and Grace Williams (no relation), the alternate who had replaced Marian Walecki. "We've been fighting for three or four weeks," Grace Williams told the *Los Angeles Herald-Examiner*. "It's very frightening what went on behind closed doors," Marilyn Williams added.

According to Marilyn Williams, two members of the panel "walked into the jury room with their minds already made up that it was first-degree murder. One of them said he decided right after the judge read the instructions," she recalled with disbelief. "I asked him, 'How can you do that without deliberating first?' Another one said he stopped listening after the prosecution put on its case," she added. "I'd never want to be a defendant with *them* for a jury. They didn't even give Rick his basic rights. They assumed he was guilty, not innocent."

Marilyn Williams says on the first poll four jurors voted for first-degree murder, six for second-degree, Grace Williams for manslaughter, and she herself voted not guilty. "Both Grace Williams and I said it was a lawful killing," she protested. "Grace said it was manslaughter . . . she didn't verbalize it. I was questioning involuntary manslaughter or self-defense, just to keep them from bugging us. We were being harassed."

After several weeks of deliberation, things got so tense in the jury that certain jurors stopped carpooling together.

Marilyn Williams said several of the jurors "thought about it over the weekend" after Marshall Lai wrote the note to Devich announcing their impasse on Friday, April 19, "and decided the next Monday to ask for more time" before the judge declared a mistrial. At the time, she said, the jurors who had voted for second-degree murder were escalating to first-degree murder to try to reach a unanimous decision. She and Grace Williams were pressured to change their votes.

By most of the jurors' assessments, it was Lew Watnick's re-creation during his closing argument of how he said the shooting occurred—regardless of whether it was supported by the physical facts or not—that finally persuaded most members of the jury that Rick Kyle shot first.

"That really stuck in their minds because it was visual," Marilyn Williams said.

It is interesting that all the jurors had some sympathy for Rick, and even liked him—a fact that worked against him, according to Marilyn Williams. "It was almost like, if they were prejudiced, they'd go the other way." Steve Sumner related that several of the jurors who voted for first-degree murder did not want Rick to go to prison.

Both Mrs. Williamses were adamant in their belief that the prosecution had simply not proved its case. "They had pieces of a puzzle that didn't fit," Marilyn Williams observed. "There were a whole bunch of missing things. I'm a nurse, and with my medical background and Dr. Bucklin's testimony, it was almost medically impossible, with the kind of wound Henry received, for him to fire that shot at the courtyard door at a six feet one inch height after he'd been shot. And some of the jurors were saying he had 'all the time in the world' to shoot! If a piece of evidence like a glove had been found . . .'' she suggested.

Williams also felt the other jurors failed to grasp important underlying issues. "They had no concept of the abuse syndrome," she criticized. "They needed an explanation. Some of them said, 'So what if he was abused? Why did he keep going back?' And that's one of the classic symptoms of abuse. You don't know what a struggle I had.''

Court reporter Jeanie Snyder, who took down every word of testimony during the six-month trial, was as surprised as the court-watchers by the jury count. "I've been a court reporter for eight years," she said afterward, "and I can usually judge a jury, and I didn't think they'd go to first degree. I assumed it was ten to two for not guilty. *I* had a reasonable doubt," she volunteered. "The high shot gives me a doubt. There just was not enough evidence to convict somebody.''

Judge Devich was tactful. "That's what makes the world go round," he said with amusement, when advised of his court reporter's opinion. "I thought it was a tremendously interesting trial. My feelings were evident from the way I handled the case.''

"I feel very frustrated," Lew Watnick said a few days later, with bitterness in his voice. "I'm not happy about it." Not surprisingly, the deputy DA was pleased with the jury. "We tried to get jurors who were not swayed by emotion, or sympathies," he related. "Strictly by the law.''

Steve Sumner was more philosophical about the outcome. "It's sort of like kissin' your sister," he said of the mistrial, with a slight grin. "It just doesn't *do* anything! We would have liked the numbers to be the other way," he said, more seriously. "But we had a lot to be proud of. We won on the glove issue.''

His attitude toward the jury was revealing. "We wanted to pick gentle, sensitive, nice people who would hate Henry Kyle and like Ricky. That happened—but they were maybe not the most intelligent and *perceptive* people. They were not as intelligent as we thought. Our case was like a puzzle. We gave 'em all the pieces, and they couldn't put 'em together. It might just be that a case like this requires a mistrial to get it all in focus," he added. "Think of it as a necessary step toward Rick being acquitted," Sumner chortled.

As for Ricky himself, according to Steve Sumner, "He called me eight times last night in the middle of the night," right after the mistrial. "Like one of my kids. It was one of the first times I ever heard him become emotional," Sumner noted. "He started chokin' up. He wished I'd been there."

Several months after the mistrial, the State officially announced it would retry Rick Kyle, with a different prosecutor. Marilyn Williams and Grace Williams, the two jurors who had voted to acquit him, showed up in court for the hearing.

"I thought the case was very interesting," Marilyn Williams said, explaining why she came back to Department 123. "But I feel badly, because I feel Rick got cheated because he had a biased jury.

"After it's all over," she remarked, "it's a hell of an experience."

27

AFTER THE DEFENSE'S REVELA-
tions about Henry Kyle were publicized, a number of people
from the millionaire's past came forward with stories about his
darker side, or to express sympathy for Ricky.

Wayne Freeland, Kyle's former SMU fraternity brother, observed that he would "hate to be his kid. We went back a long
way. Henry was not long on understanding." In business, Freeland said, "I would work *with* him, but not for him, because he
could be a miserable son of a bitch. His attitude was 'If we
make a deal and you're happy, I didn't get enough.' Henry would
get enough. That was a disappointing thing to know about him."

According to Freeland, Kyle "screwed Don Tanner around
awfully—just terribly"—because, in Freeland's opinion, he
couldn't accept the fact that most of the "important money"
he made was due to Tanner. "I'm playing psychologist here, but
it didn't fit his image of himself. Don and I talked about it a
thousand times—figuring Henry out."

Even Jim Benford, one of Kyle's champions, considered that
the "big bucks" he began making in the sixties were at someone
else's expense. "A helluva lot of it came from Jim Justice, to
be honest with you. Henry sort of screwed him around. He had
a tendency to run over you if he could. He was a good trader
and he was tough—I wouldn't say dishonest. But if he had you
down, he wasn't gonna let you up."

Don Tanner, Kyle's business partner and roommate in the
sixties and seventies, claimed he found and made the sales on

all twelve of the deals he did with Henry, and Kyle would never admit it. "It wasn't one-sided—I'm the big guy, and then little old Henry—no!" he explained. "It was a very even type of thing. Henry alienated most people 'cause he was mean to them. It was a good guy/bad guy deal: He'd go in and rough some-body up and then I'd come back and follow him and smooth it over. Worked really well for us." The reason he finally broke away from Kyle, Tanner said, was because he found out he'd been "stealing him blind" through the bookkeeping system at La Buena Vida. "When I got on to that, I decided that I was going to systematically, unemotionally get a business divorce from Henry and separate all our properties. He never knew it was coming. I didn't want anything to do with Henry Kyle at that point in my life."

Dick Traweek, who acted as broker when Kyle and Tanner finally sold La Buena Vida in the seventies, felt that the split occurred because Henry was frustrated at not being able to con-tinue to "control" Don. Traweek compared it to his inability to deal with his sons. "Henry had a difficult time dealing with people he couldn't control. He needed an impending—how can I say this properly? I read about how he held the will over his sons' heads—I really saw Henry that way. He would continue to negotiate himself into positions where you had to come back to him. He wanted the ultimate say-so. Over your deal or your life or your whatever."

In the opinion of Tom Rippey, Kyle's SMU friend and first financial backer, most of his problems could be reduced to one word: ego. "Henry was always a smart, logical guy," said Rip-pey, "but when it came to his personality, he was the most com-plete egotist I've ever known. But one who really *believed* he was completely infallible. If anyone questioned his authority, it wasn't that they were questioning Henry Kyle. They were ques-tioning *God*."

"He couldn't sustain a relationship," agreed Wayne Free-land. "He had ego problems. 'You'd rather be right than rich,' I'd tell him. He couldn't be wrong."

"He couldn't stay charming long enough to sustain a lasting friendship," Traweek analyzed. "It had to be long-distance or money. He just surrounded himself with people whose economic future was predicated on his whims. I think he was very ambi-tious and extremely lonely."

Others had far worse stories about Kyle. Don Tanner, for example, told of a time he and Henry were building a country club in Cuernavaca, Mexico, on land that had traditionally been inhabited by fifteen hundred peasants. According to Tanner, the peasants refused to move off the land when the construction crew started earthmoving for the golf course. The golf-course superintendent called a lawyer in Mexico. The lawyer called the *federales*, who in turn called the *ruralraes*, who "machine-gunned somewhere between eighty and a hundred and ten Mexicans." When Kyle got the call from the greenskeeper to report the incident, Tanner related, "Henry said, 'Fuck 'em! A hundred and ten less Mexicans . . . that's spicks. Who cares if there's one hundred ten less spicks?'" (Yet, at the same time, Kyle would refer to his mechanic friend Rudy Alvarado with affection as his "little Mexican." "I don't think anyone was closer to Henry than I was," Alvarado says.)

James Windham, a Palm Springs lawyer and former district attorney who hired Kyle to work on the Cuernavaca country-club project, supported Tanner's view. "Henry Kyle was no friend of mine," he said after the trial. "The best way I could put it is to tell you what one of the Mexican fellows who worked with him said: '*Es como tener un alacrán en la bolsa.*' 'It's like having a scorpion in your pocket.'"

According to Windham, Kyle "clogged [the project] up purposefully instead of expediting it," then tried to take over the project. "He wasn't working *for* me, he was working against me. It was a hard experience for my wife and me, because it really set us back financially."

Helen Windham said she and her husband were "impressed" with Kyle when they first met him. "He came down to Mexico with a big Cadillac convertible. He had special hangers made for his suits. He had a nice figure. Big shoulders. He seemed to know all the right answers. He was very glib." Kyle's charm, she said, was "a facade. He manipulated people very well. People who knew him in the business sense might admire him. You needed to know him personally. The man was quicksilver. He could say black is white and somehow get people to believe it." Her and her husband's three years in business with Kyle were "such a traumatic experience," Helen Windham said, that they never pursued him in court. "Kyle isn't the type of man you could confront in the first place," she explained. "You felt he was dangerous. You wouldn't want him to think you had that on him. I had the feeling he would do anything to gain his hand. People were just puppets. He had no morals."

A former Illinois schoolteacher named Les Nimmo loaned Kyle money on some farms in Georgia. Kyle arranged the appraisals through a lawyer in Georgia. When the payments were not being made on the mortgages, Nimmo said, he notified Kyle, who told him he didn't think the farms would sell for enough to meet the appraisals. "I investigated," Nimmo related, "and found that they'd been inflated about one hundred percent in value." As a result, Nimmo lost half a million dollars, and Kyle made $200,000. "I eventually had a confrontation with Kyle, and he admitted he knew the value of the farms, but said, 'What are you gonna do about it?' He outweighed me by at least a hundred and fifty pounds. He had absolutely no integrity at all."

One business associate of Kyle's who did go after him was Don Abel. Abel and Kyle shared an apartment in Atlanta in the late 1950s, and worked on several country clubs together during that period. Kyle did the legal work, Abel says, and he "put the whole ball of wax together." Afterward, Abel maintains, Kyle tried to take all the credit and all the profits, so Abel sued him. "He settled out of court. He had no defense. The only talent that Henry had was how to cheat in a business deal. Con. Cheat. He would have more fun figuring out how to cheat someone than doing it right. He didn't seem to have any fun unless he got in your britches." After the suit was settled, Abel never spoke to Kyle again. "I refused to go to the funeral. I wouldn't honor him, even in death. And if that sounds bitter, it is."

Wayne Freeland and Tom Rippey viewed Kyle's motivation more sympathetically. "In many ways the result of what he did in business was very cruel, crude, and amoral," Rippey conceded, "but to talk to Henry about it, he was doing someone a favor. It might take him a few weeks to talk himself into it, but he'd rationalize himself into screwing somebody and twist himself into thinking he was not being dishonest, he was actually doing you a favor." According to Freeland's analysis, "Henry was not a crook, but he sometimes did crooked things."

Rippey also recalled how Kyle would berate his employees "to the point where I wouldn't have taken it—call them stupid, idiotic, dumb. To make himself feel superior, I guess." Rippey,

Kyle, and George Owen were financing car washes together, and according to Rippey, Owen "got some of the worst beratings. It was embarrassing to go around there. He'd say, 'You haven't got a damn thing to your name. Without me you'd be in the street. . . .' It'd almost bring the tears to your eyes. I just couldn't take it anymore. I said, 'Henry, I'll give you a call.' "

Frances Murphy, Kyle's secretary, confirmed Rippey's account, and added, "There were inevitably bitter feelings between Kyle and all his business associates. It was always stress, animosity, problems—the way he'd treat people."

In light of some of the testimony at the trial, Kyle's relationships with women came to be seen in rather different terms.

All his friends spoke of his need to compete where women were concerned, and several—Don Tanner and Tom Rippey, among them—claimed that he was having problems keeping up with younger men, and it "got to him." Chloe Zachary,* the director of a Los Angeles art gallery, agreed with this image of Kyle. Zachary crossed paths with Kyle about the time he made an offer on the house on Stone Canyon. She and a girlfriend were introduced to him at a club in Westwood. Zachary and her friend were in their early twenties at the time. When they sat down at a table, Zachary related, "Henry held my girlfriend back so he could sit between us. He then proceeded to put his hand simultaneously on each of our thighs. We were completely repulsed."

According to Tanner and Rippey, Kyle's need to compete was so great that if someone else was dating a woman, "he wanted to take that girl out and take her away from you somehow." During their SMU days, Rippey said, if a fraternity brother was getting married, "you could bet Henry would hit on his fiancée before the wedding—to put the knife in the back and show he could."

"I *know* Henry," Rudy Alvarado agreed. "If there were any girls in the room, he would have to be the hero, the macho. His son's girlfriend . . . hell, his son's granny! It didn't matter. Henry didn't care."

In fact, Don Tanner suggested, Henry Kyle actually despised women. "We talked about that a lot," Tanner said. "He used to tell me about it. He thought they were weak, that women were good for nothing, he said, except as a sex object." Tanner

* Not her real name.

said Kyle used words such as "contempt," and "disgust," and "hatred," when referring to the opposite sex, and that he talked about tying women up and using "discipline" to show his feelings. At some point, Tanner remembers, he recommended that Kyle visit a sex dungeon in West Los Angeles, where they were licensed to perform exotic sex acts. "I told him, 'If you really hate women that much you should go up and visit this place and they will teach you some things I think you will find helpful in your expression.'

"Henry told me what he used to do with women," Tanner related. "You want the truth? It was really sick. And he didn't realize it, or else he couldn't face it. But he used to put clothespins on girls' nipples. He had a name for his cock. He used to call it 'Big Henry.' And he'd make these girls bow down to his cock and say, 'I worship Big Henry more than God. More than my parents.' And this was while they were tied up! Once he started going to these sex dungeons, he did something called 'Golden Showers,' where he would urinate on a girl, just to show her humiliation."

The reason Kyle resented women, Tanner said, "was because of his mother. The no–no was that she had been previously married before she married Henry's father, and the fact that she had had another man made her a slut.' Course, it was okay for him to have five wives. He had a double standard. We talked about that a lot. That's why he beat his mother up. Called her a whore and a slut. An eighty-year-old woman! I heard about it through some others in the family. Charlotte knew it."

Charlotte Whatley agreed that Kyle did not like women, and for that reason, she "never suspected" that he was unfaithful to her. "He'd make comments all the time, even if they were pretty: 'She's fake,' 'She probably spent half her life at a plastic surgeon,' things like that." Whatley also corroborated Tanner's account of Kyle's relationship with his mother. "Henry always told me he didn't like his mama because she had slept with another man before she married his daddy. It was a love and hate relationship. He always put her down. She was very afraid of him. As much as she didn't want to lose me—we remained friends till she died—she *told* me to leave when I left. They had a strange relationship. She was totally dependent on him."

Both Tom Rippey and Wayne Freeland, who were around

Kyle in the fifties when his mother moved to Dallas, said they "wouldn't be surprised" if he beat her, and Freeland "heard from someone way back then" that he had. Freeland described her as "pretty subservient."

"I knew he abused women," Charlotte Whatley conceded. "I *knew* that. But the kids were different. Rick told me a little bit about it, but I didn't take it seriously. Henry told me many times, 'I'm gonna kill that boy,' but I didn't take him serious because that's part of his language. . . . I have to live with that now."

John Greer, Kyle's longtime valet, had this to say after the shootings: "I just think Henry went out there, and got on those boys, and got himself killed."

"It's like one of the old Greek tragedies," Helen Windham suggested. "Where you abuse your son so much he turns against you."

EPILOGUE

AFTER THE MISTRIAL, MANY OF
Kyle's friends and followers were convinced, predictably, that
Ricky had murdered his father in cold blood.

In George Shore's view, Kyle's behavior the week before the
shootings proved he "knew something heavy was coming down
in California."

One of Ricky's staunchest defenders after the mistrial was
Rudy Alvarado, a former machinist at Jetco who had run errands for Kyle and the boys. Alvarado was one of the few people
who knew Rick, Scott, *and* Vicki. In Alvarado's opinion, Ricky
Kyle was simply not capable of premeditated murder. He sees
the shooting as "something that happened" that got complicated
by other people's ulterior motives or loyalties to Kyle. "Everyone's trying to make it so damn complicated, and it's not."

Steve Sumner maintained that "somewhere between the two
extremes" lies the truth about Ricky. "He's not the sweetest,
most artistic little journalist," he said between trials, "or a slimy
son-of-a-bitch. I've caught him conning me on little points. The
basis for my ultimate convictions is the physical evidence and
Dr. Bucklin. He may be the slimiest creep—I don't think so—
but I don't believe he pulled the trigger first."

Sue Blum, producer Harry Blum's wife, spent time with Rick
and Scott the summer before the shootings. She strongly dis-
agrees with the police that Rick murdered his father for his
money. "It was a crime of passion," she insisted. "It's the father-son relationship. It's very complicated."

A former boyfriend of Jackie's, Dale Swann, who lived with Ricky and Doug Halley at Preston Towers after the indictment, supports this view: "Rick didn't care about money when I was living with him, or when I met him. That's why the twist on the will didn't make sense to me. I've seen the boy live on two dollars a day, and not many people can do that who come from his background. He was the type person who took a bunch of shit and finally couldn't take it anymore. My own feeling is, they shoot horses, don't they?"

Rudy Alvarado agreed there was "not a thing greedy about Rick. Rick's the type of person who, if he had two sacks of money, he'd take out enough for a six-pack and give you the rest. All you had to do to get whatever you wanted out of Henry was play the little role Scott did. Then you'd get a new car and credit cards. But Rick was not that way. You can see right through him. He won't play any damn role for any damn pair of tennis shoes."

Friend Wayne Freeland saw Kyle's threats to cut his children out of the will as empty gestures. "I'll bet those kids heard a thousand times a month, 'I'm cutting you out of the will,'" he observed. "I can't believe they took it seriously."

Paula Holtzclaw, Kyle's oldest child, acknowledges that "the stories were true about the will. You never could *not* bring it up," she said after the trial, "because he always mentioned it." Paula said she was cut out of Kyle's will in 1967, when she was eighteen, because she married her high school sweetheart over his objections. "He was disappointed in me not marrying second-generation money. That was my place in life. For some reason, social acceptance was important to him." Holtzclaw says she was put back in the will in the early seventies, and later she and her father reached "an understanding" that she would receive lifetime gifts rather than a large bequest, because she "didn't want to do business with strangers," i.e., her half brothers.

Although she never spent much time around her father or Ricky, Paula Holtzclaw perceived Rick's "obsession" with Kyle. "Once I saw Hank bait Rick playing tennis, and then Rick got very upset. And I thought, 'Rick, he baited you, you fool!'" Holtzclaw said getting along with Kyle was "a game, and if you learned to play the game, then he lost and you won. I saw Rick so upset one day," she related, "and Hank laughed. He did it in such a way that it made you mad. Rick took it seriously and Hank didn't know it."

Yet, after the indictment, Paula believed Ricky should be convicted—Bob Grogan convinced her the shooting was premeditated. Grogan also "convinced" Kyle friends David Charnay, Jim Benford, George Shore, and Vicki Kyle.

Paula has not spoken to either Ricky or Scott since 1983. She and Vicki have become "fairly close friends," and she says she "feels sorry" for Jackie. The reason she entered into the settlement agreement, she says, was in part because of her bitterness toward Rick and Scott. "Once we knew it was a murder and premeditated, we tried to figure out how we could hurt Rick the worst and still not destroy ourselves. Everything in moderation. He will get his just dues in California."

Paula Holtzclaw's problem in understanding Ricky, she says, lies in the fact that he didn't break away from Kyle. "If you lived with Hank, you had to live his life. You had to leave. What Ricky and Jackie have not learned is that tragedy is what you make it. If they'd broken away—I mean, why didn't he leave? Rick *let* my dad overpower him."

Charlotte Whatley says Rick and Scott thought it was their fault they couldn't get along with Henry. "The boys never talked to me about the abuse till after the trial," she said in the summer of 1985, "and then Scott and I stayed up till five in the morning one night discussing it. Scott said they thought if they told me about it, I wouldn't let them see him anymore. They had a fixation about him—Big Henry, you know."

As people began opening up, a preliminary portrait of Scotty began to emerge. Jim Benford, for example, described Scott as "smarter and sneakier" than Ricky, an opinion seconded by Ray Hames. Hames ventured that Scotty got in just as much trouble as Rick, but "he wouldn't get caught. He'd tell me things," Hames volunteered. Hames called Scott more a "follower" than Rick, "more laid back and reserved. Like he'd never go enlist in the Marines," he explained. "He just doesn't have that kind of initiative."

Rudy Alvarado claims Ricky was "always the fall guy" for Scotty. "Most of [Ricky's] lying started covering up for Scott," Alvarado says. "Rick never, never told on Scott. If Henry'd find whiskey bottles, Rick would say, 'They were mine.' He grew up covering for him. Scott was smaller, and Rick was afraid he couldn't take a whipping, so Rick took the heat. That was his little brother! Rick always looked after his little brother.'' Did Scott ever cover for Rick? Alvarado snickered, then said, ''You've gotta be joking!''

Another family friend describes Scott as ''smarter and very naturally manipulative,'' with a ''real cold core.'' Sue Blum, like Rudy Alvarado and others, saw Scott as ''capable of doing anything for Scott,'' whereas Rick was *not* capable of doing anything for Rick, but capable of doing anything for Scott.

One longtime friend who knows both boys says it was Ricky who was Kyle's favorite, not Scott. ''I think Scott *wanted* to be the favorite son,'' she analyzed. ''The Cain and Abel syndrome. Henry was so conflicted about Rick. He was a writer, and Henry thought that was sort of a pansy thing to do, but he still said he was pretty good.'' In this friend's perception, ''Scott courted Kyle's favor, but Ricky had it. Scott saw himself very much in the footsteps of Henry, and Rick did not. I think Scott was desperately trying to curry Henry's favor, and did it by using his brother.''

Paula Holtzclaw had even harsher things to say. ''Scott knows what he's doing every minute of every day,'' she commented after the mistrial. ''Ricky's just what you see—if he's hurting, happy, stoned, that's what you see. Scott's way behind a dozen layers of fake. He's always on the con. He's a Kyle. He gets it legitimately.''

Scott Kyle refutes these portrayals of Ricky and himself. He claims Ricky was ''mean'' to him when they were growing up, and that his brother ''never got along with anybody.'' Scott contends that Ricky ''made life more difficult'' for him with their father ''because I'd be afraid he'd tear something up and then I'd have to tell Dad that it happened and watch Dad get mad.'' Scott claims that it was he who covered for Ricky, rather than the other way around. ''Just to keep the peace, I'd go along behind Ricky and straighten up what he didn't do. . . . I'd say, 'Ricky, why'd you do that?' And he'd say, 'Oh, shut up, you're Daddy's boy,' and just yell at me like that.''

According to Scott, ''there's no doubt'' that he was his father's favorite. ''My dad told me that I was the only one he wanted around. He told me even up to the month before he died that he never liked Ricky—loved him, but didn't like him. Which is a view I share.''

After Kyle was killed, Ray Hames noticed a change in Scott. "His voice lowered and stuff. He was trying to be more like his father." According to Marj Helper and Jim Benford, shortly after Kyle was shot, Scott showed up in Arland Ward's office, sat behind the desk, put his feet up, and announced he was "taking over."

A similar episode occurred just before Kyle's death, related by Ray Hames. Scott had dropped out of SMU, Hames says, and Kyle had asked Hames to find out "what he wanted to do with his life." Hames took Scott out to see the construction site he was working on for Kyle, and when they got back, he asked Scott what he wanted to do. "I'd like to do what *you* do," Scott replied. "I told him, 'Scott, you can't do that overnight—supervise multimillion-dollar construction jobs. The way to learn it is to get involved.'" Hames told Scott that a good way to begin was to go to the Stone Canyon house and take part in the renovation. Scott called Kyle "right then," Hames reports, and told him he was coming. "Scott started crying on the phone," Hames says. "Not sad, kinda happy that he leveled with Henry."

Since the shooting, Scott has become his father's champion. Only when cornered will he admit to what he calls Kyle's "strict" behavior. He says he and his dad had only one "rocky" period in their relationship—during the period he withdrew from Selwyn because a liquor bottle was found in the bathroom his room shared with another student's. Then Kyle was "threatening" and "verbally abusive," and hit him with a tennis racket when he got home.

Scott concedes that Kyle was "more violent" with Ricky. He saw his father slap and kick his brother, and "once in the kitchen," he saw Kyle pound Ricky until he was on the ground. "But a lot of times Ricky—I don't know if he deserved that to that extent—but he deserved a lot of it. 'Cause he would push you to the limit."

Rick and Scott did see each other a few times after the shooting, and spent Christmas during the first trial in Atlanta with their mother. Since then, however, they haven't seen or spoken to one another, for reasons that are somewhat obscure.

According to both Ricky and his lawyers, the estrangement came about in large part because of money. Ricky's fees for his defense in the first trial came to almost $2.6 million, he says and Steve Sumner confirms. The figure was larger than his share in

Kyle's estate. Consequently, he tried to get the money for his next legal bill out of his interest in the trust, which was encumbered by a lease and several other complicating factors. As Sumner relates it, Scott would tell Rick to his face he could get it, "then turn around and his lawyers would say no. He won't help Rick. It's the most amazing thing in the world."

"Scott took advantage of me in the whole deal," Rick claims. "Me and Scott don't talk, period. One reason is our attorneys told us not to, and he's using that as an excuse not to help me." Scott's criminal attorney, Ron Goranson, denies Ricky's and his lawyers' charges. Goranson says it was Ricky who "had a tendency to harass Scott" in the settlement of the civil suit, and that Ricky was "quite antagonistic" toward Scott and "less than gentlemanly about the situation." Goranson concedes, however, that Scott will not give his brother any money. "Scott basically is listening to his civil lawyers," who, Goranson says, are "meticulous" and have done a "super job."

Scott says the reason he hasn't seen or talked to Ricky is because he "doesn't approve" of him and "doesn't want to be around him." He claims he never discussed the trust with his brother, but acknowledges that he has given Ricky no money. "I let my lawyers handle that."

As a result of Scott's position on the trust, Ricky feared he would have to hire a public defender to represent him at the second trial. But in December 1985, Gibson and Sumner flew to Los Angeles for a hearing to set the date for the second trial. While they were there, they advised the judge they would be Rick's counsel, even though they had no guarantee of being paid. A few weeks later, Gibson's wife died of a heart attack. Sumner decided to stay on as lead counsel, with a summer trial date.

At the time, Sumner noted that the fact that Scott wouldn't help Rick with the trust to pay for his defense proved they weren't in conspiracy, "because all Rick would have to do is testify against his brother, and the DA would cut him some slack."

Shortly after the mistrial, Rick and Kelly and Justin moved in with Charlotte Whatley in Atlanta, where Kelly was taking art classes. They were doing fine for a while, Charlotte says, but eventually the pressures of the case became insurmountable, and the two were divorced in the spring of 1986.

Shortly thereafter, Charlotte stopped speaking to Rick as well.

"I talked to my doctors about [cocaine]," she explained before the retrial, "and they said it was the only way to straighten him out. It's hard. I love Ricky and I'll always love him. He's my son." She said she still believed he was not guilty, but that wasn't the problem. "I don't care what happened, really. I loved Henry. What's done is done."

On July 15, 1986, roughly a year and a half after his mistrial, Ricky Kyle's second trial for murder began in Judge Robert Altman's court in Los Angeles. This time around, the State was represented by Stan Weisberg and John Moulin, and the defense team was whittled to Steve Sumner and John Vandevelde, operating on a drastically reduced budget of $300,000.

Weisberg's case, which lasted several months, was essentially the same as Watnick's with a few significant exceptions. Weisberg changed the prosecution's theory to suggest that Ricky moved to California in the summer of 1983 not to murder his father but to "rip him off," and that after he arrived, he decided he had to kill Kyle before Kyle found out about his lie about getting into Stanford.

As far as the State's witnesses were concerned, tennis player Bobby Green was severely discredited his second time on the stand. By the time Sumner was through with him, Judge Altman threatened to hold Green in contempt. At one point, for example, Sumner asked Green if he had tried to sell a book about Kyle since the first trial, and Green denied it. Then Sumner cited a conversation between Green and a New York editor the previous December. Green did a double-take and claimed the editor had contacted him. Eventually, he was forced to admit that he had two agents, "some notes," and an outline. After the judge ordered him to produce the book materials, Green brought a complete manuscript, filled mostly with gossipy tidbits about Kyle's girlfriends—he conceded it was mostly "literary license."

The prosecution did come up with a new witness named Priscilla Ford, who had spent time with Ricky between November 1983 and February of 1984. Ford claimed that while she and Ricky and Dale Swann were free-basing cocaine during this period, Ricky told them that he and Scott had planned the shooting and that Scott "chickened out." Dale Swann, however, testified that Ricky never said anything about the shootings to Ford in his presence.

Most damaging for the State's case, however, was the absence of its former star witness, Jackie Phillips. Weisberg said he did not call her because she "could not add anything to the case," and was "highly emotional." But Sumner and Vandevelde accused the prosecution of "trying to hide" her because it would be clear to the jury she had fabricated her story.

The defense, under Sumner's direction, demonstrated this time for the jury "over and over" how the defense believed the shootings had occurred.

Sumner also introduced a new theory: Bob Grogan, he contended, had taken too personal an interest in Ricky's conviction because he wanted to retire from the detective force in a blaze of glory and then make a movie about the case. After the first trial, Sumner became aware of a book called *Two of a Kind*, about the Hillside Stranglers case, in which Grogan had participated. The author of the book, Darcy O'Brien, reported on the Kyle case in the epilogue. He wrote that Grogan had "tipped off" David Charnay that Ricky was going to be charged with the crime right after Kyle was shot, so Charnay wouldn't turn over the assets of Four Star to Rick and Scott. Charnay and Kyle, Grogan found out, had a buy-out agreement and Charnay implemented it, based on Grogan's tip. In exchange for the information, O'Brien reported, Charnay gave Grogan a production office at Four Star and a trip to Europe.

Sumner contended, and argued to the jury, that Grogan, Charnay, and Harry Blum were planning to make a movie about Kyle. That was the reason, he said, they were holding meetings at Blum's house after the shooting.

When Grogan was on the witness stand at the second trial, he admitted to Sumner that he had formed a production company called Sunny, after his boat. He also conceded that he had entered into an option contract with Four Star in mid-September of 1983. But he claimed that he and Charnay talked about working on projects "unrelated to the Kyle case." Grogan also denied being given a trip to Europe.

Sumner reminded the jury that it was Grogan who had "put the fear of God into Jackie" about the gun—"so he could get her and Henry Miller as witnesses."

In support of his new theory, Sumner claimed he had some new evidence concerning Grogan, Jackie, Henry Miller, and Frank Wright. At the first trial, Wright, Miller, and Jackie all testified that Miller had first contacted Wright to represent him and Jackie by an "emergency" call on August 7. Grogan and Wright said that Wright first called Grogan on August 8.

After the first trial, however, Sumner found a notation in the police homicide book in Grogan's handwriting—which Grogan identified at the second trial—that showed Grogan actually met first with Wright on July 30, more than a full week before August 8. This meant that Jackie and Henry Miller had to have contacted Wright to represent them before July 30 (and probably July 29, the day Grogan questioned Jackie about the gun).

Wright also told a journalist that he held on to the map that Ricky drew for "about a week," instead of the single day he had testified to at the first trial.

The question arises: Why did Jackie, Henry, Frank Wright, and Bob Grogan all testify that Jackie and Henry Miller contacted Wright a week later than they actually did?

Sumner theorized that Jackie and Henry contacted Wright on July 29 after Grogan questioned them about the gun. At that time, Sumner speculated, they told Wright of Rick's confession but said that Kyle shot first, or were unclear about that point. Wright contacted Grogan on July 30 and Grogan told him to "sit on the map," Sumner argued. Then on August 1, Jackie and Henry called Henry's estate lawyer George Nachtman, whom they met with on August 4. Nachtman advised them, Sumner hypothesized, that unless Ricky was convicted of murder, Jackie would get only $10,000 from Kyle's will. Sumner argued that this was the "emergency" that prompted Henry Miller's call to Wright on August 7. Sumner thus suggested that Jackie and Henry Miller then remembered Rick's confession somewhat differently from the way they had at the first meeting with Wright.

Armed with his new theory, Sumner introduced the same witnesses he and Gibson had used in the first proceeding to tell of Kyle's propensity for violence. He again used the two expert witnesses, Dr. Bucklin and Larry Fletcher, to argue that Kyle had fired the first shot.

On December 5, 1986, after four and a half months of testimony from both sides, the State's murder charge against Ricky Kyle went to the jury for the second time. On January 9, 1987, thirty-six days later, the eight women and four men on the panel emerged with a verdict of involuntary manslaughter, the least serious offense possible. It carried a sentence ranging from probation to six years in prison. By voting for involuntary manslaughter, the second jury showed it had accepted the defense's theory that Henry Kyle had fired the first shot.

The jurors refused to grant interviews after the verdict, but one called John Vandevelde, Ricky's California defense lawyer. By her description, nine or ten of the jurors wanted to acquit, but they compromised on involuntary manslaughter to avoid another mistrial.

After the verdict was announced, Ricky Kyle proclaimed, "It should have been an acquittal. But I'm pleased with it. I have a future now. I think my punishment has been the last three and a half years of having this hanging over my head."

On February 6, 1987, Ricky's saga took its final, ironic turn. After considering three letters from jurors urging probation (six jurors from the second trial and one from the first showed up in court to show their support), Judge Robert Altman sentenced Ricky Kyle to five years in the state penitentiary, three for involuntary manslaughter and two for the use of a handgun.

Then he went on to add that he considered Ricky to be a "cruel, callous liar," who had "put on a show for the jury." Altman said he believed Ricky Kyle "hated his father" and had "no genuine remorse." After several other stinging remarks straight from the prosecutor's case, the judge set bond for an appeal at a million dollars and said it was "deliberately high" because he didn't believe Ricky was a "trustworthy individual."

The jurors left the courtroom in shock and outrage and said they felt they had "wasted eight months of their lives." Steve Sumner described the judge's actions as "undermining the jury system." Charlotte Whatley, who had flown in for the sentencing, looked slightly dazed and fielded questions from reporters, who jammed microphones into her face.

Meanwhile Ricky Kyle, who earlier that morning was talking about enrolling at Cal Tech Long Beach and getting on with his life, sat in a holding cell waiting for the long ride to prison.

ACKNOWLEDGMENTS

I would like to thank the friends, associates, and relatives of Henry Kyle who were kind enough to share their time, information, and insights with me in the writing of this book, even when it was difficult or painful. I am also grateful to the lawyers, judges, investigators, participants, and others connected with the case who assisted me, particularly Steve Sumner, who deserves a separate acknowledgment.

This book could not have been written without the support of my friends and family, or without my editor, Doug Stumpf, to whom I am deeply grateful.

A special thanks to Linda Goodman and Dr. Jack Tracktir. They know why.

BIOGRAPHICAL NOTES

DON ABEL shared an apartment with Henry Kyle in Atlanta in the late 1950s. They were business partners until the early sixties, when Abel sued Kyle and they reached a bitter out-of-court settlement.

RUDY ALVARADO "ran the transom job" for Kyle at Jetco and took over as chief mechanic at Trencher Leasing in Grand Prairie, Texas, when Jetco declared bankruptcy. He also ran errands for Kyle and his sons, and remains close to both boys.

MARTHA ARNOLD was a secretary at Four Star. She dated Kyle and helped him manage La Buena Vida, where she lived in the late 1960s. She and her sisters moved into a house Kyle owned in Benedict Canyon in the mid-seventies. She is still employed by Four Star and lives with David Charnay.

QUINT BARNES is a friend and former boyfriend of Jackie Phillips. They were dating when his Rohm pistol was stolen from his car. He is now a practicing anesthesiologist in Dallas.

GUY BARTOLI is an architect in Marina Del Rey, California.

JIM BEARDON runs a detective agency outside Dallas. He worked with the defense on both the Cullen Davis and Kyle cases.

JIM BENFORD is a Dallas-based geologist who worked with Henry Kyle on a number of projects from 1968 to 1983.

BARBARA BISHOP is a wealthy Kansas wheat farmer who entered into a prenuptial agreement with Kyle in 1978.

HARRY BLUM is a Los Angeles attorney-producer with whom Kyle became friends in the late 1960s. His producer credits include *Obsession*

315

and *The Bluebird*. Blum lives in Brentwood. He manages the singing group Duran Duran.

SUE BLUM is married to Harry and is an aspiring writer. They have two college-age daughters, including Wendy.

WENDY BLUM became friends with Ricky Kyle the summer before the shooting.

HELEN BOEHRNS worked as a manicurist at Preston Towers and dated Henry Kyle off and on from the mid-seventies to the week he was killed. She lives in Dallas and sells real estate for the Carolyn Shamis Agency.

PAT BROWN, also known as **PAT MORRIS,** was another Dallas girlfriend of Kyle's.

DAVID CHARNAY was a longtime member of the board of Four Star. He sold his shares to Kyle in 1982 to enable Kyle to acquire a controlling interest.

I'NI CHEN, now an architect, worked for Guy Bartoli the summer of 1983.

DR. JOSEPH LAWRENCE COGAN performed the autopsy on Henry Kyle.

ALLAN CONWILL was general counsel and the director of corporate regulation at the SEC from 1961 to 1964. He was Kyle's boss in 1962. He is now retired and lives in New York.

RUSTY DUNN is a carpenter who was hired by Kyle to renovate the house at Stone Canyon. He was living there when Kyle was killed.

WAYNE FREELAND was a classmate of Kyle's at SMU and occasional business partner in the sixties and seventies. He lives in Kansas City and is a real-estate developer.

ZSA ZSA GABOR, the actress, dated Henry Kyle in the 1970s.

MICHAEL GIBSON was Ricky Kyle's lead counsel in the first murder trial. He is a partner at the Dallas firm of Burleson, Pate & Gibson.

RONALD L. GORANSON, a Dallas criminal lawyer, represents Scott Kyle.

BOBBY GREEN is a tennis pro who lived in a guesthouse on Kyle's Preston Road property from 1980 to 1983. He moved into the Stone Canyon residence a few weeks before the shooting.

JOHN GREER began as a gofer for Henry Kyle in 1970 and became his houseman and close companion.

ROBERT GROGAN has been with the LAPD for twenty-six years, nine of them in Robbery-Homicide. He also heads a movie-production company called Sunny and plans to retire from police work in 1987.

LARRY HAGMAN is the actor who portrays J. R. Ewing on *Dallas*. He was renting Kyle's Dallas house at the time of the shooting.

DOUG HALLEY is Kelly Moore's half brother and was Rick Kyle's brother-in-law between the summer of 1984 and the spring of 1986. He lives in Norman, Oklahoma.

RAY HAMES, Henry Kyle's "country boy," is currently supervising the construction of a chain of health spas for George Shore.

MARJORIE HELPER is a Santa Monica realtor who was introduced to Kyle by her friends Harry and Sue Blum. She sold Kyle the house on Stone Canyon.

PAULA HOLTZCLAW, Henry Kyle's oldest child, is his daughter by first wife, Rheba Rice. She lives with her husband and two small children in a small town outside Atlanta.

DEREK JONES is the neighbor on Sunset who heard footsteps and voices the night of the shooting.

TRESA JERECZEK worked as a maid at the house across the street on Stone Canyon. She heard voices, and a pause between the first two shots, the night Kyle was killed.

JERRY KRAMER, a former pro football player with the Green Bay Packers, met Kyle when they were both living at La Buena Vida in the 1960s. He now lives in Parma, Idaho, where he writes occasional books about football and pursues business interests.

WINK KRAMER is Jerry Kramer's second wife. They have a daughter.

DELLA KYLE was Henry Kyle's mother. She died in Dallas in 1979 and is buried in the Tennessee hills.

ERNEST KYLE, Henry Kyle's father, died of tuberculosis in the 1950s.

HENRY HARRISON KYLE, JR. (RICKY) is the older son of Henry Kyle by his marriage to Charlotte Edwards.

SCOTT EDWARDS KYLE, Henry and Charlotte Kyle's younger son, currently lives in Austin, Texas, with a girlfriend. His plans are to return to school.

VICKI YANG KYLE grew up in Taiwan, where she married John Yang and had two children, Ellen and Richard. She married Henry Kyle in a "confidential" ceremony in San Diego in 1982. She currently lives in Taiwan and works for her father.

BOB LEVINSON met Henry Kyle on the board of a company in the late 1960s, and was a business partner on several ventures. He is an executive with Andrex Industries in New York.

ANN MEIDEL is a Palm Springs decorator and socialite who lived with Kyle at 9909 Preston Road in Dallas from 1978 to 1980.

GREG MEIDEL, Ann Meidel's son, lived at Preston Road with his mother and Kyle from late 1978 to 1980. He is now married and works for Paramount in L.A.

HENRY S. MILLER III, son of Dallas real-estate mogul Henry S. Miller, is the former fiancé of Jackie Phillips. He still lives in Dallas and works for one of his father's companies.

JOHN MOULIN, a deputy district attorney in Los Angeles, assisted Lew Watnick in the State's first case against Rick Kyle, and Stan Weisberg in the second.

FRANCES MURPHY was Henry Kyle's secretary from 1968 to the early 1980s, when she quit because of a brain tumor she believes was brought on by stress from Kyle.

GEORGE NACHTMAN is a Dallas probate lawyer who represented Jackie Phillips in connection with Henry Kyle's estate.

LES NIMMO, a former schoolteacher from Illinois, became acquainted with Kyle between 1960 and 1963, when Kyle was developing country clubs in Mexico for James Windham. They had a falling out over a loan Nimmo made to Kyle on some farms Kyle and Charlotte owned in Georgia.

GEORGE OWEN is a Dallas banker, married to former exotic dancer Candy Barr.

JACK PATE, of Burleson, Pate & Gibson, represented Ricky on probate matters and moved into the Bunker Hill Towers next door to Mike Gibson and Steve Sumner during the first trial.

BRYAN PHILLIPS married Jackie Miller Kyle in 1958, after her divorce from Henry Kyle. He is an insurance broker in Dallas.

JACKIE LYNN PHILLIPS is the only child of Henry Kyle's marriage to Jackie Miller Phillips. A former model, she is currently unemployed and lives in the townhouse Kyle bought her in Dallas.

JACKIE MILLER KYLE PHILLIPS (also known as JACKIE GLENN GARRISON) was married to Henry Kyle from 1954–1957, and is the mother of Jackie Lynn Phillips. She married Bryan Phillips in 1958, and he adopted little Jackie.

PETER RACHTMAN is a former music promoter from Florida and New York. With Kyle's backing, he moved to L.A. and became an agent, living for a time with actress Karen Black. He moved into Kyle's Benedict Canyon house in the mid-1970s, then quit the business and relocated to Colorado and then New Zealand. He is currently married, and lives in Seattle.

RHEBA RICE was Henry Kyle's first wife and the mother of Paula Holtzclaw. She remarried and lives with her second husband in Atlanta.

TOM RIPPEY is a wealthy ex-classmate of Kyle's from SMU, and was his first financial backer. He lives in Dallas.

JOHN ROCKWOOD, a homicide detective with the LAPD, assisted Bob Grogan in the Kyle investigation.

MADONNA WIESE KYLE ROSENFIELD was married to Kyle for three months in 1953 and ''hid'' from him until his death in 1983. She is now a travel agent in Tempe, Arizona.

CAROLYN SHAMIS is a Dallas real-estate broker who first dated, then became ''fabulous friends'' with Kyle for eighteen years.

EUGENE (GENE) SHIPLEY was Henry Kyle's half brother, the son of Della Kyle by her first marriage to Melo Shipley. Now deceased, he worked for the Panama Police Department.

GEORGE SHORE is a longtime friend and occasional business partner of Kyle's from Kansas City.

MAJOR GENERAL RALPH W. SPANJER served with Kyle in the Marines and was headmaster at MMA when Ricky was a student. He is retired and lives in Florida.

STEVE SUMNER, a former professional baseball player and later an associate at Burleson, Pate & Gibson, was Mike Gibson's co-counsel at Ricky Kyle's first trial, and lead attorney in the second.

DALE SWANN dated Jackie Phillips on and off between 1980 and 1982. He was Ricky's roommate at Preston Towers between the indictment and the first trial, while Doug Halley was living there.

DON TANNER shared the penthouse suite at La Buena Vida with Henry Kyle from 1965 to 1975, and was his business partner and friend. He lives on a thirteen-acre tract in Bel-Air with four guesthouses, a pool, tennis court, electric gate and three-and-a-half-story waterfall. Among other properties, he owns Yesterday's, a popular club in Westwood.

DICK TRAWEEK acted as broker in the purchase of La Buena Vida from

Kyle and Don Tanner. He lives in Marina Del Rey, where he runs a limited partnership.

JOHN VANDEVELDE was Rick Kyle's California counsel at both trials.

MARY ANN VIOLA dated Kyle in the 1970s.

ARLAND WARD was Kyle's accountant, one of the trustees of the Henry Kyle Family Trust, and the executor of Kyle's estate.

LEWIS WATNICK tried the State of California's first case against Ricky Kyle. Then a deputy district attorney, he is now retired.

STANLEY WEISBERG acted as prosecutor in the State of California's retrial of Rick Kyle. He is now a municipal judge in L.A.

CHARLOTTE EDWARDS KYLE WHATLEY was Henry Kyle's fourth wife and is the mother of Ricky and Scott. She is divorced from her second husband, pharmacist Leonard Whatley, and lives in Atlanta.

STEWART WHATLEY, a half brother to Rick and Scott Kyle, is the son of Charlotte Whatley by her second marriage. He is a teenager and lives with his mother in Atlanta.

JAMES WINDHAM hired Kyle to help him develop a country club in Mexico in the late 1960s. He is a former district attorney and lives in Palm Springs.

HELEN WINDHAM is married to James Windham.

FRANK WRIGHT, a former prosecutor, is a Dallas criminal lawyer and longtime friend of the Miller family. He has represented Henry Miller III on drug-related offenses since the 1970s. He originally represented Henry III and Jackie, now just Henry.